By the author of

DETOUR ON AN ELEPHANT

A Year Dancing with the Greatest Show on Earth

CHASING CASTLES

Nineteen Years Living and Teaching Ballet in Italy

Barbara File Marangon

CHASING CASTLES
Nineteen Years Living and Teaching Ballet in Italy
Copyright © Barbara File Marangon, 2018

Some names have been changed in order to protect the identity of the people.

Published by: Ogham Books International
Category: Autobiography, Self-discovery, Ballet, Travel, Living in Italy, Dance School Business in Italy, Producing Ballets in Italy, Genealogy
ISBN: 978-0-9911731-4-3

Written by: Barbara File Marangon
Edited by: Nancy Whalen www.eyespyproofreading.com
Italian Editing: Rossana Minniti
Cover Design by: Watchmaker Design
Text Layout/Formatting by: Polgarus Studio

Front Cover: CHASING CASTLES, Painting of Venice and Bourke Castle by Barbara File Marangon
Back Cover: Portrait of Barbara File Marangon by Graziella Modanese
Part of Exhibition at CastelBrando, Italy

Printed in the United States

In Memory of Helen, Mary
And My Mother Dorothy

Contents

*"Time is measured in hours.
Life is measured in emotions."*
Antonio Curnetta

PROLOGUE

A Bronx Castle

"Remember the name Bourke," said my grandmother. "We are descendants of a noble family in Ireland, and centuries ago, great castles belonged to them."

"Castles?" I asked, like a child enchanted by a fairytale.

Ireland and the Irish Sea are far from the Hudson River and Washington Heights, New York, where I was born on a cold January day in the Chinese Year of the Dragon. Noble heritage and great, lost castles had meant nothing to me then. I had entered this world struggling to breathe. My heartbeat was faint—I was half dead, strangled by my mother's umbilical cord. Some cultures would say my entrance into the world was lucky and others that it was unlucky, but life has given me a mixture of both good luck and bad. I survived. Maybe it was the luck of the Dragon or the luck of the Irish. As one who believes in God, I think He had other plans for me that day. Sitting in my grandmother's kitchen years later, with my future yet to be written, our distant past was spread over the table, where it held a strong fascination for me.

Helen Monihan File, or Nan, as I called my paternal grandmother, would sit at one end of the table beside the window in her long, tube-like kitchen. She was shorter than five feet, round, and as wide as she was tall. Her silvery, white, wavy hair, once jet-black, was meticulously curled on the ends. Her porcelain white skin was wrinkle-free, and her blue-gray, twinkling eyes were set under heavy, dark eyebrows. She had a hearty, jovial laugh that often made her double over in tears.

Five years earlier, my grandfather had sat by the window and looked out at the trees in front of the apartment. He had told me he would not live to see the spring, and I hadn't believed him. But he died the day before spring officially arrived, so it had been true. He had been more like a father to me than a grandfather, so his death had devastated me.

After this tragedy, my grandmother lived alone. I would visit her in the Bronx on weekends, arriving by bus from Manhattan on a Friday afternoon. Her Irish neighbors kept a lookout for me while she cooked dinner. The first resident to see me was Fred. A permanent fixture in front of the apartment house door, he would call up to Margaret, who lived on the second floor, when the bus arrived at the corner. Margaret, with her powerful Irish brogue, would then yell upstairs, and the chain of announcement would continue to my grandmother's door. By the time the noisy, heavy, steel elevator door opened, the smell of meatloaf (a secret recipe that she kept under lock and key) permeated the air, and Nan stood smiling at the end of the long, dim hallway.

The door opposite to her apartment was closed and had remained so for many years. But there was a time it had always been open. Nanne, my great-grandmother, had once lived there under the watchful eyes of my grandmother. Nanne, or Mary Barrett Monihan, had been born in 1868, right after the Civil War, and was ninety when she died. There was something frail and mystical about her. Her ghostly appearance frightened me—white hair, skin, and bluish white eyes. She was blind, though to what extent we didn't know, because she refused to visit a doctor. When I was small, and with the security of my grandmother's hand in mine, I would enter my great-grandmother's apartment. All around the bedroom were huge, life-size religious statues of the saints, Mary, Joseph, and Christ on the cross. As a small child, I would look into the face of the Virgin Mary—we were both the same height—and admire her glazed, ceramic beauty. The old tradition of covering the statues in black for mourning was observed in Nanne's room right before Easter. One time, when I was a child, the phone had rung in my grandmother's apartment, and she had left me alone at Nanne's bedside to go and answer it. I had stared all around at the statues covered in black cloth and had started to tremble. Then I had seen Nanne lying on the bed, as though she were in a trance, shaking and mumbling prayers or words that were undistinguishable. The minutes had seemed to last an eternity, and I had cried until Nan walked in and found me.

"Why are you crying?" she laughed.

"I'm afraid of Nanne and the black statues," I sobbed.

"There is nothing to be afraid of," she consoled. The matter was closed to her, but I never forgot it.

One glance at the closed door would always bring back that memory. I would turn to my grandmother, who kissed me and welcomed me inside. When our eyes met, it was like looking into a mirror, but the resemblance stopped there. My height, ample forehead, high cheekbones, and profile had all been inherited from my German grandfather. I also had inherited the strain of reddish-blonde coloring that often appears in a family of dark Irish. This phenomenon is attributed to the invasion of the Vikings centuries ago, when the invaders had left their mark on the Emerald Isle forever.

After dessert, the table would be cleared of dishes and a yellowed, worn-out, cardboard photo box would come out. This box was filled with stories of our past, stories that I never tired of hearing.

"Our ancestors originally came from Normandy," she would explain, "and castles were awarded to them for their bravery and valor in war. Centuries later, they were stripped of everything, including the castles, by the English. They had chosen to embrace the Catholic religion, preferring the riches of heaven to those of earth. They lost their property and titles, spiraling to the depths of poverty."

Nan had remained a devout Catholic, and she possessed a kind of nobility that had come from our ancestors. Her palace was this tiny apartment in an Irish ghetto in the Bronx. I knew she had played the violin before I was born, but I never heard her play. However, she had already decided that I would not follow in her footsteps as a musician; instead, I would become the family's ballerina.

When I was seven, I would watch her, in a familiar ritual, place her flowered hat perfectly on her head, don her white gloves, and slip her large handbag over her arm. Then, with determination, she would take me by the hand as we marched off to Radio City Music Hall.

"Maybe someday you will dance with the Radio City Music Hall ballet company," she said with love and conviction, as she looked down at me.

We never had to wait in the long lines, where a wait of two to three hours for tickets was not uncommon. Nan would always purchase tickets well in advance, so we got to wait in the short lines. Every time the show changed, we made our cultural pilgrimage to see the ballet company in a new production. My love for dance was born there, and by the time I was nine years old, I knew I wanted to be a ballet dancer.

"Eventually, they would make their way to the shores of America," she would conclude her story, "and the hunger boats carried the Irish here with hope for a new life."

Whenever I would visit, we would stare in silence beyond the window of Nan's apartment on Sedgwick Avenue in the Bronx. The old family photos were all over the kitchen table, with the faces of our ancestors staring up at us. I had no idea then that destiny would one day take me to Europe, where I would dance in an Austrian ballet company.

The water in the reservoir across the street shimmered like a carpet of gold sequins on a stage, under the intense, theatrical light of the sun. On the other side of this immense stage stood the backdrop of Hunter College, which was the closest thing to a real castle that I could imagine at the time. The light would become gold, copper, then red as the sun went down and the stage went dark. The curtain had come down on another day, but a white spotlight from the moon remained to guide the way to the Hunter College castle. Born that night was my dream of finding out who I am and where I came from. Guided by the light, I vowed that I would go to Ireland one day to find our lost castles, if they still existed.

My grandmother Nan

From the left: My mother, me, Nan, and Nanne

CHAPTER 1

Holidays in Hollywood

"Until you carry a dream in your heart,
You will never lose the meaning of life."
Gandhi

Sixteen years later, I sat at the window of the train compartment that was carrying me to the next chapter in my life. It was August of 1987, and the heat and humidity were stifling, even though it was only eight o'clock in the morning. The train trip had begun in Munich at midnight and was going to culminate in Venice. I had made this same trip many times before.

In my early twenties, I had left the United States and landed in Germany. It was a German friend from my days of studying at the School of American Ballet who had first brought me to Germany. Later, I joined the Stadttheater in Klagenfurt, Austria. But before beginning my contract there, I had wanted to visit Venice, so I had set out to see it for the first time and had fallen in love with the mysterious, magical city.

Now I looked out at the Venetian lagoon, which had become so familiar to me over the years. This trip was different. I was not visiting: I was going home. Confirming this fact was my Yorkshire Terrier, Charlie, sitting on my lap. I had bought his one-way ticket, *hund,* in Germany, along with mine. The train slowed on the Liberty Bridge, giving me time to think and reflect on where I had been and where I was going. *How had I gotten here? What chain of events had brought me to Venice now?* Oddly, it was a production called *Holidays in Hollywood* that had given me my ticket here.

***

It had all begun the year before, in the late summer of 1986. I was living in Los Angeles and teaching ballet, when I was offered a project to choreograph a fundraising show for an organization of designers in L.A. Each year the fundraiser raised money for a scholarship, awarded to an aspiring design student. That year, the organization had decided on a dinner/show fundraiser.

The board had deliberated whether to use professionals or amateurs and had decided on the latter. The organization was filled with talented people, many of whom were former singers and dancers. An audition, directed by me, was scheduled at the ballroom of the Beverly Hills Hotel where the show was to take place. The event was scheduled for before Christmas, so we had three and a half months to prepare.

The audition moved along, and when it was over, I had a funnyman, a tenor, a dance partner, a singer/dancer, and a pianist, all from the male tryouts. Two of the women were ex-Las Vegas dancers who were still in great shape. The most talented among the women was Verna, a tall, big-boned singer, with a strong, gifted voice and the character of a diva.

The board of directors decided that the production would be called *Holidays in Hollywood,* since it was to be a variety show in December, and I chose a selection of pieces from Broadway for the performance. The costumes were designed and made by a woman named Sandy. The rehearsals were underway and the songs and dances were coming along nicely. However, the complexity of the different personalities working together began to heat up, starting on day one. Immediately, the former Vegas dancers, Jean and Beth, had taken a strong disliking to me. They were constantly chewing gum and wearing sour expressions, complaining that the dance was too difficult.

"This choreography is impossible!" complained Jean, who was always the spokeswoman for the two of them.

Beth kept chewing gum and rolling her eyes. But the problem with Jean and Beth was the stiletto high-heels they insisted on wearing while dancing. I didn't know how they could walk in those shoes, much less dance in them! From the beginning, they left each rehearsal angry, constantly threatening to quit. Everyone, including me, secretly wished they would, but they didn't.

For a while, we rehearsed at a couple of recreational centers in Los Angeles, but then we switched to the Falcon Studios in Hollywood. The Falcon Studios had a brilliant, noteworthy past. The owner, Ralph Faulkner, was a legend in Hollywood. An Olympic fencing champion and silent screen actor, he had continued to act and fence in films until the age of ninety. He had been the fencing coach to many actors and had choreographed the sword fight between Errol Flynn and Basil Rathbone in *Captain Blood*. Mr. Faulkner's niece had arranged everything with me, and we worked exclusively at night, after the working hours of the cast.

"One other thing," the niece said. "Please keep an eye on Mr. Faulkner."

The first night rehearsing at the Falcon Studios, I arrived a half hour earlier and was greeted by Mr. Faulkner himself. He was a tall, charismatic man, even at his advanced age. His stern expression seemed to say, "I don't want you here in my studio." Then he held out his hand and I gave him mine. He gripped it tightly, as though he had caught me in some criminal act.

What's happening? His grip tightened and then he suddenly burst out in laughter.

"You see. I'm still as strong as a young man!" After that initial test, he became very friendly, but my hand hurt the rest of the night.

It seemed as though the ghosts of Errol Flynn and other famous Hollywood stars floated through the rooms and embodied the space—the place was like a museum to Hollywood's golden years. That first night, Mr. Faulkner would walk by the door of the studio constantly and look in on us with skepticism. I asked him if he would like to come in and watch; reluctantly, he accepted. As the night went by, I could see he was enjoying the rehearsal. After that, he became a regular presence at our meetings. When we finished rehearsing, two performers, Dean and Jerry, would drive Mr. Faulkner to his home. This became our routine, and the show united all of us together like a family.

The nights we didn't rehearse, I went over to Sandy's house to help with the costumes. We drank a lot of coffee to keep us awake late, so we could work as long as possible. Patterns were spread out on the wooden living room floor, and I cut the fabric with them. Sandy did the sewing, and we moved along quickly and efficiently together. As we worked, we shared some stories of our lives and experiences.

Finally, the big night in the Beverly Hills Hotel arrived. The ballroom was elegantly decorated for Christmas and packed with people. It was like something from a film of the golden era of Hollywood. Everyone was dressed in their finest gowns and tuxedos. We had dinner by candlelight before the show, but I barely ate because I didn't want to have a heavy stomach while performing. After dinner, all the performers slipped away to change into costumes, while the audience finished their meals with coffee and after-dinner drinks.

The stage went dark and our emcee Jerry came into the spotlight to warm up the audience with some jokes. Then the show officially began with Verna, Val, a singer/dancer, and Jerry singing "Wilkommen," from the musical *Cabaret*.

The finale of the show was the same as that of the musical *A Chorus Line*. With loud applause echoing in the ballroom/theater, the cast brought me out on stage and presented me with an enormous bouquet of red roses, which I had difficulty holding in my arms. Inside the bouquet was a long white envelope with a card inside. I struggled to hold the flowers as I opened the envelope, and I was dumbfounded when I found a plane ticket to Venice for Christmas! That instant will remain in my heart forever. Along with the great satisfaction of a successful show, I had been given love and appreciation from the entire cast. That is what I will always remember.

Why Venice? How had they known? During the coffee and costume-making nights I had spent with Sandy, we had talked about many things, and I remembered that one of them was Venice. I hadn't realized then that she was putting something together for me, based on our discussions.

***

The day after the show, I experienced a sense of relief that months of work were over and everything had gone so well. But there was also a sense of emptiness, as though I had given birth. The project that had developed and grown inside me was now separated from me forever. The process of creation had finished with the performance.

The gentle waves of the Pacific quieted these turbulent thoughts as I looked out to sea, sitting by the window of my favorite Malibu restaurant and enjoying the view before me. To make the scene even more spectacular, an occasional whale emerged from the ocean in the far distance. Though it was December, it was like summer along the California coast.

Why would I want to be any other place? I had chosen to live here for the warm climate and the ocean. Then I pulled the coveted plane ticket to Venice out of my handbag and stared at it. *Why would I want to leave this sunny, summery weather to go to cold, dark, and damp Venice?*

I thought that maybe I should cash in my ticket to Italy and save the money for the dance school I dreamed of having someday. But the ticket money would never come near the amount I would need for a school; it would be a drop in the bucket. So I chose to go to Venice. Because a part of me seemed always to be there, I wanted to see if the other part of me belonged there too. Only then could I decide if I was meant to live in California or in Italy. I put the ticket back in my bag and vowed to call my friends in Venice to let them know I was coming for Christmas.

***

Before I left for Venice, Sandy gave a cast party at her home so we could officially close the triumphant *Holidays in Hollywood* chapter and say goodbye. Verna had been discovered by a record company producer and was thrilled to be negotiating her first record contract. Jean wasn't able to come because she had broken her ankle getting out of her car in her high-heeled shoes. Sadly, I understood that I would probably never see most of these people again.

Before the evening was over, Val, the singer/dancer, took me aside and said that she had a small present for me. I opened the package and stared, speechless, at a carved, brass elephant. During the period of rehearsals, we had been on the phone every night. She would cry that she didn't have the courage to go through with the performance. But by the end of the call, I would convince her to continue.

"I will never forget you and the courage you gave me," Val said. I never saw her again, but the brass elephant still reminds me that I was able to help her achieve her dream. And the ticket to Venice, the fantastic gift from the *Holidays in Hollywood* cast, would help me travel the path to my own dreams.

Beverly Hills Hotel, *Holidays in Hollywood* rehearsal with my partner

CHAPTER 2

A Ticket to Venice

"The journey of a thousand miles begins with one step."
Lao Tzu

I took a flight from Los Angeles to Europe in December of 1986. Instead of flying directly to Venice, I changed my flight plans to go first to Munich, where I stopped to see some old friends. Snowy, cold Munich gave me a shock after the warm California weather I had left behind. After visiting friends, I took the train, an eight-hour trip, down to Venice. The midnight Dolomite Express always reminded me of the first trip I had made there in 1975. Italy had no snow on its plains, and it wasn't as cold as Germany. By eight o'clock in the morning, the sun was up and the train was making its slow-motion approach across the Liberty Bridge.

Going back in time on this bridge, I would always lose myself to the surroundings. An occasional gondola could be seen from my window in the second-class *carrozza* compartment. Stepping off the train at the Santa Lucia station, I was hit by the piercing chill and damp air that made Venice seem colder than Munich. But I was immediately warmed by the sight of my friend Katia, waiting for me. We hugged each other—we had been friends for the past thirteen years. She had been eleven when I first met her, two months before I signed a contract to dance in the ballet company of the Stadttheater Klagenfurt. Her uncle Paolo, a local artist, and I had been romantically involved for almost a year. After the romance was over, I had remained friends with his family.

Katia had been studying English at school when we first met, and her parents were happy that she had had someone to practice with. She wrote letters to me in English for years, and I had especially enjoyed reading them when I was touring with the circus. Her knowledge of English eventually landed her work in the tourist industry. After I left the circus, I had decided it was time for me to learn Italian. So, between the two languages, we managed to communicate and learn from each other. I hadn't seen her since my move to Los Angeles. Now she was married to a gondolier.

We took the *vaporetto,* a kind of water bus, to Giudecca, across the Canale della Giudecca, on the other side of the main island. Rather than seek the heat inside the boat, we couldn't resist standing on the deck outside. The winter sun shone on us like a gift, though it gave little warmth. This trip by boat was always exhilarating, even with the icy, cold wind blowing against our faces. I felt very much alive, with the biting, sharp, even painful sensation touching my skin. Though we moved through the water in a powerful, modern boat, buildings from centuries ago ferried us back into the past.

The anticipation was great as we came closer. I hadn't seen Katia's family in a few years. The huge Redentore Church, with its enormous cupola that could be seen as far away as St. Mark's Square, was our boat stop. The magnificent structure came closer and closer as the vaporetto arrived at our final destination. We disembarked on the small dock and walked through the wooden, windowed shed that serves as protection against bad weather for the waiting passengers. The building rolled in the wake of the boat, and we struggled to keep our balance. The doors of the church were in front of us, but instead of entering, we made a sharp turn to the left, following the sidewall of the church. An iron gate squeezed between two buildings led to a beautiful garden. Next to the gate was a column of buttons with residents' names etched in brass. Katia pressed one button that opened the gate, just like a magic password, into the garden. To the right, parallel to the garden path, was a two-story, modern structure with windows. A curly-haired redhead popped out of one window on the first floor and smiled.

"Ciao Barbara!" Katia's mother Sonia cried out.

"Ciao Sonia!" I returned.

This same exchange had repeated itself every time I had visited her in Giudecca for the past thirteen years. We embraced each other and studied the physical changes that the years had made on both of us.

"Sei sempre uguale." (You are always the same.) We exchanged these words to each other with approval.

Katia's father Tony greeted me, along with other family members. Then I was led to the table. It has always amazed me how a weary traveler can arrive at an Italian home and find a hearty meal awaiting her. The plate was set and I was welcomed into the family. In the next few days, we celebrated Christmas together. I alternated my stay between Sonia in Giudecca and Katia on the main island of Venice, where she lived with her husband Fabio in the area named Giardini. Both of them made me feel at home. I had constantly moved around in California, so I had no sense of permanency in my life. I had been homeless at various times in the five years I had lived there. Fortunately, there had always been a kind friend who had given me temporary lodging, so Charlie and I had never had to sleep in the car. Venice represented stability to me: it never changed.

***

The last time I visited Venice was five years earlier. Again, it was Christmas, and I was the guest of a friend, the Austrian artist Frederick Hundertwasser. I had received an invitation a couple of weeks earlier from Frederick, inviting me to attend a party to be held at the United Nations in his honor for designing a special stamp collection for human rights. After the reception, we met for dinner one night while he stayed in New York. I asked him where he planned to go for Christmas, and he said he was going to Venice.

"I wish I could be in Venice for Christmas," I replied.

Then a few days before Christmas, I received a surprise telephone call from Austria.

"A ticket is waiting for you at Alitalia. Hundertwasser is expecting you in Venice," said his secretary Janine. There had been no place for me to go that Christmas, so I was thrilled to accept his gift.

I lived a fairytale week in a decadent villa on the island of Giudecca. The Venetian villa had been the former home of Igor Stravinsky and had once been owned by the King of Greece. There was a private bridge to the entrance door and a high brick wall surrounding the grounds. The magnificent, enormous garden within these walls contained a small guest house where Frederick painted. There was a large swimming pool that had become a dark, muddy pond with wild flowers growing in the water. Trellis-covered paths were entwined with green vines that bore flowers in the spring. We often associate Venice with canals, but hidden behind many Venetian doors are incredible gardens. I was able to spend time with Katia and her family on Christmas Day. The place where I stayed and the home where they lived were separated only by the Redentore Church. At night, Fredrick and I sat reading books by the warm fireplace. Because he was a man of few words, I remember everything he ever said to me.

"Read this," he commanded, as he handed me a book about the famous painter Grandma Moses.

It was his way of saying that it was never too late to find inspiration, which I had yet to find. When I returned to New York after that Christmas, I packed for the move to California.

***

Now I was back to where I had left off five years earlier. I cherished the time I spent alone in Venice, drifting through the tight streets, or *calli*. The street artists that I knew so well collected in groups along the waterfront. We reminisced about the nights we had danced away our youth until the early hours of the morning. The owner of the nightclub would serve us a plate of *spaghetti, aglio, olio,* and *peperoncini* at four o'clock in the morning, the closing time of the club. The artists had aged quickly from their constant exposure to the outdoors, day and night. Their youth was gone, and many had become hard-working family men.

History had imprinted the Byzantine architecture on Venice, giving it the look of an exotic Arabian fairytale. But the historical occupation of the Austrian Empire would leave something of its own: the elegant Viennese cafés in Saint Mark's Square. The cold weather made me crave hot chocolate, so I decided to splurge at one of the famous Viennese establishments, Café Quadri, where the musicians stayed inside in the winter. While I was enjoying hot chocolate, they began to play the melancholic "Anonimo Veneziano." The music is from a romantic, Italian love-story film. I had seen the film from the outside in and from the inside out. The apartment of the two lovers, with its incredible view of Saint Mark's Square, had been the first home and studio of Hundertwasser. Many times I had had the privilege of seeing this spellbinding view, just as the lovers had seen it together in the film. For the entire year I spent traveling on tour with "The Greatest Show on Earth," my little tape recorder had played the movie theme. It had accompanied me in my roomette on the circus train and reminded me of Venice. Now my eyes filled with tears as I once again heard it played live. Every time I listened to the piece in Piazza San Marco, I would think about how fortunate I was to have another opportunity to see my beloved Venice again.

By the end of my vacation there, I knew I wanted to stay forever. California was beautiful, but it held nothing for me. I had found my other half. I knew I was meant to live my life in Venice. *But how could I stay?* Unless I could find work or marry a Venetian, it would remain a romantic fantasy.

"If only I could get a teaching job here, I could stay permanently," I told Katia.

There was nothing she wanted more than to help me stay in Venice, so we sat down and made a plan. We wrote down the addresses of all the dance schools in Venice, the Lido, Mestre, and Mogliano, and I planned to send a resume to all of them as soon as I returned to California. It was a long shot but worth the try. The day of my departure came, and after goodbyes to Sonia and her family, Katia and I left for the train station and my long trip back to Germany. From Munich, I would catch my flight back to Los Angeles. We looked at each other as we said goodbye, but something was different—we both felt it. Katia was the first one to speak.

"Barbara, I feel as though we will see each other soon."

There was a good feeling as we said goodbye, as though it wasn't really a farewell.

"I feel the same, so let's not say goodbye but see you soon," I said.

The train pulled away, and we smiled as I waved to her. There were no tears of sadness or any uncertainty that we would see each other again.

***

I flew back through time and weather changes, a difference of nine hours and sixty degrees, to the land of sunshine, California. Looking around at the streets and buildings in Los Angeles, I felt as though I had traveled in a time machine. The cultural shock took a couple of days to wear off. I was back to driving my old Honda long distances, rather than walking or taking a boat. My ballet classes were full, and a couple of the schools had waiting lists, so I was always busy. Nevertheless, I sent out a resume and letter to each school in and near Venice.

Work kept my mind focused on the present. There was a small amphitheater in Topanga Canyon, named after the well-known character actor Fritz Feld who lived in that small community. I had been invited to perform the *Dying Swan* at night in this simple stone arena, surrounded by forest and mountains. What added to the beauty of the performance was the sound of the mountain lions and other wild animals, along with the piano version of "Dying Swan." It was here that I had the pleasure of meeting Fritz Feld for the first time. He loved ballet and felt that all children should have the opportunity to study this art. As we discovered common ground, we became friends.

The months passed, and I had all but forgotten about the resumes I had sent to the different dance schools in Venice. Then in April, I received an excited call from Katia. A school in Venice had called her about my resume and said they needed me for September. The owner of the school, Dina Marcielli, didn't speak English, so all negotiating would have to be done by Katia. I was numb—it was a dream come true! I had to be there by the end of August, so I made a one-way reservation to Munich. Again, I would take the Dolomite Express from Munich down to Venice.

Along with my happiness about this wonderful news, there was also sadness to reckon with. I would have to say goodbye to my faithful students. Then there was my preoccupation for Charlie, my mother's Yorkshire Terrier, who was very old and had lived with me since my mother had died. *Would he live through a trip across the ocean?* I asked the veterinarian, and he thought that Charlie would live through the trip but he wouldn't live much longer because of his advanced age, blindness, and arthritis. I had to face his mortality when I made the decision to leave the United States and the last living connection to my mother: Charlie.

***

The original plan had been to fly to New York before flying to Munich and then to go on to Venice by train. There were things that I had left unfinished in New York when I moved to Los Angeles five years before. All my personal possessions were in a storage room in a warehouse on Twenty-Third Street, and I needed to check on everything. I decided I would ship everything over to Europe once I was settled there. The other thing that I had left unfinished was the relationship with my father. Five years before, we had had a terrible fight, and I had not spoken to him since. Now that I was stopping over in New York, I wondered if I should contact him. We had never been close—he was distant, both physically and emotionally. He had always chosen jobs that required him to travel all the time or to live in another state. As a result, I had had a close bond only to my mother. When he came home, he would make our lives miserable. But there were also good things I remembered about my father. When our terrier Suzy had died, my mother was crushed and my father wanted to give her another puppy to substitute for her great loss.

"I couldn't love another dog so soon after losing Suzy," she had said.

But when my father had brought Charlie home for the first time, the puppy had jumped into her lap and she had loved him immediately.

When my mother had had to have a mastectomy, my father had gone out and found another woman right away. My mother died of breast cancer ten months later, and he had remarried within a couple of months. This is what had triggered our last argument. I remember the words so well. "Why wait?" my future stepmother had asked.

My mother's body wasn't even cold, and my father married another woman. I hated him for his betrayal.

"She will never know," he had whimpered.

Was it possible that a person could change? The man I wanted to find again was the one who had given Charlie to my mother, not the person who had done terrible things to us. I decided to see a counselor to explore my feelings and make a decision about whether to see him or not. After a few sessions, a therapist helped me come to terms with the past.

"You are stronger than you think. Your father can never hurt you as he did when you were a child," she told me.

So I wrote a letter to my father and sent him my phone number, thinking that if he didn't call, then I would know he wasn't interested in seeing or hearing from me again. But he did call. It was awkward and strange at first, but eventually we agreed to meet at the airport in New York.

I promised everyone that I would come back to Los Angeles if, for some reason, I wasn't happy in Venice, but saying goodbye to my students was painful. I sold my faithful Honda Civic for the same price I had bought it for, eight hundred dollars. It had been my dependable companion across the desert many times, and I had accumulated enough mileage to cross the country five times. It had taken me everywhere, without any mechanical problems, but I certainly wouldn't need a car in Venice. Then I went to say goodbye to Fritz Feld and his wife Virginia in their Topanga Canyon home.

"We want to hear that you found your true love in Italy," said Virginia.

"We hope you find a handsome count and live happily ever after in a beautiful castle," said Fritz, with his German accent.

I doubted the part about the handsome count, but the part about the castle reminded me of the promise I had made in my grandmother's kitchen years before.

***

This is how it came to be, in the summer of 1987, that I found myself moving to Italy. Beyond the train car window and the Venetian Lagoon was the Adriatic Sea. Though I loved Italy, I have no Italian blood in my veins and no link to the country. I knew *how* destiny had brought me here, but not *why*. It occurred to me that the Irish Sea was a mere two hours away from Italy by plane. I had made it across the ocean and to Europe, but would I get to Ireland and find the castles of my ancestors? *Would I chase after those castles until I found them one day or just give up the dream?*

I understood then that I still had a long way to travel before finding the answers. This train was carrying me to a new life, just as the hunger boats had done for my ancestors.

Hundertwasser's villa in Venice

CHAPTER 3

The Anonymous Venetian

"No artist tolerates reality."
Nietzsche

My new home was down in Via Garibaldi, at the extreme tip of the island of Venice toward Lido beach. Ironically, this area was named *Castello,* or Castle. I had never been to this part of Venice. It was off the tourist beat. The street was wide, with shops and restaurants on both sides. At a certain point, a canal divided it down the middle. Katia and I took the left side, passing a small bridge that connected the other half of the street. Immediately after the bridge was a door. She rang the bell, and a very nervous, swaybacked, fiftyish man by the name of Antonio opened it. He was the caretaker for the apartment. After introductions, he led us down a seemingly endless hallway. Even from the entrance, I could see a lush garden beyond.

The large room at the end of the hall was partitioned. Two bedrooms had been created, making the living room smaller, by the addition of Japanese shoji paper walls. The dining area, with a large table for many guests, was parallel to the huge ceiling-to-floor window overlooking the garden. On the same side was a small, narrow kitchen, with a door opening into the garden. Next to the kitchen was the bathroom, also with a door to the garden. From all doors, there was a step up to go outside, where a terrace with a roof offered protection from rain and sun. Another long table was placed on the terrace for outdoor dining. Extending outward was a marvelous garden, with a small path and a couple of large, old trees, all surrounded by a high brick wall. On the other side of this wall was a canal. This was my new home!

Antonio gave me his phone number in case I needed anything and left us. Then Katia looked at me and asked,

"Well, what do you think? Do you like the apartment?"

"I love it! I've never lived in such a beautiful place."

Katia had to return to work. Before leaving, she showed me the provisions and supplies that she had packed in the cupboard and refrigerator so that I wouldn't have to worry about shopping the first day. I continued to walk around my new home in disbelief. The garden, shoji walls, and the openness resembled a tropical getaway rather than an apartment in the ancient city of Venice. It was definitely a far cry from my roomette on a circus train, where I lived on tour for a year, traveling all over the U.S. with the circus.

"What do you think of our new home?" I asked Charlie. He couldn't see his environment, and I noticed the trip had taken a toll on him. He moved slowly and carefully around the rooms.

My employer, Dina Marcielli, was away on vacation, so I had time for myself until she returned. One day I strolled aimlessly around Venice and soaked up the humidity, along with the idea that this was now home. I stopped for a cool drink in a small café and almost choked when I looked up and saw my name in huge letters on the wall. *Oh my God!* The poster was a large black and white photo of a dancer dressed in practice clothes. The ballerina was in the middle of a jump, and in the background was the island of San Giorgio. There was the name of the Dina Marcielli dance school, with my name under the words *Insegnante Ospite,* which means guest teacher. Everywhere, on every wall, in every piazza, there was my name on gigantic posters. I was famous! But the publicity became overkill after a while. I put on dark glasses and hoped no one would recognize me because I felt exposed. But since it wasn't my photo on the billboard, only my name, I was guaranteed some privacy. I felt notorious, as though my name were on a "Wanted: Dead or Alive" poster. All that fame was a bit embarrassing in the beginning, but I quickly became used to it.

I had unpacked the two large suitcases of clothes and emergency items that pertained to work, in case the gargantuan traveling trunk I had sent from Los Angeles arrived late. But on the day prearranged, Katia's husband Fabio pulled up by boat in the canal that faced my front door and unloaded the trunk into the apartment. Now I was truly settled in, as far as living quarters, but there were many unforeseen problems ahead.

***

When Dina returned from her vacation, she was eager to meet me. Katia took me the longest, but easiest, way to the school in Barbaria de le Tole. Beyond the door to the school from the street was a courtyard, with a mossy garden and an old, unused well in the middle. There was a door across the courtyard, which opened to a low reception area, then into the main studio. The studio was small, but it had a high, windowed ceiling that allowed the sun to stream into the crowded, damp space. Dina and her husband Fulvio greeted us. They examined me from head to feet.

"Che bella!" said Dina, as Katia presented me.

My new employer was under five feet tall, even with high spike heels. Her hair was short and bleached blonde, and her skin was heavily tanned. When she smiled, she displayed a set of buck teeth with a large separation between them, which made her look like a rodent. I found out later that Italians put little importance on their teeth. They spend an enormous amount of money on clothes, jewelry, and plastic surgery, but their teeth are left natural. Her husband Fulvio was tall, loud, and totally bald. He reminded me of Daddy Warbucks from the musical *Annie*. Dina made an appointment with me for the following afternoon to begin working on the syllabus for ballet classes. I would begin teaching professional dancers in the morning of the following week, then all of the students in September.

"Devi mangiare molto," she said. (You must eat a lot.) She explained that I would be teaching so many classes that I would become all bones if I didn't eat enough.

***

After the first visit to the school, I was determined to find a short cut for getting there. The distance was shorter from my apartment, according to the map, if I took a myriad of inside streets rather than the way I had first come. Equipped with a map, I began exploring a new route to work, which would save me time and energy. The *calli*, or streets, became more desolate and abandoned as I penetrated deeper into the heart of the area behind the Arsenale. Here was the shipyard where Venice had once built great ships, when the Venetian navy had commanded the seas of the world. The streets there were unmarked at one point. Then I found myself standing in a small piazza, overgrown with grass, in front of an abandoned church. *Where do I go now?* I followed the direction toward the school, but the unmarked calli often carried me in another direction. By the time I arrived at my destination, I was exhausted.

Every day until classes started, I carried the map and headed out by foot to find a shorter way to the school. Again, I found myself in the same piazza with the same dilemma: where do I go now? I would try another street, which would take me off into another direction, and sometimes it would connect me with a street that I had taken the day before. Years later, when I thought about it, the piazza with the empty church came to symbolize the crossroads of my life. *Which road or street would take me to my goal?* Some people discover the right road immediately, but for others, it's a matter of trial and error. I had to try them all to find the right one, but in doing so, I learned a lot. This was a roundabout way of getting to where I wanted to go, and there were many detours along the way. The strange thing was that the piazza was not listed on the map and no one seemed to know about it. Finally I planned a compromise route. I followed the route that Katia had taken me the first day, but midway along, I took the streets through the Salizada dei Greci, the Greek section of Venice, and this cut out a big portion of the distance to the school.

***

As far as eating, I couldn't find my favorite foods. This sounds crazy in a country known for its fantastic cuisine. Growing up in New York, I had experienced ethnic dishes that had become a part of my daily diet. I started to cook from scratch what I couldn't find, like bran muffins. There was an international grocery store near the Rialto Bridge where I was able to find certain ingredients and spices (at a very high price) that Italians didn't use in their cooking. The supermarket, which was a way of life in America, was just being introduced back then in Venice. However, the size was not so "super." It was just a self-service grocery store, with carts so small they looked like toys.

Fruits and vegetables were sold in the open markets at the Rialto Bridge, Strada Nuova, and in small shops dedicated to produce around Venice. I learned the hard way that the vendors could be terrible swindlers if they didn't know you. Produce was handled by the vendors, not the customers. When you chose something to buy, they would take it and turn away to wrap it. While wrapping the items, they would substitute them with produce that was rotten. The first time this happened, I burst into tears at home. The second time it happened, I became angry. The next time I bought fruits or vegetables, I had the vendor open the package so I could see what I was getting. Again, it was rotten, and the vendor was embarrassed.

"Questa verdura è marcia!" I shouted. (These vegetables are rotten!)

He said it was an accident but exchanged them for the freshest vegetables and added extra portions to calm me down. "Mi scusi, Signora," he apologized.

After that, I was never tricked again. I always checked on what I had bought after it was put in a bag. In supermarkets, I could pick the produce from the shelf. However, unlike in America, customers had to put on plastic gloves, provided by the store, before touching anything.

***

There were two curious customs in Italy that took a while to get used to, along with other oddities. When the cashiers at stores or markets ran out of change, they would give the customers either hard candy or *gettone*. I found the candy useless, but the *gettone*, which reminded me of a subway token, was absolutely essential for making telephone calls from a phone booth. So it was good to have some of them handy in my pocket. The other custom had to do with waiting in line. I liked to read while waiting in a line, but I had to give that up. People always cut in front of others. It was not considered cheating, but a game of intelligence. The attitude was that the smart ones moved up, while the stupid ones remained behind.

In August, most of the stores were closed, especially in Via Garibaldi where I lived. The shops didn't need to worry about tourists buying souvenirs, because only native Venetians resided in this *borgo*. Everything was closed during that period, with the sign *"Chiuso per Ferie,"* meaning Closed for Vacation. I found out quickly that shopping in Venice would be a nightmare.

The terrible, humid climate was something I wasn't used to either. The tile floor in my apartment was always damp because of the humidity and the moisture, which came from living in a *casa* on the ground floor. Poor Charlie was slipping all over the place. California was never so hot, and the climate was dry; and New York had air-conditioning. But Venice felt like a tropical jungle. There was no air-conditioning anywhere, except for the five-star hotels. The climate was so different that the little silver elephant necklace I had worn for ten years produced a horrible rash on my chest, something I attributed to the change in the quality of the air.

I didn't have a washing machine and there was no launderette in Venice, so I hand-washed everything. I discovered it took days for clothes to dry in that climate. Dryers were rare, costly, and they needed hours to do their job. There was no such thing as tumble-dry. The items would come out of the machine packed in a dry, wrinkled ball that only heavy-duty ironing could fix. So it was less time-consuming to let nature do the work of drying laundry, even if it took her days to do it. Progress was years behind the United States there, but in the beginning, these things seemed almost romantic to me.

It is sometimes amazing to discover our worst fears. Nagging at me was one worry: How would I explain myself in a medical emergency? I imagined being in an operating room, trying to describe my pain to an

Italian doctor. Only English words would pour out because I was too nervous to speak the Italian language. *What would happen to me?* I was afraid I could die, trying to explain what my problem was. Someday I would have the opposite problem, where I could only remember the Italian language when I became nervous.

***

I began teaching the morning professional classes, which consisted of a small group of dancers, mostly from a company in Mestre. The director, Gianfranco, also took classes with his company. The students were friendly, hardworking, and seemed to enjoy my lessons. I fumbled and stumbled with the Italian that I had studied years before at New York University. The universal language of dance is French, so this part was easy. But corrections were hard to explain in Italian. By the end of the day, I was always mentally exhausted. I wanted so much to relax and speak English, but no one understood or spoke a word of my language.

The afternoons I spent at Dina's apartment where we prepared the lessons for September.

"Vuoi una Coca Cola?" (Do you want a Coca Cola?) She always asked this before we began our work, even though I had told her I never drank it. "Don't all Americans drink Coca Cola?" she would repeatedly ask.

Communication was difficult for both of us, so I always kept a dictionary with me. One afternoon, Dina informed me that I would have to teach aerobic classes at the school. At first I thought there was a misunderstanding with the language, but she repeated this statement over and over.

"I've never taught aerobics," I explained in miserable Italian.

"Devi imparare," she responded. (You must learn.)

So I began taking her aerobic classes to learn for teaching. At first it was alien to me, but then I began to feel and look better. Within a short time, I had lost weight and my body had become more toned. The studio was packed at night with women taking the classes—the exercise trend had just arrived in Venice. This was the bread and butter of Dina's school, and it supported classical ballet, which had lost popularity over the years. Unfortunately, in the crowded space there was something very unpleasant to deal with in every class: the strong smell of body odor, which was overwhelming and sickening. The windows were always kept open, even in the winter, to ameliorate this problem. At the end of the class, there was a mad dash for the showers.

When I embarked on teaching aerobics, I learned the disadvantage in having the last class at night. The teacher would have to wait for all the students to shower, dry their hair, and dress before closing the school. Sometimes this could take hours. I wondered why they didn't shower at home. Later, I discovered that it was customary for some students to wait for the aerobic class in order to use a shower. I was informed that hot showers at home were considered a luxury, so a hot shower was a bonus included with the lesson.

While I hated closing the school late in the evening, it had certain advantages. The beauty of Venice at night was breathtaking. I could walk the long distance to the other side of the island and not encounter a soul. However, on three occasions, there was an electrical blackout in the *sestiere,* or district, where the school was located. With all the street lights out, it was totally black outside. I was terrified! The only way to get out of the dark was to finger my way slowly through the sestiere. My hands followed the walls until they found a break where another calle began. A few steps more, and the wall continued, all the way to the canal. Then I heard the soft sound of water slapping against the canal wall or rocking a boat. I knew approximately where the bridge was, and I felt for the first step with my foot. My feet and hands guided me from there, and I continued this way until, with great relief, I saw the lights of the next sestiere.

There was always a mist over the canals at night, and when autumn came, the fog set in. Later, when I moved next to the Santa Lucia train station, I would take the boat on the Grand Canal from the Rialto Bridge. Usually, at that hour of the night, I was the only passenger, and it was as though the boat were mine. I stood on deck with the boat captain and line operator, commanding my ship. The Grand Canal was filled with boats during the day, but at night we were alone. We glided along slowly on the water, through the vaporous mist. Lantern-style lights gently illuminated the buildings and created the impression of an antique gold veil of tulle over everything. The moon would cut a dancing spotlight in the rippled waters of the canal. I sensed the city was all mine, and in those moments, I was the nameless Venetian of another time.

***

The classes for children and teens commenced the middle of September. The schedule was terrible. The lessons I taught were scattered all throughout the day. I was the last teacher to be hired, so I had the worst hours. It also became apparent that my relationship with Dina was not good. She treated me like a Martian at first, but her attitude seemed to go in the direction of antipathy, with frequent anti-American remarks. As my Italian improved, I began to feel the pain of her sharp tongue. She spoke negatively about me to friends and family in my presence, using the Venetian dialect. *What did I get myself into here?* I started learning the dialect as quickly as possible, though I never spoke it. The original pay agreement was not respected either, so I had to look for other teaching possibilities. Friends of hers called me to offer extra hours teaching at their schools. Beginning in October, I set about working outside of Venice, in Mestre, on the mainland.

"Ricorda. La mia scuola viene sempre prima," Dina threatened. (Remember, my school always comes first.) My dream of Venice was turning into a nightmare. One day at lunch, I confessed to Sonia my disillusion with Dina and her school.

"Tutti non sono bravi come nella nostra famiglia," she said. (Everyone isn't good like our family.) I thought about returning to the United States, but I decided to give it more time. The romantic adventurer in me would always override the realistic one.

Charlie and I traveling

CHAPTER 4

An Italian Love Story

*"Nothing wounds, poisons,
sickens, like delusion."*
Oriana Fallaci

I will always remember the date September 17 because it was the day I met Ovidio, my first husband. It was Dina's birthday, and I had been invited to a party at her home. The evening was unbearably hot, especially in her top-floor apartment above a stagnant canal. The odor of the canal reminded me of rotten eggs. From the terrace, you could see the Grand Canal, but there was no breeze to break the stifling humidity. Inside, Dina introduced me to everyone at the party. The guests were using whatever method they could to fan themselves because the heat and stuffiness were intolerable.

She presented her brother, Ovidio, who couldn't get up from his chair to shake my hand because he had torn a ligament in his lower leg while playing tennis. Though he was seated, I could see that he was small and wiry. Ovidio, or Ovid in English, looked like the actor Roy Scheider, with a receding hairline. His huge, sad brown eyes enraptured me. He had studied ballet at the Teatro La Fenice with his sisters Dina and Lorella and still carried the upper part of his body like a dancer. His occupation was *rappresentante* for wines, liquors, and chocolates for restaurants and bars in Venice. That night I was bursting with conversation, and he politely but continually laughed at my mistakes in Italian. I asked for his help in pointing out my errors so that I could learn the language faster. By the end of the evening, we were both laughing at our awkward method of communication.

"Vorrei accompagnarti a casa, ma non posso con la mia gamba," he said. (I would like to walk you home, but with my leg I can't.) He asked me for my phone number and said he would call. Because I had always believed in love at first sight, I fell head over heels for this man named after a famous poet.

That night, I stood on the deck of the vaporetto and looked at the magical city of Venice with a different eye. It was more romantic now because I had a part in its romance. I experienced the giddiness a lover feels at the beginning of a love story. When I touched solid ground, I jumped up and down the steps of the bridges and danced all the way to my apartment. At home, I prepared a cool drink and sat in the bamboo swing that had been mounted on a tree in my garden. There I sat, rocking back and forth, looking at the stars that seemed to dance to my dizziness all night. I was high on love, a potion stronger and more dangerous than any drug. My spirit was flying, never touching the ground. However, as the weeks passed and Ovidio didn't call, my happiness turned to depression. Again, over lunch, I asked Sonia what she thought.

"Call him and ask how his leg is." But a voice inside me said not to call, so I didn't. Venice began to look like a lonely place instead of a romantic one.

***

At the same time, I had immigration problems to deal with. After one month living in the apartment, Antonio informed me that I must register with the *Questura*, Italian police headquarters, as a resident. Katia came with Antonio and me, in case there was some problem translating. The *Ufficio Straniero*, or foreigners' office, at the Questura had a long line of people waiting for permission to stay in Italy. They came from all parts of the world. Finally, it was our turn. The man who took care of the permissions was the personification of the devil. He wore a beard that came to a point at the tip, and he had a sharp widow's peak at his hairline. His face was pale, his deep-set eyes dark and cold. He studied my passport, then asked a few questions that I was too terrified to answer, so Katia replied for me. The blood rushed to his face and he began to shout at me. I didn't know what he was saying, so he stood up, as though this would somehow make me understand. With his hand, he made a gesture for us to get out, and with his voice, he continued to scream. We scurried away from the scene, trembling.

Down on the street, we were all shaken. Katia was so upset that she began to cry. I asked her to explain what he had said. "He said you can't stay in Italy!" she cried.

Back then, the European community was being formed, and only citizens of countries in Europe could get permission to live in other European countries. Those from other continents were classified as *extracomunitari*, or community outsiders, and it was difficult, if not impossible, to get permission to remain.

"Only a contract from your employer will give you the right to stay in Italy," explained Katia.

"Well, if that's what I need, I will get it from my employer." But Katia looked doubtful. I had assumed that these papers were in order before I came.

We arranged a meeting with Fulvio and Dina at the school. I couldn't follow the excited discussion in the Venetian dialect, but Katia tried to translate. Dina couldn't place me under contract because she collected a pension from the Teatro La Fenice, where she had worked as a ballet soloist. In Italy, once you collect a pension, you cannot continue to work. Her school was under a non-profit umbrella, so technically she wasn't working, even though she was making a lot of money *in nero*. The term *in nero*, or money under the table, is a way of life in Italy. A great part of the country works illegally, earning undeclared money to avoid taxes.

Fulvio decided he would use his connections to fix the problem. He was a good friend of the police chief in the Questura, so he made an appointment to see him and we went together to his office. Vincenzo, the police chief, was a small, dark, mild-mannered Sicilian.

"Unfortunately, I can't help on this," he said. "I have no power in the department of immigration. I can only put in a good word."

After a brief phone call, he directed us to the immigration office, and there at his desk sat the devil, or *Il Diavolo.* This time, we were cordially invited to sit down. Fulvio had been carrying a long tube under his arm. After a few pleading words, he stood up, and opened the tube, and unrolled the poster with my name as *Insegnante Ospite,* explaining that he had spent a fortune on publicity. Il Diavolo was in shock, and I was embarrassed, though I had a hard time not laughing out loud. Fulvio thought Il Diavolo would give me permission to stay in Venice out of pity for all the money he spent on publicizing me. Instead, he came to his feet and angrily dismissed us from his office.

"We'll find a solution," said Fulvio optimistically. But I started having nightmares about Il Diavolo.

***

I had almost given up hearing from Ovidio when he called. He apologized for not having called sooner but explained that he had been recovering from the injury.

"I couldn't walk, so I couldn't invite you to go out with me," he said. His voice was sexy and mysterious. He invited me to dinner at Dina's apartment, which I thought was a strange first date. I called Sonia to tell her the good news.

"He is taking things slow by inviting you to dine with his family." However, at dinner, Dina spoke only about the school. My reluctance to talk business at the table was viewed as a lack of interest, and she continued to pressure me. Exasperated, she yelled,

"Lei non capisce niente!" (She doesn't understand anything!) She proceeded to complain about me in the Venetian dialect, saying that my Italian was a *principiante,* or beginner's level, so I understood nothing.

Both Fulvio and Ovidio shouted, *"Basta!"* The discussion about work ended there, but the evening had been ruined.

We took the vaporetto to Arsenale, and then he walked with me the rest of the way to my apartment. I offered him something to drink before he set off on his long journey home. My apartment was at one extreme of the island and his was at the other, so he had a long trip ahead of him. He was amazed by the size and beauty of my apartment.

"Aren't you afraid to live here alone?" he asked in Italian.

"Why should I be?"

"There is a canal on the other side of the wall. Someone could climb over it from a boat and enter your house." That thought made me feel uneasy.

Ovidio said he had to leave immediately to catch the vaporetto to the train station or wait another hour for the next. He lived on a street that was parallel to the *ferrovia,* or train station. Venetians seemed to have memorized the boat schedules all over the city. We said goodnight at the door and he started to turn away. As if he had an afterthought, he made a smooth pirouette in my direction and, embracing my body like a tango dancer, he softly kissed me. It was brief—a small sample or taste—but passionate.

"Buona notte," he said. Then he walked away.

Ovidio and I continued to see each other, though it was usually over dinner at Dina's place. She was careful not to discuss work, but the conversation always came back to the school. Invitations to dinner from outside the family started coming in, and he began to present me to his friends.

During that period, I started teaching ballet classes for his cousin Sandra every Tuesday afternoon. Her studio was in Favaro, a suburb of Mestre, and it was in a *palestra,* or gym, that was part of a public school. Sandra was very different from Dina, both physically and in her personality. She was calm and articulate, and she expressed warmth toward me by frequently putting her arm around my waist or shoulder. Her large frame and age had not robbed her of a charismatic beauty. It was a pleasure to teach Sandra's students because they had had excellent training from her. Part of my work was to choreograph a ballet piece for her intermediate class, so I decided to teach them the finale of Fokine's *Les Sylphides.* I simplified the steps to accommodate their level. The students didn't respond to me at first and seemed to be distracted. Sandra could see that I had a problem. In the beginning, I thought it was my Italian, but Sandra placed her arm around my waist and smiled like a wise mother to a child.

"Sei troppo buona." (You're too good.)

"Voi Anglo-Sassoni siete molto calmi, purtroppo," she declared. (You Anglo-Saxons are too calm, unfortunately.) Everyone from Northern Europe was considered Anglo-Saxon in Italy.

"Devi frustare gli Italiani o non hanno respetto per te!" (You must whip Italians or they have no respect for you!) This sounded rather extreme.

"Alza la voce è diventi cattiva!" (Raise your voice and become mean!) I raised my voice and became more commanding, but I didn't whip anyone. The students paid more attention and were more respectful.

Now the first chill of fall could be felt in the studio, and I was introduced to another difficult aspect of life in Venice: the pervasive lack of heat. I would have to shop for warmer clothes.

The next stage of my relationship with Ovidio came on rather quickly—the introduction to his eleven-year-old son Lorenzo. Without his approval, apparently, our future was doomed. Lorenzo lived with his mother Stefania in Mestre, after a bitter separation between Ovidio and her. I got along well with Lorenzo when we met, but from that first moment, I became entangled in their family drama. After dinner invitations from his friends, their wives would invite me to meet them in Venice. They recounted the family story over lunch and warned me not to let Lorenzo or Stefania destroy our happiness. In the beginning, I couldn't imagine this happening, so I didn't worry about it.

One month after we met for the first time, Ovidio invited me over to celebrate our one-month anniversary. The marriage proposal came over dinner, in the small kitchen of his apartment. I was taken by surprise, but since I believed in love at first sight, this didn't seem odd or crazy to me. It was unceremonious and unromantic, but to me it was special because, at thirty-seven years old, no one had ever proposed to me. Even though we had known each other a short time, I loved Ovidio, so I felt everything would be fine. But there were other important factors that weighed on my decision: I didn't want to go back to the United States because I was happy in Venice, though not so thrilled with my teaching job. There was no family I could return to in America. "Back home" did not exist because I had no home there. My home was now here in Venice. So I said yes.

A few days after he proposed, he came to meet me at the school.

"Dina gave me your pay for September," he told me. I thought it was very odd that Dina had given Ovidio my pay.

"Let's go shopping," he said. The weather was getting colder each day, and I had mostly light clothing from life in California. I needed to shop for the fall and winter, so we went on a clothing hunt. Venice is a myriad of small shops and boutiques, and I was used to big department stores. There were no shopping malls, so a person had to know where the shops were or stumble on them by accident. I appreciated that Ovidio was with me because he knew where to go. He knew every corner of Venice, not just because he was Venetian, but also because of his work. By the end of the day, I had bought a winter coat, some sweaters, boots, and a bag.

I received compliments on my new purchases, but what I didn't like was that Ovidio told everyone that the clothes were his gift to me. After all, it was my pay that he had used at the cash register. *Maybe I misunderstood the language?* But the reality was that I refused, in the beginning, to accept that he would lie. He would show me off to everyone, like a special treasure he had found. He made me feel important, so I overlooked his shortcomings. Among these shortcomings was a morbid obsession he had with Lorenzo.

"Can't you see I'm talking to my son? Don't interrupt us!" Ovidio snapped. This would happen when all three of us went out together on Sundays.

It was my job to be invisible when Lorenzo was present. In the beginning, Ovidio was hostile and rude to me when his son was around. After Lorenzo had gone home, he would apologize for his actions but, at the same time, try to justify them. As Lorenzo's future stepmother, I was considered a threat, the big, bad monster lurking in the shadows. Divorce and the concept of extended families were not a part of the Italian way of life, so it was difficult for Ovidio to handle.

One time Lorenzo asked me about chili con carne, because he had heard about it in Western films. I promised to cook it for him when he came over for dinner. That's when I made the discovery that stores were not only closed three to four hours at lunch time and all day Sunday, but each type of business was closed half a day on a predetermined day of the week. I had all the ingredients but the meat, so I went to the Rialto Bridge where there was a butcher store. The butcher and Ovidio had known each other a long time, so I had been presented to him a week before. But when I got to the store, it was closed. I went to another store and it was closed also, so I kept looking for one that was open. They were all closed. Lorenzo was coming over that night, so I was desperate about the chili, but there was nothing I could do.

"I will have to prepare the chili Saturday, because I couldn't get the meat," I told Ovidio.

"Everyone knows that the *macelleria* are closed on Wednesday afternoons!"

"I didn't. In the U.S., they were open on Wednesdays."

"Get America out of your head. You are living in Italia."

But the worst part of all this was that I had promised Lorenzo chili con carne—no rain check was acceptable. Having no chili for dinner was treated as a terrible, unforgivable betrayal. Though I prepared it on Saturday and Lorenzo enjoyed it, Ovidio never seemed able to forgive me for this.

The move to Ovidio's apartment was planned for the weekend before the end of the month. Because I was teaching six days a week, I could only do it on a weekend. At the last minute, Ovidio told me he couldn't help with moving because Lorenzo was staying with him. I would be on my own, hauling bags on boats. This is when I had serious doubts about our living together, much less marrying. At that moment, I realized I wasn't ready for such problems. Maybe neither of us would ever be ready and it just wasn't meant to be, though it was too soon to know that. After my Saturday classes, I sat down and cried. Parents of my students were worried when they saw me break into tears, but I didn't tell anyone the reason.

"Sto bene." (I'm okay.) I went home and thought about returning to California. Probably I could get my teaching jobs back, and I could pick up the other projects that had been suspended. Then the phone rang, and it was Ovidio. He wanted to know when I would arrive at his apartment with my suitcases, and I told him the truth: I wouldn't be coming there—not later, not ever.

"Please, don't do this. I will help you tomorrow with moving." The next morning he was there with Lorenzo, and we each took a bag to the boat dock. To me, this was a sign that Ovidio was able to compromise and that our relationship was important to him.

The following day, Charlie and I took a final look at the beautiful home that had briefly been ours. We had walked halfway to the end of Via Garibaldi when I realized Charlie didn't want to walk any farther. He was one hundred years old in canine years, and his arthritis had finally conquered him. So I carried him to the vaporetto station and found that the boats were on strike. With him in my arms, I walked from one end of Venice to the other, a forty-five minute walk. He could no longer see, so I described to him everything that I saw on this last trip together. We had traveled so often and so far. The rain began to fall, and the drops mixed with my tears. I wept as the rain fell harder. We were both soaking wet, and people stared at me, crying and speaking English to this little dog in my arms. The veterinarian's prediction that Charlie would die soon came true shortly after I moved into Ovidio's apartment. He went to sleep one night in an open suitcase, as though he were preparing for another trip somewhere. But he never woke up again.

***

One obstacle that could have changed my entire future in Italy was Ovidio's divorce from Lorenzo's mother, Stefania. They were legally separated but not divorced. She had refused to give permission for a divorce over the years, even though she had left him for another man. Again, he asked her for a divorce. His lawyer, however, tried to persuade him not to marry me.

"Don't marry a foreigner. She could be a criminal. What do you know about her family?" He proceeded to tell the story of a Venetian client who had married an Australian.

"She came from a background of criminals." He was referring to the penal colony in Australia hundreds of years ago! Most Venetians, especially Ovidio's family, did not approve of him marrying a non-Venetian, and a fate worse than death was marrying an American. Thanks to the slow postal system in Italy, even from Venice to Mestre, the divorce papers arrived after the date that Stefania could have contested it. So Ovidio was free to marry me, except in the eyes of the Church.

One Sunday, we went to visit the Basilica of San Antonio in Padua, known for miracles. We weren't there to ask San Antonio for a miracle, but simply to find a priest who would approve our marriage. Maybe we *were* asking for a miracle. We asked a young priest whose answer was ambiguous: marry in a civil service if you both love each other, but the church won't recognize your marriage. Then we found an old priest and asked his opinion.

"Definitely not! You will always be married to the woman you gave your vows to in front of God."

It was six months from the time Ovidio had proposed and the date of our wedding, April 5. During this time, I came to believe that he wasn't sincere about marriage. Whenever I would mention my feelings, he would shrug it off and tell me that we would marry in time. It seemed like he kept postponing the wedding date. Even his friends were dismayed. By then I was fluent in the Italian language and understood the Venetian *dialetto*, so when they discussed our marriage plans, I knew what they were saying,

"Do you love this woman?"

"If there is a woman at home, my son will leave his mother and live with me." This was his response—not exactly a declaration of love.

"Do you love me?" I asked him more than once.

"Of course I do," he would always answer.

Finally, I was on the verge of deportation, and I had only one more month to stay. Immediately, he went to the city hall and made the appointment for our wedding. All the arrangements had to be done quickly. When we officially announced the date, Lorenzo moved in with us. Ovidio was thrilled that Lorenzo had left his mother to live with us, but I needed to sit down when I heard the news. The prophecy of his friends was unfolding before me.

***

I don't have fond memories of our wedding day. My father and his wife flew to Venice for the occasion. We were like strangers, so it was awkward and uncomfortable, especially because they slept on the sofabed in our living room. We had met at the airport in New York before I came to Italy, but they had not invited me to stay at their apartment in Queens. Charlie and I had spent the night in a hotel, and then an old friend had invited us to stay at her place. Since I was merely a relative who was getting married, it gave them an occasion to visit Italy. Their wedding present was a modern purple Murano glass vase, the kind sold as souvenirs to the tourists in the streets. My stepmother confessed that they bought it at the Rialto Bridge market. That same day, she was furious after making a discovery.

"We paid fifteen dollars at Rialto, and downstairs they sell it for nine dollars!"

The morning of the wedding, the Marcielli family arrived at the apartment for breakfast. I had my jacket on, but I was still in my slip so my skirt wouldn't wrinkle. The wedding hat that Sandra had given me became lopsided as I baked croissants for everyone and made one cappuccino at a time with the expresso machine. It was crazy! *Why couldn't they have a croissant and cappuccino at the café downstairs?* Pina, my future sister-in-law, touched the cappuccino cup and said with disgust,

"You could have heated the cup." As if I had time for this small detail. *Why couldn't Ovidio help me?* He was doting over Lorenzo as though *they* were getting married. Finally, everyone left, and I ran to finish dressing.

Downstairs, the family waited to get a glimpse of the bride. In my navy blue suit, I looked like I was dressed for a funeral, but dark blue was *la moda* at the time, so I had no choice. The day was as dark as my suit, and

I could feel some raindrops. Our gondola waited on the Grand Canal—it was *black*. The custom is a white gondola for weddings and a black one for funerals, but we had chosen the black one to save money. As we were about to walk to our black gondola, a gypsy came up to me, grabbed my arm, and shouted her prediction that the marriage would be a disaster. Fulvio pulled her away, but she warned of a *maledizione*, a bad omen or curse. Everyone told me not to listen, but I was left trembling.

The gondolier helped me into the gondola, along with my father, stepmother, Lorenzo, and Ovidio. The rain became heavier but tolerable. Years later, I came to the realization that everyone in the boat that day hated me for some reason, except for the gondolier. They had done terrible things before, and they would do them again as time went on. As I looked back, I wondered why I hadn't jumped into the Grand Canal and swum to safety. I was wet anyway! The warnings of the gypsy extended beyond the marriage—the relationship I had with all the people in the black gondola was a curse of great magnitude.

The civil ceremony was conducted in English and Italian. Many of the students I taught at Dina's school attended the ceremony, which gave me joy. My students gathered around and hugged me. They had all chipped in and bought Murano glassware as a wedding gift. We didn't receive any presents from Ovidio's family. After the matrimony, I insisted on going to San Marco Church. Though we were not married in the eyes of the Catholic Church, I placed my bouquet of flowers at the altar of Mary. Ovidio and I lit a candle there and prayed together.

The marriage died on our wedding night. My new husband decided to sleep with his son in his room, to help him adjust to the fact that his father had married a woman who wasn't his mother. Sadly, I already had a stepmother who didn't accept me, and now I had aquired a stepson who refused to accept his father's marriage to me. Ovidio promised that things would get better and we could be together soon. But this would never happen. Alone in an empty bed, I cried myself to sleep.

Wedding Day with Ovidio

CHAPTER 5

Canvas Castles

"Something is always born of great excess; great art was always born of great terror, great loneliness, great inhibitions, instabilities, and it always balances them."
Anais Nin

I was teaching a marathon of lessons. The years became divided and recorded by the ballets I had produced those years. However, before I had my own school, the days were underscored by the cities where I taught. If it's Thursday, it must be Pordenone, or if it's Friday, it must be Treviso. Sometimes I would teach in the morning in one place and the afternoon in another. All my employers were friends and enemies to each other at the same time. They would compare notes about me. Did I give more time to one school than another? Was the choreography I prepared more beautiful and interesting for Dina's school?

Work went well with Sandra, who was now my cousin by marriage. At Teatro Toniolo, a small jewel of a theater in Mestre, I presented the *Les Sylphides* piece with Sandra's students. The ballet was a success, and it was a great experience to restage classical repertory in a theater older than the original piece. Things did not go as well in Treviso, where I taught ballet classes. Once a week, I worked for Dina'a friend Loredana. Six weeks before the school show in Treviso's Teatro Comunale, Loredana asked me to choreograph eight dances, seven solos and one group ballet. I went there every Friday, so technically I had only six lessons in which to teach the choreography. I was able to prepare and teach the seven solos, but the group dance was impossible. Groups take longer, especially when working around absent dancers.

After the second rehearsal, only one third of the dance was ready. Loredana called Dina and complained that I didn't work fast enough. The following Friday, I went to her school and found that the choreography was finished. Loredana nervously explained that her friend, a teacher from France, had arrived the weekend before and completed my choreography. She had had all week to work with the students. The solos went very well at the performance, and I will always remember Teatro Comunale as one of the foremost and spectacular of the theaters I worked at in Italy. But I decided not to work for Loredana again.

***

My first year of living and teaching ballet in Venice was coming to an end. Il Diavolo had granted me a *permesso di soggiorno,* or green card, the moment I became Ovidio's wife. I had some stability, at least for two years. Lorenzo continued to live with us until July.

After the wedding, Stefania and Ovidio had started a contest to win over Lorenzo. Each parent competed for him by giving him whatever he wanted. I was an accomplice, along with Antonio, Stefania's boyfriend, because my pay, as well as his, contributed to the competition. After the summer classes, I was unemployed until September, so I had no more money to provide. Ovidio bought an expensive bike for Lorenzo, but Antonio was able to offer a better one. Lorenzo moved back in with his mother, traded in the bike that his father had given him, and accepted the one from Antonio. The parent with the most money won. Ovidio, however, needed to blame someone, and I was his scapegoat.

"He left this house because you were a lousy mother!"

I kept my distance and waited for his next move. We had hit a very low point, but things slowly began to improve and we gradually became friends. One reason for this was that we were finally alone together, so we were able to discover each other. The other reason was that I worked more often outside of Venice, so we saw each other less frequently.

***

One thing about traveling constantly by train from one city to another was that delays were guaranteed. Strikes were unpredictable during my first years in Italy, but later they were announced in advance so the population had time to prepare. Each week, a strike "menu" was proclaimed on the news. The list detailed the strikes that would take place, whether they were for transportation or services, and the times and motives. Other times, a train could be blocked because of the discovery of a World War II bomb, placed by the Nazis years ago under a bridge or railroad track. It was a constant reminder, almost half a century later, of the war that had taken place here. Sadly, there were also suicides on the tracks or accidents that blocked the trains for hours.

My second year in Italy, I had added Portogruaro to the list of places where I taught, to replace teaching for Loredana. During the summer, a teacher by the name of Gilda had brought a group of her students to study with me for two weeks at Dina's school. At the end of the course, she had asked me to come and teach at her school one day a week. One of my memories of teaching there was a particular train strike that I got caught in. The train left Portogruaro for Venice, and within a few minutes, we were in the country, with fields all around. Suddenly, the train stopped in the middle of nowhere, and all the passengers were hustled off the train.

"Sciopero!" announced the conductor. (Strike!) We began our procession along the train tracks to the next station. It was a long walk, skirting the fields, but at least the weather wasn't bad. A couple of miles later, we arrived at the next town and train station. Two buses were parked outside the entrance of the station to haul all the unlucky passengers to Venice. As we began boarding the buses, our train slowly rambled into the station.

"Lo sciopero è finito!" shouted the stationmaster. (The strike is over!) All of us got back on the train, and off we went to Venice.

***

The most outstanding recollection of the year I taught in Portogruaro was the choreography I did for the children's show "Piccoli e Grandi Fans." It was a popular program that occasionally invited a dance school with small children to perform. Schools all over Italy were invited to audition for the one spot. Gilda desperately wanted her school to participate, so she asked me to mount the choreography. When the children were ready, she requested an appointment with the RAI TV talent scout. With six little girls, I prepared a short, simple dance to music from the ballet *Coppelia.* The talent scout was a young woman who came from Milan to see the presentation at Gilda's school. After the dance, she didn't seem to be too impressed. "We will let you know what we decide," she said in Italian.

I boarded the train home to Venice and spotted the scout in a compartment. She had to go to Venice first, before catching another train from there to Milan. We spoke about the audition on the trip. She confessed that she loved the dance but thought it lacked *something.* I tried to discover what that *something* was, as she explained how she envisioned it. By the time we arrived in Venice, I discerned that the missing piece she described and was looking for was a cartwheel.

"That's it! A cartwheel in the beginning would be dynamic!"

While a cartwheel in a ballet seemed inappropriate, I added it to the choreography. The little girl who was the soloist performed a cartwheel as an introduction before the dance started. We were accepted for the TV program and on our way! Gilda insisted on taking the children to Milan and told me it wasn't necessary for me to be there. I was okay with this because I had other teaching obligations that I couldn't cancel.

The Sunday morning show was finally broadcast in March, and I watched the program with Ovidio and some family members. The actress and host, Sandra Milo, announced my name on TV, as the choreographer. Immediately after, Ovidio called Lorenzo to see if he had seen the show. His mother angrily took the phone and told Ovidio,

"Now that your wife is a famous television choreographer, you can give us more money!"

This dampened the success of my work. The worst part was that Ovidio felt that his ex-wife was right to ask for more money from me for her son. The irony of it all was that I didn't receive a *lira* from the job! A week later, Gilda took me to lunch and told me that, unfortunately, the TV did not pay anything. The school had gotten publicity, and that was that. However, the truth came out later. The school had been paid a lump sum to cover the expenses for the choreographer and dancers, but Gilda had kept all the money.

I related this discovery to Dina, and she said she would have done the same and kept the money!

"And furthermore, I wouldn't have allowed the TV to give you credit for the choreography. *I* would take the credit because you work for *me!*" I recognized that I needed to think about going out on my own, becoming free and independent and having my own school.

"You will never have your own school because you have no money to start one. You will always work for someone else, so get used to it," said Ovidio. My strong will and determination would eventually prove him wrong.

***

In April, after the broadcast of "Piccoli e Grandi Fans," I experienced a train sciopero that lasted a few days. Dina called me and asked if I wanted to stay three days in Pordenone while the strike was on; otherwise she would ask the conservatory to cancel our classes. I jumped at the opportunity because I sensed that some time alone would be therapeutic. Ovidio and I had once again become distant after the TV program, so this three-day separation came at the right moment. I arrived in Pordenone the night before the strike commenced. The conservatory gave me a room in the best hotel, the Hotel Moderne, in the center of the city. The hotel was renowned for its restaurant, which was recommended as one of the best in Italy by the *Michelin Guide*. All of this was paid for by the city of Pordenone for the Conservatory of Music and Dance, which was very important to them.

The first day I had an afternoon of Dina's classes, and I rehearsed her dances as she requested. The next day, I was free to explore Pordenone. Then the following afternoon, I had my own lessons. Both days the students were the same, because they studied twice a week. I repeated the finale choreography of *Les Sylphides* for the intermediate class, which I had prepared for Sandra's school. In addition, for the advanced class, I adapted my own version of the opening of Balanchine's *Symphony in C,* and called it *Sinfonia.* The girls learned fast, so later on, in addition to this piece, I choreographed the Arabian Dance from the *Nutcracker* for them to perform barefoot. Each of the five girls had her own repertory solo from *Sleeping Beauty,* which I had learned from Alexandra Danilova, as a student in the School of American Ballet. We had been working on these pieces for six months, and they were all in good shape. My meals were cooked and my bed was made at the hotel, so I could think only about choreography and teaching. It was truly the perfect sabbatical for me! On the third day, the strike ended and I went home that night. Ovidio and I were happy to see each other, another bonus of the *sciopero.*

June came, and the Pordenone Conservatory, along with Dina's school in Venice, came together for the end-of-the-year show. Both schools performed in Teatro Goldoni in Venice and in Teatro Verdi of Pordenone. I contributed eleven dances, which I had prepared during the year. In addition I performed and choreographed one piece with a student. After the show in Pordenone, the mayor gave a dinner party for Dina and me to honor the work we had done for the conservatory and the city.

***

The performances ended the school year. We were closed for vacation, and I made plans to return to the United States. I was studying for the test to become certified with Dance Masters of America and planned on taking the exam in New York. One day Dina and I sat down together to discuss the future.

"I know you want your own school, and I heard about one for sale outside of Venice," she told me.

Her friend Simone knew a woman from Treviso who owned a ballet school in Conegliano and wanted to sell it. I jumped at the opportunity, and Dina arranged for me to talk to Simone.

"It is better for the family if you have your own school," she admitted. We had always had problems and disagreements when we were working together.

Simone arranged the appointment with Tiziana, the seller. She was a beautiful, petite, young blonde who was determined to finish her university studies and change her career. The studio was in an elementary school where her mother was the principal. There were eighty-five students, and the rent was low, though the monthly tuition was very cheap. The price of the school in lira was the equivalent of fifty thousand dollars, which was two years' gross pay. I had done my homework on buying and selling dance schools, so I knew it was overpriced. From my calculations, I figured that the value of the school was about half that, and my accountant figured it was worth one fourth her asking price. I made my offer for half the asking price, but Tiziana wouldn't consider it. We were both disappointed, but I held firm on my offer.

I passed the Dance Masters of America examination in New York and became a member. It was the summer of 1989. In September, Simone notified Dina that a buyer hadn't been found yet for the ballet school.

"Tiziana would like to meet with Barbara. I think she will come down in price."

We agreed on the price, but the big problem was that I had no money. We went back to the table to negotiate. I offered to pay her twenty thousand dollars over a period of two and a half years, with a deposit of five thousand right away. The deposit I put down was a loan I had requested from a bank. I signed all the *cambiali,* or certified checks, for the payments. It was risky, but I was convinced that I would succeed. After making the monthly payments, I would still be left with more money from the school than what I was presently earning by freelancing. Before anything was finalized, however, I had to go and see the students.

***

The Venice to Vienna train stopped in a small Italian town with a long name that was difficult for a foreigner to pronounce: Conegliano. Years before, when I had danced with the Stadttheater of Klagenfurt, I had often traveled on this same train from Klagenfurt, Austria, to Venice; more recently, I would pass it on my way to Pordenone. The city of Conegliano marked one hour before arrival in Venice. This was all it had meant to me at the time. The medieval village was known for superb wine and the artist Gianbattista Cima. The town is surrounded by a beautiful, prosecco-producing countryside, which was the subject of Cima's paintings from 1459 to 1517. However, it was the castle that had mesmerized me every time I traveled back and forth between Italy and Austria, and I had admired the castle with lights at night, on my way home to Venice from Pordenone. It was a real castle, not a canvas backdrop for a ballet or a painting in a museum. Cima's paintings, with the castle of Conegliano, could be seen in museums all over the world. I had never imagined, years ago, that one day this town with the castle would become a long chapter in my life. Now, for the first time, I stepped off the train in Conegliano and was welcomed by Cima's castle.

By the end of all the classes that day in Conegliano, I had a splitting headache. Tiziana had left the school in the hands of two incompetent substitute teachers for the past year, while she pursued her other ambitions.

"Are you the one that's buying this school?" asked one of the teachers, who looked like a high-school student.

"Don't bother. It's a huge *bidone*, garbage disposal!" With that comment, she walked out of the school forever.

When Tiziana arrived, she was furious to hear what had just happened. The other teacher remained and taught a terrible class. Tiziana was somewhat embarrassed, but as she had promised, there were eighty-five students that day. The dress code was "anything goes," and there was absolutely no discipline. When one group wasn't dancing, they sat in a circle on the floor, talking. My mouth fell open when a student came to take class in a mini-skirt and sneakers, with her long, waist-length hair covering her face. She couldn't *see*, much less dance! I knew I had my work cut out for me, but I was up to the challenge.

We agreed that I should be presented to the parents as the new substitute teacher. The mention of a new owner might send people running, especially if that owner was an American. A Saturday meeting was planned, and I was presented to the parents, who were skeptical.

"You have so much professional background, but we don't want our children to be professional dancers," said one mother.

"We don't want a foreign teacher to change our customs and traditions," said another.

"Americans have a different mentality. We are Italians."

But in the end, with reassurances from Tiziana, they all agreed to continue studying at the school with me. All of these negotiations took place in the month of September, while I continued to teach for Dina in Venice and Pordenone.

"Ricorda. La mia scuola prima!" Dina reminded me. (Remember. My school comes first!) I changed the schedule of my school so that I could continue teaching classes for Dina until she found a substitute.

***

In October 1989, I was the owner and teacher of my own ballet school in a small, medieval town in Italy. At thirty-eight years old, I had long awaited this moment. I had had no money and no moral support, but alone I had managed to make this dream come true, after many years of hard work. I proudly placed my Dance Masters certificate on the wall and looked around at the dance studio. The *sala gialla,* or yellow room, as it was referred to, was a space the size of a large stage. The ceiling was very high, which eventually would be an advantage for pas de deux work. Along one side of the room was a long metal ballet barre. Across the dance floor, on the opposite side of the room, were huge windows overlooking a courtyard. The sun bounced off the buildings outside the school complex and fell on the windows, so the studio was always cheerful. The light would constantly change with every season. It reflected the seasons of my life over the years—and the hopes I had for the future. The only negative feature was the yellow linoleum floor mounted over concrete, which was harsh on muscles and joints.

The students were fascinated by my accent—most of them had never met an American. Immediately, I made a strict dress code of black leotards, pink tights and shoes, and hair pulled back from the face. The students were so interested in my classes and learning that I didn't have to enforce discipline. They followed the rules and didn't challenge them because there was also the element of fear. They were not comfortable with foreigners, so they were slightly afraid of me in the beginning. After one month, their work had improved immensely. We started working on a demonstration for the parents for Christmas. The *Nutcracker* would be the end-of-the-year performance. I hoped to repeat it the following Christmas and initiate a new tradition there.

"Che cosa è Lo schiaccianoci?" (What is the *Nutcracker*?) This question came from Giorgia, a tiny twelve-year-old girl with big brown eyes. The girls knew nothing about the *Nutcracker*, and most of them had never even seen a ballet. It was not part of their Christmas tradition, and ballet companies never came to Conegliano back then. I narrated the story of the ballet and showed them pictures in the books I had. They became excited about the whole project and couldn't wait to learn the dances.

Occasionally, Ovidio would make a surprise visit to the school. He had been trained well at the Teatro La Fenice, so he could recognize talent right away.

"Che brava!" he exclaimed. "Quella bambina salta molto bene!" (That little girl jumps so well!) He pointed to an eight-year-old named Elena, who had incredible feet and a high jump. Ovidio was the first to discover her ability, even before I had. Years later, she would represent Italy at the Prix de Lausanne, the highest ballet competition in the world.

Except for classes in Venice and Pordenone, I didn't teach in any other schools. When I passed Conegliano on my way to Pordenone, I could see my school from the train. *There is my school,* I thought with great pride. The elementary school was located close to the railroad tracks in Via Kennedy, a street named after President Kennedy, who was loved by the Italian population. The school was named Scuola Elementare Kennedy, and now, coincidentally, an American was teaching ballet there. I had named the school the School of Classical American Ballet, or *Scuola di Danza American Ballet,* but most just called it American Ballet. However, it was always Cima's castle on the hill that gave the new school prestige.

One day I decided to climb the hill and visit the castle. I walked an old, narrow, cobblestone street, with stone walls on each side, leading straight up to the top. There wasn't another soul on this ancient road that day. Once again, I experienced the sensation of being in a time machine that had transported me back several centuries. The steep path was named *Calle della Madonna,* or the Street of the Madonna. After an arduous walk to the top, I discovered a small chapel, the *Madonna della Neve,* or Madonna of the Snow, culminating the passage.

The castle was built in the twelfth century, according to ancient documents that described peasants digging moats and constructing walls. The walls that protected the city within the confines of the castle still remain intact today. However, the Bell Tower and the Church of San Leonardo are the only remaining structures left to visit, along with the grounds. After the Hungarians were driven back in 1412, the other structures had been allowed to decay. I remember the castle grounds were green and well-kept, offering the peaceful atmosphere of a park. There was an incredible view of all the hills around, with a background of the Dolomites, and on a clear day, it was possible to see as far as Venice. I took a deep breath from the tower of the castle and thought: *the dream of my own dance school has finally come true.*

CHAPTER 6

The First *Nutcracker*

"He came to the David....began taking off the papers,
reading them one by one....his eyes began to mist:
for they were messages of love and acceptance."
The Agony and the Ecstasy (p.362)
Irving Stone

"You're going to need sponsors for the *Nutcracker*," said Tiziana, who continued to help with advice for the school. Dina had never needed sponsors for her shows, so I hadn't thought I would either. Between the costumes, recital payment, and tickets, she usually made a fortune. She often sold more tickets than seats in the theater, and people would scramble to find places to sit. One time, Ovidio and I had given up our seats to ticket-holders and had sat on the floor in the aisle. Even Vincenzo, the chief of police, had wandered around the theater, looking for a seat. When I mentioned this oversight to Fulvio, he laughed, but things became stricter after the Teatro La Fenice burned down. After the show, Dina would offer a dinner party in a top restaurant to her friends and family. That was the only big cost to producing her show: the dinner party.

Things were very different between Venice and Conegliano, as far as the money needed to produce a show. Teatro Goldoni charged a mere one hundred dollars, which was probably the same price centuries ago. The lighting technician and stage crew were included in this ridiculous price. On the other hand, Teatro Accademia charged one thousand dollars, and everything was extra. A lighting technician, along with his crew, had to be hired. Unlike at Goldoni, all of the stage lights had to be installed. This was another one thousand five hundred dollars. I needed scenery, and stagehands to operate the scenery, for a full-length ballet. There was also scenery that had to be built, so Tiziana was right about finding sponsors.

"The secret to finding sponsors is to have an exemplary program for their publicity," she explained.

She showed me her dance programs from past shows, and they were beautiful—all color, large, many pages, and quality paper. They were more like books than programs. So my fundraising career began with the realization that I needed to raise a lot of money if I wanted to do full-length ballet productions on a high level.

Tiziana introduced me to the most important sponsor, the Bank of Tarzo. They had sponsored the cost of printing her entire program and the *locandine,* or posters. Tarzo is a tiny village, much smaller than Conegliano, in the wine and prosecco hills only a few miles away. The modern bank was in the center of the main piazza. We decided that I wouldn't be introduced as the new owner, but as a teacher and choreographer working with Tiziana. The director of the bank was middle-aged, wore glasses, and was very businesslike. He recognized Tiziana right away, and after a brief exchange, she presented me.

"We need your sponsorship this year for the *Nutcracker* ballet. Barbara will be doing the choreography."

"Bene. Mandami il conto della tipografia," said the banker. (Good. Send me the bill from the printer.)

Outside the bank, we looked at each other and breathed a sigh of relief. The most substantial sponsor had agreed to support the *Nutcracker. It was so easy,* I thought; but I learned quickly that finding sponsorship, particularly such a large contribution, would never be so easy again. Now the drive was on to fill the program pages, but I didn't know where to begin.

In the meantime, Tiziana took me to the scenery workshop/warehouse in Quarto d'Altino, *La Bottega Veneziana,* or the Venetian Shop, as it was called. We met with one of the owners, Willi, who would become a good friend over the years. I rented a backdrop of vast windows from *La Traviata* for the party scene and a solid blue one for the snow scene. The *Nutcracker* Christmas tree that would grow in the dream would be made by the *bottega,* along with the grandfather clock. At the school, Tiziana had the set for *The Magic Flute,* which she had made into a ballet. One backdrop was the interior of a palace in sky blue, highlighted with glitter. The exterior backdrop was the perfect fairytale canvas castle on a hill, and I used this for the "Kingdom of the Sweets." Both would be a part of almost every ballet that we performed in the school. They had been made by the bottega to fit the dimensions of Teatro Accademia.

A couple of weeks later, I received a list of prospects for sponsorship from Tiziana's friend who worked in City Hall. One sponsor on the list owned an insurance company, and it was pointed out that he was prepared to make a generous contribution. After the bank, this would be our largest sponsor. The director of the insurance company was Luca Gallina, and I decided to ask him to help us pay for the *Nutcracker* Christmas tree. I called for an appointment with Signor Gallina, and his secretary gave me one for eight o'clock. The problem was that the trains were not always regular, so I had to get a train very early in the morning.

I was bleary-eyed when I arrived in Conegliano, but I saw the sun rising and the castle on the hill glowing with life as we rolled into the station. I headed to the *pasticceria* near the station for a pastry and cappuccino. The insurance company was upstairs, next door to the pasticceria, and I went there at the appointed time.

"Mi dispiace, ma Signor Gallina non c'è," the secretary informed me. (I'm sorry, but Signor Gallina isn't here.) He had been called away for the day, so the appointment was rescheduled. Signor Gallina had to break many more appointments, but I never gave up. One day I was lucky.

"Il Signor Gallina è nel suo ufficio. Attenda, per favore." (Mr. Gallina is in his office. Please wait.) I waited for an hour and mentally prepared for my speech. When the encounter came, I was so excited after waiting so many weeks that I blurted out my sales pitch to Signor Gallina before I had even sat down. It was one long sentence—I never came up for air! He looked startled, and when I had finished, there was a long silence in the office. "Who is this crazy foreign woman?" said the expression on his face.

"Va bene." (Okay.) He agreed as though he was too frightened of what I would do if he said no. The insurance company paid for the Christmas tree, and their position in the program was on the back cover, which is the prime place for publicity.

There is always one prop that launches everything. It can be large or small, cheap or expensive, but its purchase is the first step in making the production. I walked past a toy store named Piovesana on my way to the ballet school, and my eye caught a shiny silver toy trumpet in the window of the shop. One day I went into the tiny store and bought the trumpet. The owner of the store was always polite and wore a pleasant smile, but he looked surprised and confused, as though I had fallen out of the sky. He must have been wondering, "What is an American doing in Conegliano, buying toys in my shop?"

The item was the beginning of everything and is still with me today. Now it is retired from the *Nutcracker* ballet, but the horn looks as new as when I bought it. The little trumpet is my private museum piece: it reminds me of where I started and how far I've come.

***

The train after three o'clock would have gotten me to Conegliano after four o'clock, when my classes started, so I had to take the one scheduled before lunch. I had to find a place to hang out for coffee and a light snack before work. Everything was closed at lunch except for two pricey restaurants in town. There was a *gelateria* on the main street named Darling, and it was open at lunch time. The café that served gelato was owned and operated by a mother and daughter. I would dine on a five-scoop gelato, two chocolates and three vanillas, followed by a cappuccino, before leaving. Only a crazy American would eat gelato for lunch! The Italians were at home eating a healthy pasta dish. I was usually the only customer until the end of lunch, when people came in for an espresso before the shops and businesses opened. The owners generously gave me an occasional free coffee or gelato.

The gelateria became my office for two and a half years. When I finished my work, lesson plans, choreography, or business, I would read to relax before teaching. Often the owner's daughter, Lorena, would sit down, smoke a cigarette, and talk with me when the café wasn't busy. After the first year, parents would call me at the gelateria because they knew I hung out there, and it became known as the studio office.

***

I continued to hunt for props and sponsors to pay for them. Each and every student wrapped the Christmas presents under the tree. It was homework for the Christmas vacation—not the easiest of projects for them, since the selection of ribbon, bows, and paper was limited in Italy. The most important prop was the nutcracker itself, but in Italy, this wooden doll did not exist because the story was not part of their culture. Germany was practically next-door, and there you can find nutcrackers everywhere. I called a friend in Munich and asked him to send one, after explaining the type and size that I needed.

Some props were not so easy to find. Venice was fascinating to explore in depth, and there were calli that even Ovidio had never walked. On these lesser traveled streets, there were shops that had somehow remained frozen in time. The owners were usually long past retirement age, and the products in the store belonged to the past. Under layers of dust, a person could find something that she had been searching for for years. In one of these forgotten stores, I found metal and wooden toy-soldier rifles that were practically antique, and I paid the original price from years ago.

The most challenging and costly props in the battle scene were the rat masks. Venice has always been famous for its masks, but they are very expensive, especially if bought in quantity. The rat masks had to look authentic and scary—I refused to compromise. Ovidio helped by investigating stores off the beaten track that didn't cater to tourists, where the prices were cheaper. Many of these shops, or *botteghe,* as they were called, had workshops on the premises. Very few artisans did animal masks, because they were less popular and more complicated to make. Finally, Ovidio found a young artisan who specialized in animal masks in the labyrinth of calli on the other side of the island. He offered an inexpensive price for the stamp or mold for the mask and a discount for the number I needed.

***

Back in Conegliano, I returned to the search for sponsors. I had to find one who would buy a full-page ad to sponsor the masks. One of the names on the list was a sofa and chair upholsterer, *Corinto*. Signor Corinto was a smiling, grandfatherly man with enormous hands. He looked like a strong bear that could lift the sofas and chairs he upholstered over his head, so I was surprised when he spoke so fondly of classical music. In the end, he agreed to a full-page sponsorship. Signor Corinto would go on to sponsor every ballet my school would perform, and he always requested to sit in the same place.

Before I left his office, he suggested,

"Perché non fai un balletto di Stravinski?" (Why don't you do a Stravinsky ballet?) The *Nutcracker* was the best ballet to start with because the dancers had very little experience technically.

Once I had the sponsors in place for certain expenses, I concentrated on finding the people for the key roles. The oldest student in the school, Marta, was nineteen, and she continued studying with me. Her experience on pointe was limited, so I decided to have her dance the role of Clara. Marta would dance a simple pas de deux on pointe with the Nutcracker. *But who would play that role?* Marta's neighbor and friend was a champion in wu shu kung fu, and he was interested in learning how to dance with a partner. However, he was worried that classical ballet was too feminine.

"Lui non vuole calze di danza o trucco," Marta told me. (He doesn't want dance tights or makeup.) I promised Moreno, the wu shu champ, that he could wear pants instead of tights and no makeup, so he agreed to work with us. Moreno was handsome, charismatic, and had the presence of a male dancer. He didn't want to look feminine so there was resistance in his movements, and the usual mistakes in partnering were made. However, they would spend hours together at the studio, practicing each new lift and the choreography, and soon I could see they were making progress.

For the Christmas party scene, I needed adults with some experience on stage to portray the guests. Marta knew of a talented acting company named Colonna Infame that performed locally around Conegliano, and they agreed to work with us. I chose one character actor, Roberto, to play Herr Drosselmeyer and the Rat King, and he would fight Moreno in the battle scene. They would have no dialogue in the scene, only mime and music. It was important that their actions be coordinated with the music, so I worked out a script based on the music.

The most important and difficult role was the Sugar Plum Fairy, and I decided to dance the part because none of my students was ready yet. Gianfranco, who had taken classes with me when I first arrived in Venice, agreed to be the Cavalier, and we started rehearsing. Teaching and practicing aerobics had given me the strength to perform the role after so many years. I went to Mestre several times a week to rehearse with Gianfranco, and then I boarded the train to Conegliano or Pordenone.

The beautiful ballet tutus, long and short, all came from a company in Florence named Fantechi. Most of the Italian ballet schools in Veneto used them. At that time, it was customary to go to Florence to make the order, so I went alone and met the proprietor of Fantechi, who was rather cold and snobbish. After her icy reception, I enjoyed a hot lunch in a local trattoria. With a few hours to kill before my train, I went to see Michelangelos' *Davide*. It had been fifteen years since my last visit to Florence, while on vacation from the Austrian ballet company, when I had seen this incredible masterpiece for the first time. I cried with emotion when I saw the *Davide,* because this great statue had ignited Michelangelo's career and was his favorite creation.

***

Before leaving Florence, I went to a café and gelateria where I had had a funny experience fifteen years earlier. While I had been eating a huge gelato there, ten young Italian men had each tried to hit on me. One by one, they left my table, frustrated because I had continued to eat my gelato and hadn't spoken to any of them.

The last one said, "Number nine is very upset that you didn't talk to him. You hurt his feelings." With that remark, I burst out laughing and explained to him that I had a boyfriend, so I wasn't interested in meeting someone there. This reason seemed to have satisfied them, so they had waved from their table and smiled before looking around for new prey. Two days later, Katia's uncle Paolo, who was my *fidanzato,* or boyfriend, at the time, had made a surprise visit to Florence to check up on me. He was extremely jealous and hadn't believed I was there to see the art.

"You know, Venice has wonderful art too," he told me.

"Are the men in Florence more interesting?" he testily asked.

I had laughed and told him about my encounter with ten Florentine gigolos at the gelateria.

"Take me there. I want to see the place."

We had gone there, and sure enough they had all been sitting at the same table. I was uncomfortable, but Paolo had suggested we eat gelato. The group had stared at us, and finally their representative had come to our table.

"You are a lucky man Signor. Your *fidanzata* would not speak to any of us," he had said, indicating the table of young men.

Now, fifteen years later, there were no gigolos in the open-air gelateria, just families eating gelato.

***

There were many costumes that needed to be made by a dressmaker. Marta's mother, Adriana, was an experienced *sarta* who had made costumes in the past for Tiziana and her shows.

"Her work is fantastic, but her prices are high," warned Tiziana.

I drew the costume designs for the *Nutcracker* and then met with Adriana. She would make the Spanish, Arabian, Chinese, Russian, and Mother Ginger costumes. The tallest actor, Gianni, would play the latter, with six small children. Adriana was an artist when it came to costumes and was easy to work with. We went beyond the outskirts of Conegliano in her little Fiat and explored the hidden fabric shops known only to the locals. She saved money on material but asked me if she could splurge on decorations, lace, and borders.

"Un po' di pizzo?" she would plead. (A little bit of lace?) I never said no because I knew her work was remarkable.

Fantechi made the soldier costumes, but they didn't include hats and they didn't make them either. *What could I do?* Something so simple caused me sleepless nights. Ovidio could see my distress and called a few friends to see if they knew someone who made hats for costumes. Finally, someone suggested a woman named Giacinta, who lived in Martellago near Mestre. In Italy, many of these villages are called a *frazione,* or a fraction of a place every couple of miles.

We took Ovidio's old burgundy BMW, which he always parked in some remote place in Mestre, and drove off to find Giacinta. When Ovidio drove, he always got lost. Venetians are usually bad drivers and have no sense of direction on land, because they are more familiar with boats and water. There was a terrible, thick fog in Mestre, and it was impossible to see beyond the front of the car. All I knew was that we were driving in circles. I pointed this out to him and said that the directions we had been given were useless. We were lost! Just when we were about to give up, we saw a sign that said Martellago. Then we began searching for the house number, which didn't take long in a small village. Giacinta was a strong farmwoman who spoke only *dialetto* and worked out of her kitchen. When I explained to her what I needed, she pulled out three different pairs of potential soldier hats, undecorated, dusty, and rather beaten up. In a short time, she decorated the hats and made them presentable. From a distance, they would always look better than up close, but they served the school for a long time. Every time I looked at them over the years, I thought about Giacinta and the adventure in Martellago.

What was the one important thing I learned, living and working in Italy? The answer to this is *improvisation.* Finally, all of the costumes, accessories, and props were ready for the ballet.

The parents of my students were involved in the production, and I remember their help with great affection. One parent, Franca, was always there for me, finding sponsors, driving me everywhere, transporting scenery, or problem-solving. The list of support she gave me was endless, even after the ballet. Franca's son Paolo was ten at the time, and he helped me carry two pieces of scenery that didn't fit into the van: the clock and Christmas tree. We carried them across town from the ballet school to the theater and back after the performance. It made a curious sight in a small Italian town.

***

Months before, I had reserved the Teatro Accademia for May 27. The theater had an impressive history, but back then, it was also a cinema from Friday to Sunday. Finally the day arrived, after months of preparation. Ovidio was with me to help and give some moral support. I could see the theater from the train as we descended onto the station platform. The street in front of the station was the path that swept straight to the stairs, the *Scalinata degli Alpini,* which carried visitors to the Old City. Immediately, I could see our posters announcing the ballet all over the place. Two weeks before, Ovidio and I had placed two hundred posters in every shop and on every wall we could find in the city and on the outskirts of town.

Three great arches at the top of the stairs created an open-door view of the imposing theater. There was a large, open space in front of the theater, Piazza Cima, which had been painted like a huge chessboard for the Renaissance festival they held every fall. The piazza wasn't flat; it inclined uphill toward the theater entrance. Two stone-carved sphinxes were poised, guarding the main facade to the temple of art, music, dance, and film. The theater marquee had a large glass window for posters, announcing the film featured that week or other productions. Today the Nutcracker posters filled the window and advertised the ballet. I was presenting the first *Nutcracker* to be performed in Conegliano.

We walked through the lobby and to the dark interior of the theater *platea.* The stage had a dim light, and two men were rolling out the portable dance floor. The original stage floor was made of wood, which had rotted with age and the jungle-like humidity of the Italian summers. There were holes everywhere and nails that sprang up like weeds in the wood planks. The gray portable dance floor resembled a troubled sea of waves—it refused to lay flat.

"Perché il pavimento è cosi?" I asked Bepi, the chief stagehand and carpenter. (Why isn't the floor flat?) He explained that it probably needed time to settle, but it remained that way throughout the performance. The next step was to install the lights and sound system, followed by the backdrops. By nine o'clock that night, we were ready for the performance. The shows are scheduled for nine o'clock in Italy because everyone eats late, which is the consequence of everything being shut down so many hours for lunch.

Right before the performance, an angry man came backstage and waved the program at me. Signor Bertolini said he was with the SIAE, which is the organization for music rights in Italy, and was furious that I had sold his special seat. I said I was sorry, but I hadn't known he had a special seat in the theater. I tried to calm him, but he threatened to charge me a monstrous fine because I had sponsors for the show. Apparently, the SIAE could ask for a percentage of the sponsors' contributions because it was considered money earned. The organization always took one third of the money from the ticket sales. His last words were unpleasant, and I was quite shaken, but I took a deep breath. *The show must go on!*

The theater was sold out and the performance was going perfectly. Months and months of tireless preparation were executed in two hours, which seemed to fly by. The moment came for the Sugar Plum Fairy pas de deux. It felt strange dancing on a raked, or slanted, stage, which is common in the Italian theaters and makes dancing far more difficult; but the pas de deux with Gianfranco went smoothly. We took our bows and felt satisfied with our performance. The applause was thunderous! It was all over, and the first *Nutcracker* in Conegliano was a huge success.

The finale was filled with a cast of ninety on stage. The appreciative dancers and actors called me from the wings and presented me with an enormous bouquet of red roses, along with a beautiful gold bracelet. I threw a thank-you kiss to my audience, and the red velvet curtain closed. I looked toward the wings where a long line had formed, with the dancers first and then the audience. Each person had come to thank me for the gift of bringing the ballet to them. It seemed like the whole town had come to show their appreciation with flowers, gifts, cards, or a simple but sincere *grazie*. There were moments I was almost moved to tears, because wrapped in their love and acceptance, I knew I had brought something beautiful into their lives.

Teatro Accademia, Conegliano, Italy

Sugar Plum Fairy pas de deux

CHAPTER 7

High Water

*"Forget not that the earth delights to feel your bare feet and the wind
long to play with your hair."*
Kahlil Gibran

"Quattro, sei, nove!" I gasped and sat up in my bed. Never had a dream been so vivid—every detail crystal clear. Nanne came to me during the night, and it seemed as though her power still coursed through my veins.

"Four, six, nine!" she said in Italian.

"You can save many lives knowing this," she advised me in English.

I had been in a profoundly deep sleep in which I was a four-year-old again. My body felt so small in the backseat of my parent's car. In the front seat, my father drove and my mother sat on the passenger side. We were on a trip across the United States, and I was drawing with my tiny hand, carefully choosing scenes from outside and selecting different colored crayons. Suddenly, my hand began to tremble and shake, and I was possessed by strength that didn't belong to a child. Terrified, I became aware that my hand was no longer mine. Then I heard Nanne's voice within me, and she comforted me with the knowledge that her blood flowed through my body and gave me great strength. My eyes began to see things beyond the car window and the west. I could see into the past, as though her memories flowed through my veins, along with her blood. Her memories became mine! In the dream, I hid behind a bush and watched a two-story, colonial house burn to the ground in the dark. *Who lived in the house?* Then men on horseback raced toward the house. Their style of dress belonged to the mid-1800's. Everything became a blur, and then I heard Nanne's voice with the numbers and the warning. I woke up with a start, breathless, and slowly began to breathe normally. The journey by car across the U.S. when I was four really had taken place. *What did the dream mean?*

Everyone I told about this was excited for me. A dead person had given me numbers in a dream—even better, the dead person was a relative.

"Go out and by a lottery ticket with these numbers!" It was considered lucky to receive numbers from the dead and advisable to play them in the lottery as soon as possible. Venetian superstition dictated this. I was horrified. The numbers meant something more important: I was certain of it.

"What could be more important than money?" asked Ovidio. Unfortunately for friends and family, I was the only one who could play because the numbers had been delivered to me.

I didn't buy a lottery ticket, but I interpreted the dream as my great-grandmother pushing me to find my heritage and roots in Ireland. Nanne was the bridge to the past, and she was beckoning me to cross the bridge. "Don't stop searching," she was saying. "Cross the bridge and look for the castles!"

***

While learning the Italian language, I had found it useful to watch American films dubbed in Italian. The dubbing was so well done that it was often better than the real voices of the American actors. When I came home from work, usually around ten o'clock, I would watch a late-night film before going to bed. One night I watched an American film that I had never seen before, and I understood the entire dubbed dialogue! This was a turning point for me, and I was ecstatic. After that accomplishment, I challenged myself by watching Italian films.

The Gulf War came, and once again the United States was involved in armed conflict. In my twenties, I had gone to an audition in an old, rundown Broadway rehearsal hall for a show that would open in Baghdad.

Before the audition had started, the assistant choreographer had explained that there might be a war between Iraq and Iran, and if so, the show would be canceled. I remember that I was dancing when the assistant walked into the studio and excitedly announced that the war had begun, so there was no point in continuing the audition. Now, in 1990, the U.S. was fighting the Iraqi forces in Kuwait.

I was interested in following the developments as much as possible every day. So I started to read *Il Gazzettino,* the Italian newspaper. Once I began reading, I made enormous progress in speaking the language. I would even dream in Italian, not in English! Whenever I would return to the U.S., I needed time to feel comfortable speaking English.

The only thing I couldn't seem to change or improve was my accent. My New York accent was always present when I spoke Italian. People I had never met knew me without even an introduction, thanks to my accent that had become famous in Venice and Conegliano.

"Prego, Signora File."

"Conosciamo?" (Do we know each other?)

"No, ma Io conosco te dal tuo accento." (No, but I know who you are by your accent.)

I desperately wanted to sound like everyone else. Then one day I was stuck in a train strike and was forced to go to Conegliano by bus. On the long bus ride, I spoke with an elegant, friendly, elderly *signora* for the whole trip. When we arrived at our destination, she complimented my Italian. I thanked her but apologized for my accent, which I said I was trying to change. She told me that I should keep my accent because it was charming and unique. From that day forward, I stopped trying to change the way I spoke.

***

It was November of my third year in Italy when the phenomenon of *Acqua Alta,* or High Water, took place. A combination of winds from Africa and the Adriatic tides is responsible for this extreme flooding event in Venice. Wooden tables are constructed in the streets and in the piazzas so that people can climb up out of the water, which can be very deep. Venetians usually own a pair of fisherman-style boots for the Acqua Alta, and so did I. Sirens in the city would warn people that the water was rising, in order to prepare them for the inconvenience.

The first time I walked out of the apartment when the siren went off, there was no flooding in Calle della Misericordia, the street where Ovidio and I lived. As I walked closer to Strada Nuova, the water became deeper, until it was up to my thighs. I stepped up on the table in the center of the street and walked as far as it would go—to a bridge that emerged from the water. *Carabinirei,* the Italian military police that also perform police duties, lined the canal because it was impossible for a pedestrian to know where the street ended and the canal began. After I crossed the bridge, I shopped at a grocery store in thigh-high water.

Another time, Ovidio and I went to our favorite fish restaurant for dinner. We had just ordered when the sirens went off.

What should we do now? Ovidio asked the owner if the restaurant flooded with Acqua Alta.

"Si, ma abbiamo gli stivali." (Yes, but we have boots.)

He asked us to come with him and demonstrated a small storage room near the entrance, filled with boots.

"Ho tutte le misure." (I have all sizes.)

Fortunately, the Acqua Alta did not elevate enough to make us sit in water up to our knees while eating our fish dinner!

***

The first *Nutcracker* had been a success, though it had been done in May, not at Christmastime. After expenses were paid, I had some money left over from the ticket sales, so I was ecstatic. In September of my fourth year in Italy, enrollment in the ballet school increased due to the success of the *Nutcracker* at Teatro Accademia. There was a line waiting outside the elementary school for registration. I was determined to repeat the ballet with a larger cast that danced even better. As soon as the school year began, I was casting the new students in *Nutcracker* roles.

Back then, I was a regular at a gelateria in Strada Nuova, close to the bridge near Santa Lucia Church. It was a five-minute walk from where I lived and the gelato was good. Like the gelateria in Conegliano, this one also played an important part in my life. The owners, Marina and Fabio, were both around my age. Marina bore a startling resemblance to the actress Leslie Ann Warren, and Fabio, who wore glasses, was tall, mustached, and handsome. I frequented their place often for conversation and gelato, along with some philosophy for the soul sprinkled on top. Marina and Fabio were elated for me over the new ballet studio. After successfully presenting the first *Nutcracker,* my imagination flew to my next dream: presenting the ballet at Christmas in Teatro Goldoni.

When the school started rehearsals, I went to the Teatro Goldoni and reserved a date before Christmas for the *Nutcracker.* A month later, the director notified me that the date would have to be postponed. I was devastated! This meant that the show would not be performed before Christmas, but after. The date was set for the middle of January. Then there was another snag—my partner Gianfranco couldn't dance with me. He had had a serious thrombosis in his leg and would be recovering for many months. Dina had a tall, handsome lambada instructor from Senegal on her staff at the school, and she suggested him as a partner. She said he had studied classical ballet. His name was Alain, and we met at Dina's school after he taught class.

"Do you have experience in classical pas de deux?" I asked.

"I worked with the Paris Opera, so I have experience partnering," he replied.

He negotiated a high fee for the performance and the rehearsals, but there wasn't anyone else in Venice. Then there was another problem: where would we rehearse? With Gianfranco, I had worked at his dance school in Mestre. I asked Dina if we could use her studio and reluctantly she agreed. However, she wanted me to pay an exorbitant hourly fee. Alain spoke with the owner of a rival school, where he also taught classes. I was able to rent her studio, which was twice the size of Dina's space, for much less.

Before beginning the rehearsals, I had an injury at the school. My muscles got cold, and when it came time for me to demonstrate a jump, I was not sufficiently warmed up. I suffered a terrible pull in my Achilles tendon. I limped to the train station that night, but by the time I got to Venice, I could hardly walk. The following day I went to the hospital emergency room to have it checked, and the doctor took X-rays.

"Non è rotto," he said. (It isn't broken.) Without further discussion, he wrapped my foot in a tight bandage and told me to stay off my feet as much as possible.

"Ho bisogno di lavorare!" I cried desperately. (I have to work!) He told me to keep my leg propped up as often as I could. He looked at the medium-heel boots I had worn to the hospital.

"Tieni gli stivali adosso," he ordered. (Keep your boots on.) He explained that they would elevate my heel so I would use it less. He also recommended a crutch, but it would be too cumbersome on trains. The doctor gave me a request for three foot-therapy sessions a week at the hospital until the inflammation went down. I figured out my schedule and how I would work around the injury.

Eventually the tendon healed, and Alain and I began rehearsing. I could see that he had never done any pas de deux work. We had to simplify steps and lifts, after trying to perform them without success. Several times we were both in a heap after a missed lift. One day I received a call from the director of the Goldoni, telling me that the January date had been cancelled and moved to the end of February, during *Carnevale*. The Venetian Carneval brought thousands of tourists, so this was a good time to present a ballet. Then a week later, the *Nutcracker* was postponed indefinitely. The floor fell from under me; I didn't know what to do. A five-scoop gelato was what I needed, along with words of consolation from friends, so I went to the gelateria. Marina prepared a gelato as comfort food, and Fabio gave me some optimism. He and his friend Enrico had started an entertainment agency.

"Enrico and I know some people in City Hall, so we can try to pull strings," he said with encouragement. I didn't believe that they had this much power, but I had nothing to lose. It was my only hope. One week later, I received a phone call from Fabio.

"The date has been confirmed for May 29 in Teatro Goldoni." I was thrilled to receive this news! I would have preferred the ballet be at Christmas rather than the spring, but at that point, I was happy we were doing it at all. I agreed to meet Fabio at the gelateria for more details.

My enthusiasm was deflated when I heard about the compromises. The performance would take place at ten-thirty in the morning and the City Hall would sponsor the event, so it would be free. Working people would not be able to attend at that hour. The department of education was responsible for bringing the ballet to the public as an educational outreach program. Fortunately, we had the scenery, props, and costumes; however, we would need to rent the backdrops again. A truck and boat were necessary to transport scenery and props, but Enrico knew someone with an old fruit boat who would do the job for a small amount of money. The City Hall would pay the fees to the SIAE for music rights and the tax required for hanging posters in public. Without sponsors to buy ads, we decided to eliminate the program and have more and bigger posters made for publicity. All of this expense could have been covered by the sale of tickets, had there been tickets to sell. Fortunately, I had funds left from the first *Nutcracker,* so I could cover the backdrops and truck. The rest of the money from that performance went to Alain and the studio rental for rehearsals with him. The posters were the only things that had to be paid for, and there was no way around this: I would have to find a substantial sponsor. I asked Ovidio for help with this. The wine, prosecco, and chocolate companies that he represented often sponsored events.

"Can you think of anyone who could sponsor the ballet?" I pleaded.

After some thought, he remembered that one of the wineries that he represented in the region of Friuli had been sold to a new owner. He called a friend of his who was the assistant director for the company and asked for an appointment to discuss an eventual sponsorship. We met his colleague at the winery and were introduced to the new owner. He was a handsome count, half English and Italian. The count reminded me of an old English painting from the seventeenth century. His long, dark hair framed a pale face, and his green eyes were brushed with long, thick, black eyelashes. The cut of his moustache and beard gave him the look of a swashbuckling musketeer.

"We are a new company, so I don't think we are ready to sponsor a production right now," he said in a sincere, noble manner. With that, he invited us to join him and the assistant director for lunch. On the way out, Ovidio gave me a look of disappointment.

"Mi dispiace," he whispered. (I'm sorry.) It was a huge letdown.

The restaurant was elegant and expensive.

"Almeno mangiamo bene oggi," Ovidio confided when we were alone. (At least we'll eat well today.)

During the lunch, the food kept coming and the wine kept flowing. At least three bottles were consumed! As usual, I drank only mineral water. After lunch, we went back to the winery and the count's office.

"Would you like me to take you on a tour of the winery," suggested Ovidio's colleague.

"Tell me more about the ballet," said the count, looking directly at me.

"As a child in London, my mother took me to see the *Nutcracker.* "

This was my cue that he would like me to stay and talk about the arts. Ovidio and his friend left me alone with the Count. When we were alone, I noticed that he was a little drunk. He looked at me seductively as he said, in perfect English,

"I would never leave a beautiful woman like you alone for a minute if you were my wife." I let this comment pass and returned to the subject of the ballet at the Goldoni.

"We are printing eight hundred posters for the ballet, and they will be all over the city of Venice." I explained that a new company like his could benefit from this publicity and he would be helping the arts at the same time. Then I outlined the graphic design, colors, and layout of the poster. He was captivated by what I said, as though I spoke of love.

"Okay. How much money do you need?" He opened the desk drawer and took out enough cash to pay for the posters. I promised to send him the *bozza,* or copy of the poster, for his approval when it was ready. Ovidio and the assistant director walked in at that moment, and I announced the good news about the Famiglia Pasini sponsorship.

"How did you get him to change his mind?" laughed Ovidio after we left the winery. I recounted that the count had been a bit tipsy and even a little flirtatious.

"I hope he doesn't regret sponsoring the show when he's sober," he chuckled.

I kept my promise to send him the bozza, and he approved it. The poster was large, red and black, with the *Nutcracker* and Famiglia Pasini dominating the advertising. The City of Venice agreed to distribute the posters for the ballet. Years after the performance, I would still see the posters glued to the walls in Venice. They were never taken down; only time would fade them away. I'm sure the count was pleased and had no regrets about his sponsorship. However, I almost got myself in high water with a lecherous count and under water financially for the ballet!

CHAPTER 8

The Sugar Plum Fairy On The Grand Canal

"Your vision will become clear only when you look into your heart. Who looks outside dreams. Who looks inside awakens."
Carl Jung

With the date settled and the money problem solved, I could dedicate more time to resolving other issues. The Colonna Infame was short two actors for the party scene. Enrico, Fabio's partner, replaced one actor and Ovidio the other. Ovidio was excited to be back onstage in a ballet. We practiced the Adult Dance every night when I came home, and he was perfect for the scene. Moreno presented another casting problem. He was busy at the time, preparing for a martial arts competition in China, so he couldn't practice with Marta. Roberto, from the Colonna Infame, expressed a desire to learn pas de deux and had more time to rehearse. So Roberto became the *Nutcracker* prince and Moreno our Rat King. The fight scene between the two could be prepared in a few rehearsals, and they worked late in the evening without me.

***

In the midst of the *Nutcracker* preparation, my personal possessions arrived in Italy. While my marriage to Ovidio and our future were rocky, the ballet school gave me a sense of security, so I could send for my possessions. The previous summer, I had gone back to New York to get my things out of storage and bring everything to Italy. They had been left untouched for seven years, while I had been living in California and Italy. While living in Italy, I had to send a *vaglia internazionale,* or international check, every month from the post office to a storage center on West Twenty-third Street in New York. It was the only way to send a small amount of money from Italy, where it was converted from *lire* into dollars.

Each month that I sent them money, the company sent a letter saying that they hadn't received anything. I had to go to the post office and file a complaint. They discovered that the money was sitting in Rome and had never been sent! The *vaglia internazionale* was nothing more than a legalized scam. The money would sit for a time in Rome and then, if no one claimed it, the government would keep the money after the expiration date. I quickly wired several months of rent through the bank because I was desperate to save my possessions. They contained all the memories I had left of my family. The storage company received the money just in time, because everything I owned was about to go to auction. After that frightful experience, I wasted no time in having everything shipped to me.

The subsequent scam came when everything arrived in Italy. I was notified that the colossal wooden box that contained the shipment had arrived in Mestre. The customs authorities told me that art appraisers wanted to examine my art collection. *What art collection?* I had declared some paintings that I had done, among other things. Ovidio and I had an appointment with the appraisers in Mestre one night. The wooden container was placed on the side of the railroad tracks, where a customs official came to break open the box. The two appraisers dutifully examined my art work and agreed that there were no stolen masterpieces. Then we were told that the boxes in the wood container would have to be sent separately by train to Venice.

The size of the wooden box that contained all the other boxes was too large to be allowed to go by train into the city. Additional money was required to transport the boxes into Venice. The cost was equal to what I had paid for the container to be packed, cross the ocean, and travel from Genova to Mestre! The shipping company confirmed that I had paid door-to-door service when I called them. But the Italians refused the five-minute train trip to the train station in Venice unless I paid the hefty fee. It was extortion, but if I didn't pay, my things would be stolen or left to rot on the side of the tracks! So I paid them, but when the boxes arrived, they were deposited in the baggage claim, not delivered to the apartment. *At least they were safe.* Ovidio knew a *facchino,* or porter, and made a deal for transporting each box to our place. Again, I paid more money. After I had payed three times, the boxes were finally in our home.

***

It was time to meet my lighting and music technician. I left messages at the theater, but he never returned my calls. Luckily, he answered the phone one day, and we made an appointment at the theater, but he never showed. I asked the director of the Goldoni when I could find the technician, and he told me that he was there for two hours every morning. The following morning, I went there and waited. He walked in and seemed surprised, then angry, that I had waited for him. His antipathy was clear, and it was obvious that he was trying to avoid me. I desperately needed to talk to him about the lighting and music, because the ballet was only a couple of days away. He opened his arms to the side and shrugged his shoulders.

"Sono qua adesso, parla." (I'm here now, speak.) He looked annoyed and listened with disinterest as I explained what I needed. Then he looked at his watch.

"Devo andare," he said abruptly. (I must go.) He didn't give me even five minutes of his time to discuss the details of the lighting and music! It was scary that the ballet would go on stage without a dress rehearsal. Our only rehearsal was the performance we had the year before.

The day before the show, we were allowed to bring the scenery and props to the theater. In Venice, stage equipment was brought to and from the theater by boat. We were given time to set up the dance floor, all backdrops, and everything for the party scene. In the morning, Ovidio and Enrico went to Conegliano and picked up the rental truck. The scenery from Quarto D'Altino had been brought to the school the day before that.

Franca met the men at the school with her dining room chairs, which she had graciously loaned us again for the party scene. Everything was loaded onto the truck, and a stop was made to pick up the dance floor. Things proceeded on schedule until the truck stopped halfway to Venice because they had forgotten to put gas in the tank! Enrico had to stay with the truck on the highway, while Ovidio walked to the nearest gas station. The inconvenience set them back hours, so the fruit boat that was to meet them at Piazzale Roma didn't wait. When they finally got there, they had to find another boat that would take everything to the Goldoni.

I arrived at the theater before the boat and met with the custodian who opened the doors. He was a loud, vulgar, bullish man with an angry, red face. Furious with the delay, he plodded all over the stage, cursing and screaming in the Venetian dialect. It was obvious that he had been drinking. Finally, the boat pulled up to the back of the theater, and all of us, including me, helped to unload everything quickly.

The portable dance floor was the first thing we put down. Two stagehands opened a part of the floor and looked at each other, baffled. Then they burst out laughing. I asked them what was wrong.

"Sei stata fregata," said the larger of the two stagehands. (You were cheated.) They said the floor was nothing but a piece of worthless, worn-out linoleum, certainly not a dance floor.

"Guarda i disegni," he said, referring to the brick design on one side. I had rented the floor from a dance teacher, Carmela, who had a school on the other end of Conegliano. I had been dubious the first time I'd seen it, but I couldn't imagine that Carmela would cheat me.

"Nessun pavimento è fatto cosi." (No dance floor is made like this.) I had to agree.

"Quanto hai pagato per noleggiarlo?" (How much did you pay to rent it?) I said two million lire, the equivalent of one hundred dollars.

"Non vale una lira a compralo." (It was not worth one dollar to buy.)

The men refused to put the floor down and told me that the theater had a portable dance floor. I asked them to install it and used the money I had intended to give Carmela to pay the rental fee. The day after the performance, Ovidio told her that we didn't use the floor because the Goldoni wouldn't put it down. She wanted the money anyway but I refused to pay her.

"Hai fatto una brutta figura," she yelled into the phone. (You made an ugly figure.) This Italian expression is used to describe a person who has been caught doing something sleazy, compromising, or embarrassing. I responded that *she* had made the brutta figura, asking for money after trying to cheat me. After that, we became enemies.

The boat was gone and the truck was parked at Piazzale Roma. Everything was ready for the *Nutcracker*, so the custodian closed the theater and we went home. The next morning, I went down to the train station to meet students, parents, their relatives, and friends. I couldn't sleep the night before, so at dawn I decided to have breakfast and put on my stage makeup. I was ready to go. There were one hundred students, and with at least one parent each, there would be a minimum of around two hundred people coming to Venice by train. However, with family and friends, the number was closer to three hundred! Some of the students had never seen Venice, so it was an adventure and an honor for them to perform there. The train came to a slow halt at the Santa Lucia station.

Masses of people began overflowing onto the platform. Among the crowd, I could distinguish many of my students, holding colorful costumes. I frantically waved my arms so that everyone could see me and then motioned for them to follow me. Like the captain of an army, I led the troops outside the station. Immediately I cancelled the idea that my army could get on a vaporetto. The lines were long and the boats were full, so we would walk.

I marched the troops through Strada Nuova, which was very wide and straight. I was like the Pied Piper in Venice! The walk was the only warmup that the performers would have before the ballet. We converged on the theater twenty minutes later, and everyone hurried to change in the dressing rooms. An hour before curtain, everyone was ready. Fabio, Enrico, and Ovidio arrived, along with Sandra, now my cousin, who was an enormous help backstage. Adriana, the seamstress, came with her daughter Marta and her sewing kit.

There was a full house in the theater, thanks to the posters distributed all over Venice by the City Hall. Many tourists flocked to the free performance out of curiosity or to rest their tired legs while soaking in the beauty of the historical Teatro Goldoni. We started the *Nutcracker* on time, and the first act flew by without any problems. I was touching up my makeup and changing into my costume when Alain knocked and walked in.

"I couldn't find the tights to my costume, so I figured you wanted me to wear these." I looked down in disbelief—he was wearing Mother Ginger's pantaloons! At first I thought it was a joke, and I burst out laughing. Then I realized that he was serious, which made the whole scene even more hilarious. Adriana walked in and her jaw dropped.

"O Mio Dio!" she said. (Oh my God!)

The intermission was almost finished, so we had to address the problem seriously and quickly. Adriana came up with a solution. The rat costume was a black Lycra jumpsuit, so Alain could wear one under his Cavalier jacket. The jumpsuit was too short, so Adriana had to sew the arms, like suspenders, under the jacket. His costume became a white jacket with black, makeshift hose, rather than white dance tights.

When the costume crisis was resolved, I went out to the stage. Ovidio had brought a vacuum from the apartment to pick up the Styrofoam snow. In the first *Nutcracker,* he had dropped the snow from the theater catwalk, but it had come down only on center stage. We had thought a couple of brooms would clean up the snow quickly, but we were wrong. Much of the slippery Styrofoam remained on stage. This time, Ovidio's friend Loris helped on the catwalk. With two men up there, the snow was divided more evenly. The home vacuum was noisy but better; however, there was still snow on the floor. I grabbed a broom, and in my tutu, I frantically swept up any bits and pieces that the vacuum had missed.

We opened the second act. Everything was moving along beautifully until the *Marzapane* solo. During the solo, the music suddenly changed track and reverted to the Party Scene in Act One. The change in music was a mistake executed by the lighting and sound man. I remembered his indifference to discussing the music and lights for the ballet, and it came back to haunt me. After a few seconds the music quickly returned on the right track.

For the first time in my life, I was nervous about going on stage. Alain was not an experienced partner, so I had visions of being dropped. But his fantastic stage presence covered his inadequacies, and everything went smoothly. The audience gave the entire cast a huge ovation at the finale of the ballet. Crowds of people came backstage to compliment and congratulate us. The Teatro Goldoni transformed the quality of the show into something more professional.

Alain thanked me for teaching him the art of pas de deux. He admitted to having no prior experience, although he had claimed that he did. It reminded me of the dance floor. The fee was negotiated, and then the surprises came. It was like buying a car and then finding out there was no motor, but you couldn't get your money back. Alain had kept his commitment to being there, so I couldn't complain. The lighting technician was embarrassed and apologized for the music deviation in the second act. I had been furious when this happened during the ballet, but I recognized that anyone could have made this error.

I dressed, cleaned out the dressing room, and walked on stage. I was speaking to a friend downstage when I heard people shouting and a commotion behind us. Fabio and the theater custodian were in a heated argument. The custodian wanted to go to lunch, so he angrily ordered us out of the theater fast. His face was red again, and his language was vulgar, to say the least. He hurled insults at Fabio, and before we knew it, punches were flying. They were on the stage floor when the actors and stage crew separated them. It was a great finale to a successful show that had overcome months of difficulties and problems.

The big stage door of the Goldoni closed with a slam. The vibration of the door caused a ripple in the water of the canal. All the scenery, props, and costumes were packed by the stage crew and loaded on the big, old fruit and vegetable boat. The unusual cargo vessel was stacked high in the middle with heavy backdrops. The huge doll boxes, the Christmas tree and grandfather clock, the rifles, swords, and Mother Ginger's enormous skirt were lighter, so they were distributed around the center. I sat like a princess on top of the windows backdrop of *La Traviata* and the *Magic Flute* castle, all folded under me. This was my throne! The final touch was the huge bouquet of red roses that I held in my arms. Dressed in ordinary clothes but still wearing full stage makeup, I was ready to sail the Grand Canal. There had been months of hard work, but now the best part of the end of this long journey was about to begin.

The May morning was clear and sunny. I could feel a damp, cool breeze against my face as we pulled away from the dock. The magic had not gone at the end of the *Nutcracker* performance. Instead, it continued on the waters of the Grand Canal. Ovidio was at the helm, along with two other friends of his who had come to help. As usual, there was heavy traffic on the Grand Canal, especially at that hour of the day. I sat majestically on my makeshift throne, high on the paint-peeling banana boat, and a total satisfaction with life swept through me, along with the spring breeze. The ancient palaces looked down on me with approval as we glided along. I imagined the ghost of Robert Browning applauding me from the terrace of his palace, Ca'Rezzonico. From the Palazzo Ca' Doro, Shakespeare's Othello observed me from his own stage. My fantasies mixed with the bizarre reality of the moment.

A vaporetto full of people passed us on the canal, and everyone stared at the pirate queen on her strange boat, holding a mass of beautiful roses. Loud applause broke out from the passengers and soon it became contagious. People applauded from other boats in the canal. As the Sugar Plum Fairy, I gracefully nodded and smiled, taking bows as I had earlier at the Goldoni. But somehow these bows were more unforgettable from my backdrop throne on the banana boat filled with *Nutcracker* scenery, cruising along the Grand Canal. On my fairytale ship, I awakened to the thought that many of my dreams had already been achieved that day.

The Sugar Plum Fairy

CHAPTER 9

Death of a Marriage in Venice

"Strength does not come from physical capacity.
It comes from indomitable will."
Gandhi

The second-floor apartment where I lived with Ovidio was large and modern. The French doors in the *salotto,* or living room, opened to overlook an enormous garden, which reminded me of a French impressionist painting of a park in Paris, rather than a scene in Venice. One could imagine ladies with long dresses and parasols, strolling hand in hand with small children or lovers. But fog imprisoned the park in wintertime. Flowers, trees, and everything that lived wore a death mask, and no one ventured out in the gray garden. I would shudder from the coldness of the scene.

Ovidio had tastefully decorated the three-bedroom apartment. In Italy there isn't openness in a home, but a series of rooms off a long hall. The peach-colored living and dining room were one, and antique furnishings were strategically placed to create more space. The kitchen was disproportionately small, and made smaller by the choice of dark red walls. There was a new dishwasher and microwave.

Next to the kitchen was a bedroom that had been converted into an office for Ovidio. Down the hall, there was a long bathroom, with a door leading to a terrace that extended over the front courtyard. At the end of the hall, there were two bedrooms.

***

"Why did you marry a poor American when there are so many rich ones to choose from?" inquired Dina's son Davide of Ovidio one night at dinner.

The Marcielli family had taken a look at my possessions, Nan's silver and family jewelry, and had decided I was poor. But it didn't matter what Ovidio or his family thought. *These things held my memories.* The wife of his friend had warned me that Ovidio had the habit of overspending for Lorenzo and Stefania, so he would sell the silver and jewelry at home to pay bills. After seeing how extravagant Ovidio was with Lorenzo, I was worried. I couldn't imagine losing things that had belonged to my family in order to pay for his ex-wife and son. The woman had suggested that I sign a *separazione dei bene,* or prenuptial, when we went for the marriage license, to protect me from his ex-wife.

When I had started earning money from the ballet school, Lorenzo and his mother had taken an abnormal interest in my business. I called the lawyer who made the contract for the sale of the school and asked him if I could have problems with them. He said that the separazione dei beni included any business that was in my name only. If I hadn't signed that prenuptial contract, Ovidio would have automatically owned half of the business, along with Lorenzo; and Stefania, as Lorenzo's mother, would be beneficiary. He congratulated me for doing the right thing legally. Otherwise, I would have had to give them half of the money I earned, even if we divorced!

On one antique credenza there were photos of Lorenzo, Stefania, and Ovidio, as a family. In another corner, there were photos of me as the Dying Swan and one of me taken together with other circus performers. An outsider would immediately pick up on the relationship of all the people in the house, just by seeing the display of photos. I was on my own island, separate from the Marcielli family. Admittedly, marrying me had alienated Ovidio from certain friends who didn't favor Americans.

***

Through Italian films, I learned many things about Italian life, which was different from that in any other society. For example, in one film with the comic Alberto Sordi, I received insight into how health care functioned in Italy. What fascinated me more than anything else was how a woman could hold a job and never have go to work, as long as she kept having children. This was the storyline in a comic film in which a woman had nine children and held a job, but never went to work. She spent years on maternity leave! While the story was an exaggeration, the concept of maternity leave was true.

"La maternita è tutto!" (Motherhood is everything!) So an employer had to pay two employees for one job, one at home and the other at work. One prima ballerina at the Teatro La Fenice had been pregnant four times, so she practically never set foot on stage. She received full pay for years and an excellent pension from a very young age. The dancers were required to attend a certain number of classes so they could collect their pay. A dancer could go on maternity leave and return before the next performance a year or so later. With three months of unused vacation she was entitled to after two years, she had time to get pregnant again without returning to work.

I wanted more than anything else to have a child. Ovidio had planned a vacation with Lorenzo, so I went alone to the Greek island of Rhodes that summer to visit my friend Dora. Her daughter Eleni, at age four, was the first student I had ever taught in California. Rhodes was spectacular! The small village where Dora lived faced the coast of Turkey. There were always strong winds, rough waves, and cerulean blue water mixed with dark patches of marine blue. But the most incredible view of the sea was high above, on the rough-pointed peak of Tsambika mountain on the other side of the island. It overlooked Kolimbia beach and the ancient city of Lindos. There was a tiny white Greek Orthodox monastery at the top of the mountain. Dora told me about the tradition that was connected to this mystical place. When a woman wanted a child, she would make a pilgrimage there and pray to the Virgin Mary to become pregnant. One day we went there by car and arrived halfway up the steep road. Beyond that point, it was accessible only by foot, climbing around three hundred and fifty stairs, with each one numbered. I turned to Dora and said, "I want to climb the mountain." It would have been another Immaculate Conception if I had become pregnant! Dora had her new baby Katerina in a stroller, so she waited, but eight-year-old Eleni accompanied me.

Hand in hand, we climbed the rough terrain. I wanted a miracle, and finally we arrived, breathless, to the top. The little white Byzantine church, with its gold icon, was illuminated by the bright sun. The clouds hung low, giving the scene a heavenly atmosphere. I prayed for a child—somehow, some way, and with someone. The emptiness I felt pierced my heart. I wanted to know the love of a man and the warmth of his child inside of me. I believe there are places so sacred in their beauty that the presence of God is felt more strongly there than anywhere else. I wasn't alone in spirit because God was here. Inside the chapel, which was as big as a closet, I lit a candle for my mother. I would never have a child, but I came to understand, years later, that all of my students were my children. This was the blessing I received that day. Ironically, it was my very first student who was God's messenger.

***

As time went by, it became clearer and clearer that my marriage to Ovidio was nothing more than a convenient arrangement for the family. Reflecting on it later, I realized that when Ovidio had proposed to me, we were in different places as far as our hearts were concerned. While I had flown above the clouds the night he proposed, his feet had remained solidly on the ground, as he mapped out his plans. He had subtly laid out all his intentions with the proposal, but I had been deaf to his words. I understood afterward that the family must have sat down and decided how I could be an advantage to them, with as little commitment as possible on their part.

It was obvious to everyone that I was nothing more than an American money machine. *How could Ovidio possibly see me in any other way?* This was the attitude of family and friends, and they made no effort to hide their businesslike sentiment. It was clear even to Lorenzo. One day he asked me how many lessons I had to teach to earn the equivalent of one thousand dollars in Italian lire, and I gave him the number.

"La mia madre non deve fare niente per quei soldi ma chiedere." (My mother doesn't have to do anything for this money but ask for it.) The innuendo was stunning: I worked for the money, then handed it to Stefania.

***

In Italy, each town, province, or region has its own set of *feste* in addition to the national holidays. They could be either a nuisance or a welcome day off. The celebrated day was often near a weekend, so it became a *ponte,* or holiday bridge. Instead of one day, it became three, or even four, days. Ovidio and I used this opportunity to visit his family in Milan. His two brothers and one sister lived in Milan with their families. Dina was the only sibling who lived in Venice.

The plan was that I would take an early train to Milan and Ovidio would come later, after working in his office at home. Milan is an ugly city, but I enjoyed the sense of freedom away from Venice. I would go to the Gothic Duomo Cathedral in the center of the city, admire La Scala Opera House, and drink hot chocolate at the famous Biffi café in the Galleria Vittorio Emanuele II. I dressed elegantly and imitated a successful European enjoying an afternoon in the city. The reality was that I didn't feel Italian or American, but more like someone who didn't come from anywhere or belong to any particular place. I felt unique and different—and sometimes very lonely. But Milan reminded me of New York, so I was comfortable there.

Later, I would meet Ovidio at the apartment of his brother Gino and his wife Pina, where we would spend the night. One evening before dinner, Ovidio was drinking excessively. A phone call from his ex-wife preluded his behavior. Stefania had told him that she needed the equivalent of one thousand five hundred dollars for middle-school books for Lorenzo. Ovidio was more worried about where to find this money than by the absurdity of her request. I told him that I had never heard of such expensive books in middle school. But Ovidio was drunk and my comment only added fuel to the fire. He shouted that I was not to dispute any amount of money that Stefania needed for their son. He added that it was my job to work for the money that she asked for and to *stare zitta,* or shut up. I didn't see his fist coming until the last minute, when I turned away in time to save my nose. His fist hit my cheekbone but didn't break it. *I must have cheekbones of steel.* I ran to Gino, who protected me from my husband. The humiliation of being struck was worse than the throbbing pain. Gino and his wife managed to calm Ovidio, and when the alcohol had worn off, he asked me to forgive him. He said it was the alcohol that made him do it, that he usually drank only a glass of wine with his meal. Pina told him that the next time she would throw water in his face to calm him down. Back in Venice, he asked his friends with children at the same school as Lorenzo's, how much the books cost. They all agreed that the cost was around one hundred and fifty dollars. He apologized to me and was angry with Stefania for trying to trick him.

The next time we were in Milan, Ovidio again started to drink heavily at dinner in their apartment. He began to complain to Gino and Pina that I didn't understand his financial obligations to Stefania and Lorenzo. I could see his anger mounting, so before he hit me again, I threw a glass of water in his face. Magically, the water washed away the spell of alcohol, and he apologized to everyone.

"Non ti do più vino a casa mia! " Pina warned Ovidio. (I won't give you wine again in my house!) We continued to eat dinner as though nothing had happened.

***

People often ask why a person being abused doesn't leave her abuser. It isn't that easy, especially if that person was abused as a child and couldn't get away from her abuser. I remember that my father took all of his anger out on me. He would take his belt and beat my legs with it—I can still see the fury in his eyes. While beating me, he would grit his teeth and tell me he would make my legs hurt so badly that I couldn't dance. But the burning pain never stopped me. It made me more determined than ever to pursue my love of dance. One time he took a bag of my pointe shoes and ripped every one of them to shreds with his bare hands. Later my mother and I laughed, because those shoes were old, broken, and about to be discarded. The good shoes were wrapped carefully in my dance bag.

My father was a bully, but his power over me came to an end when I was about thirteen. One day we argued, and he came after me with a vengeance. I ran into the bathroom and locked the door. I was afraid for my life. Survival was my one thought, and to accomplish this, I couldn't run. I had to face my enemy. I grabbed the metal rod that held the shower curtain and flung open the door to face him. With the threatening rod in my hand, our eyes met. He looked at me and understood he could never hurt me again. And then he walked out of the apartment.

As a child who was beaten, I had unconsciously fallen for another abuser when I became an adult. My subconscious wanted to rewrite the past and make everything right. If I were to leave Ovidio rather than forgive him, I would acknowledge the pain and humiliation that I had suffered with each beating. But the reality is that forgiving doesn't cancel the permanent, deep, psychological wounds. So I accepted Ovidio's excuses as I had once done with my father. This way, I could treat the violence against me as an accident. It's called denial, and though I embraced it, the scars remained below the skin.

***

In the midst of so much unhappiness, there was a time that we shared some laughter. One morning Ovidio wore an outrageous gold, bell-bottom suit that made him look like Elvis at a fifties rock concert.

"Cosa pensi?" With great pride, he asked me what I thought.

"Sembri un pimp!" I laughed and explained that a pimp was a *magnaccio*. He was offended and told me that Americans had no taste in clothes. Again I laughed and said that I wouldn't be surprised if the Carabinieri arrested him in San Marco.

At lunch time, he came home and sheepishly entered the apartment.

"Avevi ragione. La polizia mi ga fermata in San Marco." He told me I was right about the suit. The police stopped him in Piazza San Marco and asked to see his identity card because he looked like a suspicious character!

The gold Elvis suit brought some laughter into an otherwise sad marriage.

Another time, early in our marriage, we had a discussion about shopping at the market near Rialto, and I told him my story about the vendor there and how I had been cheated the first time I had bought vegetables.

"Mi ha dato della verdure marcia." (I told him the vegetables were rotten.) The ones I had chosen had been switched when the vendor wrapped the purchase in paper. Ovidio didn't believe me. Then one day he said he would stop at the market for eggplant on the way home from work.

"Buona fortuna!" I said jokingly. (Good luck!)

When he came home that night, he opened up the paper with the eggplant from the market. Rotten eggplant cascaded onto the table.

"Cosa? Sono stato fregato!" he said. (What? I've been cheated!) The unscrupulous practice wasn't reserved for foreigners only. It could happen to a Venetian. I explained how I always checked on what was wrapped up before I paid, but nevertheless we had a good laugh about the episode. Again, he apologized for not having believed me.

***

Ovidio controlled the finances at home, and we pooled the money we earned. I wasn't comfortable with this, because all my life I had taken care of the money I made. Dina told me that Fulvio took care of paying the bills in their house. It was easier because, in Italy at the time, a person had to go to the office of each utility and wait in line to pay. Some bills could be paid at the post office or bank, but the wait was the same. They didn't accept checks. I was always out of town or teaching, so it was inconvenient for me to make the payments. On the other hand, Ovidio could make his appointments in Venice before or after he went to an office. I never even saw the money I earned from Dina because Ovidio collected my pay each month.

One time, a few days after he had picked up my paycheck, Lorenzo came over with a new coat. The coat had a huge fur collar and hood, which looked very expensive. Ovidio was very uneasy talking about the coat he had bought for his son. One day I walked by a shop near the Rialto Bridge and saw the identical coat. I gasped when I saw the price, which was the equivalent in lire to almost two thousand dollars! It was all the money I had earned teaching that month. I confronted Ovidio, and we fought about it, but nothing changed.

The issue of overspending for Lorenzo kept chipping away at our marriage. However, the worst part wasn't the spending. It was the lack of respect that Lorenzo showed me. The moment came when I reached my limit. He came to stay with us a few days, and I prepared lunch for him in the dining room before I left to teach in Pordenone. He kept ordering me to get something for him when he could easily get it himself. I would bring what he asked for to the table, and then he would send me back to the kitchen on another errand. I was packing my dance bag in the bedroom when he yelled for me to bring him a bottle of ketchup.

"Hai due braccia e due gambe, vai e prendila," I told him. (You have two arms and legs, go and get it.)

That night when I arrived at home and Ovidio opened the door, I could see he was furious. He slammed the door shut without a word, then grabbed me by the throat and pinned me against the wall. Referring to what I had said to Lorenzo at lunch, he told me I would do whatever Lorenzo ordered me to do because that was the custom in Italy. He was strangling me! He repeated the warning and tightened his grip on my throat. Then he let go of my neck and went to Lorenzo's room. I remember sliding down slowly, with my back against the wall, and when I hit the floor, I sat there for hours, silently sobbing. *Did I want to live or die?* The choice was mine.

I was desperately unhappy and I cried continuously. I was turning into a skeleton, and I had lost hair from all the stress. One night I dreamed that I stood at the balcony of our apartment and looked out at the park. It was sunny, and the garden was filled with colorful flowers. In my dream, I didn't want to live another day, and I looked at all the beauty in the world for the last time. In that moment, a blinding white light came through the door of the balcony, and I backed into the living room. There on the balcony was my mother, moving toward me. She smiled and shook her head, as though she thought that it was a very silly thing that I wanted to end my life. I don't remember her words, but she convinced me to live, and when I woke up, I realized that Ovidio was not worth dying for. I made an appointment to talk with a therapist, who suggested I speak with a marriage counselor. It is never easy leaving someone you once loved.

***

We came together as a couple for the funeral of the son of his best friend. It was late autumn when they found the sixteen-year-old boy dead in the street one night from an overdose. This was not a common thing in the small, provincial city of Venice. Everyone wept for the life that was taken at such a young age, in a place where people lived to be old. His funeral at San Michele left me with a vivid impression of death that I will never forget. I had visited the island cemetery on a sunny, summer day as a tourist, many years before the funeral. I had wanted to see the tombs of Igor Stravinsky and Sergei Diaghilev, because I had seen Stravinsky many times as a student at the School of American Ballet. The cemetery was a beautiful garden then, rich with cut and planted flowers everywhere.

The day of the funeral was gelid, gray, and foggy, completely opposite to my summer excursion. San Michele is the island of the dead, one stop on the vaporetto from the other side of Venice. All those attending the funeral were on the same boat because there was only one trip to the island every hour. At the vaporetto stop, the entire funeral entourage of priests came to meet us, and we all marched silently through the foggy cemetery into the cold, damp church. The small church, which was hundreds of years old, had no heat whatsoever. The chill added to the poignancy of the scene. My attention fell to the feet of the priests at the altar. They were wearing sandals! I squirmed in my heavy socks and boots at the thought of bare feet on that frigid stone floor.

After a solemn mass, the procession left the church. Outside, a grave had been dug in the cemetery, and the reality of death suddenly hit the boy's mother. It was as though she had awakened from a trance and was overcome by desperation. I can't imagine the pain of losing a child. As the coffin descended into the ground, she had to be held back from throwing herself into her son's grave. The sharp sound of her piercing wail will echo in my ears forever. She understood at that moment the bitter truth: her son was gone forever.

The end of a marriage is like losing to death someone you love. But it is said that the heart forgets the bad memories and remembers the good ones, enabling us to accept the past.

Visiting Tzambika Church, Rhodes, Greece

CHAPTER 10

Cinderella Combats Cancer

"No matter how hard the past,
you can always begin again."
Buddha

It was the beginning of the end. My marriage to Ovidio was over. Some said it had never existed—our marriage had only been on paper. But there is almost always one event or argument that makes everything final. His harsh, painful words made everything clear, and the next, inevitable step was a legal separation.

It was September, and the office for divorce procedures was in City Hall at the Rialto. Downstairs, we had signed a marriage license, and now, upstairs, we would begin a long, complicated divorce, which in Italy takes five years. The couple first observes a three-year separation so there is plenty of time to rethink everything and maybe decide to remain together. However, this rarely happens. I remember signing the papers in the office with Ovidio and then, without a word, I ran down the long, winding staircase inside the building. The warm September sun was shining like a beacon though the huge windows along the staircase—light symbolizing the beginning of a new life. At the time, I was in too much emotional pain to understand the significance of the light. Ovidio and I had to continue living under the same roof for convenience, which I thought would be more difficult. But once we had signed the papers, our lives went back to the way they were before. We were friendly, but in the end, nothing changed.

***

Now the ballet school had been under my direction for three years, and the enrollment was up to one hundred and fifteen students. *Cinderella* was the next ballet I wanted to produce in Teatro Accademia for the students. Making plans and preparing the choreography helped take my mind off the separation. I tried to keep up appearances, which wasn't easy, but I didn't want parents or students to know my situation. In a small, bourgeois Italian town, I didn't want to be judged by the people and lose students. But I confided to the *bidella,* or school custodian, Noemi, about my *separazione;*

"Voglio buttare il mio anello dal Ponte di Rialto," I cried. (I want to throw my ring from the Rialto Bridge.)

"Non fare cosi! E oro!" (Don't do that! It's gold!)

"Melt it down for money, but don't throw it away," she insisted. So I took her advice and didn't throw it from the bridge, but I never had it melted down.

The ballet *Cinderella* was known better as a fairytale than the story of the *Nutcracker. Cinderella* sparked a great deal of enthusiasm, so it was easier to find sponsors. When my cousin Sandra heard about the project, she asked me if I could give the role to her finest student, Arianna. She had studied at La Scala, which was quite an accomplishment. A weak foot had kept her from continuing, but she was still a beautiful dancer and the perfect Cinderella. She had never had the opportunity to dance an important role, so I offered it to her and she was ecstatic. She was to be our guest soloist.

There were not as many props needed for this ballet. However, Cinderella's carriage was an absolute necessity. The production would fall flat without this important piece of scenery. The coach would have to be one-dimensional due to its size and expense. Teatro Accademia had very small wings, without enough space for any maneuverability. This problem had first presented itself with Mother Ginger's skirt in our production of *Nutcracker.* In Accademia, we had had to close the curtain for her entrance and tilt the skirt sideways to pass through the wings. The *Liquirizia,* or Bon-bon Children, had been placed under her skirt on the stage.

After deciding on a one-dimensional carriage, I had to decide on the style. *Should it be in the form of a pumpkin?* I didn't want the ballet to look Disney-inspired, so I modeled it after King Ludwig's carriage in Bavaria. I made a sketch from the photos I had taken of it in Munich many years earlier. The door would open so that Cinderella could enter the coach, and the whole piece would be mounted on a narrow base with wheels. A box seat would be attached to this so that Cinderella could sit inside. Visually, the giant wheels would not turn. However, the carriage would move along because of the wheels under the base. It would seem to float magically when fog was released from a machine in the wings. For the dimensions, I used the frame of the entrance to the living room in our apartment. I could imagine everything as far as size and measure it against the frame.

The golden cupola of the coach was too high to transport in an ordinary van, so I designed it to be removable. This would save money on transportation; otherwise I would have to rent a large truck. Later on, when it was constructed, an innovative idea of using hinges simplified the removal of the cupola, but it created additional height. So I had to rent a large truck anyway, which was the compromise I had to make to keep the beauty and smooth line of the carriage. When the sketch and dimensions were ready, I took them to Willi at the Bottega Veneziana. There I also selected two backdrops, the *La Traviata* windows again for the palace scene and the *La Sonnambula* set for the first act. This backdrop had two large, dreary windows and a huge, free-standing, gray fireplace.

The theater company, Colonna Infame, was with us again. Paolo and Gabriella from the company portrayed Cinderella's father and stepmother. Roberto, the Nutcracker, had worked with Marta for a year, but she had gone to Rome to dance professionally. He wanted to continue partnering, so I chose him for the role of the prince. He would drive to Mestre to rehearse with Arianna, and Sandra would help them with the rehearsal. This helped me because I already had a full plate due to my separation from Ovidio.

Moreno had just returned from China as the world champion of wushu kung fu. The *Nutcracker* experience had been positive for him, so I asked if he would like to join us for *Cinderella*. I wanted to choreograph a variation for him, transforming the art of wushu into the art of ballet, because so many of the steps were similar. Moreno's specialty in wushu was the *drunk*, which is the technique of combat using staggering movements. I decided he would be a drunken guest in the palace scene, and I used the music of the prince's variation in the pas de deux. Moreno began the variation with the wushu drunk movements, then classical ballet steps. He finished by running on a diagonal and making a somersault in the air, which he performed as though he had tripped from drunkenness. He landed on his knees in front of the prince and gulped a drink from the plastic champagne bottle that he held as a prop during the entire solo. Two actors dressed as foreign princes, portraying guests at the ball, carried him off the stage. Moreno's costume was a military jacket with white riding pants and black character boots. He still refused to wear tights, but he agreed to wear stage makeup this time.

"Dové hai trovato quel ballerino?" everyone inquired. (Where did you find that male dancer?) He was a hit! The public had no idea that he was performing a deadly, ancient martial art.

Only two costumes, the fairy godmother costume and Cinderella's rags, would be made by Adriana. All other costumes were tutus that I ordered from Fantechi in Florence. I decided to put the smallest children in white tutus—the first time I was up against resistance by the mothers. I had always left my door open to any problems or complaints by the parents, but there had never been any. The mothers of the preschool class organized a meeting with me to complain about buying the tutus. Each white tutu cost the equivalent of twenty dollars, but they wanted to spend less by taking a piece of pink tulle and attaching it to the child's black leotard. The budget for this was ten dollars, but it would have looked terrible and unprofessional. I looked at them in disbelief and said no. They vehemently protested, but I stuck to my principles. I was working hard to produce a high-quality ballet, and I wasn't going to ruin it. Unfortunately, every Thursday I had to face their sour expressions and coldness. I stepped into a candy store on the way to my train after that first meeting, and I bought the largest bag of *Baci,* chocolate-covered nuts. I needed the chocolates every Thursday after the preschool class, like someone who needs a drink to relax. The chocolates were my martinis, and the candy store became a sponsor in our program.

***

I had another four months until the school payments were done, but already I was doing well financially. The school was making money. Ovidio and I had to look for separate places to live, which would be extremely difficult.

Almost all Italians have their own *casa.* This can be an apartment, *villa a schiera,* which is a townhouse, or a single home. When a child is born in Italy, parents save to buy them a casa, as parents in America save for a college education for their children. With marriage, the new couple has two houses, his and hers, so they rent the less desirable one. The renters are usually foreigners, and rents are very high. It fascinated me that the average person in Italy didn't have to do anything, yet they received the keys to a fully paid house, or in some cases, houses.

Families that were poor could ask the government for a *casa popolare,* or low-income housing. There were also rent-controlled apartments for people who declared low income. Often, though, they weren't low-income at all, but simply defrauding on their taxes. It wasn't uncommon for doctors or lawyers to live in the case popolare because they had the right *conoscenze,* or connections.

Our apartment in Calle della Misericordia was rent-controlled and owned by a German man who wanted to live there when he retired. Two years before, he had informed us of his plans to retire soon, meaning that we would have to move. We were already moving in different directions and couldn't agree on where to live. The only thing we both agreed on was that Venice was outrageously expensive. Now it was absolutely necessary to look for separate living arrangements. I had two options: I could live in Conegliano or stay in Venice. The idea of living in a small town in Italy was a little scary. It was one thing to work in a place, but another to live there. Conegliano was convenient because my school was there, and it was cheaper than Venice. On the other hand, Venice was home. I came to Italy to live in Venice, not in Conegliano. But Venice could be a lonely place, and the thought of occasionally running into Ovidio bothered me.

Adjacent to the gelateria Darling was a real estate agency, Immobiliare Tinto, which had apartment listings in the window. They were closed when I arrived by train and opened when I began my classes. The prices for rentals were higher than Venice, and they had few listings. Then, one day, an apartment for the equivalent of seven hundred dollars a month was advertised. This was half the cost of the other apartment rents, and it was across the street from my school. The owner of the agency, Signore Tinto, met me at the apartment address. Signore Tinto was tall, handsome, and looked like an actor from a Roman film. The apartment was one room over a pizzeria, where I sometimes ate lunch. It was so small that the refrigerator was kept on the terrace, and there was a leak in the ceiling! It was depressing, especially for the price they were asking, so I kept looking. I began to think that buying an apartment might be a more economical solution. With the payments to Tiziana ending and the ballet *Cinderella* projected for the spring, I would probably have enough money for a down payment. Walking through San Lio, between Rialto and Dina's school, I found a real estate agency with a small apartment for sale in Venice. It was beyond my budget, but I was curious, so I made an appointment to see it.

I was told approximately where the casa was located in San Lio. The agent arrived late and didn't even apologize. He threw the cigarette he was smoking on the ground and stamped it out, then disgustedly motioned me to follow, without presentations. The door to the place was half-broken, and with a kick you could open it, but instead he used a key. It was a private entrance, and we walked up a rotten staircase on a dangerous slant. The apartment was one large room, and with both arms open, he made his presentation: this is it. I asked about the large, enclosed terrace advertised, and in silence, he showed it to me. It had a great view, but it was falling off the side of the building. One step on the terrace could result in a long fall down into the canal! My last question to the agent was about the location of the heater. He opened his mouth for the first time and told me there was no heater. It would have to be installed. In fact, it was missing everything.

"I'll let you know what I decide," I said. He gave me a weak smile and walked away, lighting another cigarette.

***

I decided to have a small footman in the third act. A child would hold a red cushion with Cinderella's lost shoe and accompany the prince on his search. It was January, the month before Venetian *Carnevale,* and the shops were filled with costumes, especially for children. There was a small toy shop on a narrow calle, which displayed a beautiful footman costume for a child. The costume could be the perfect, elegant outfit from the Baroque period. The long jacket was sky-blue and gold brocade, trimmed with lace, and the knee-length pants were aqua-blue satin. The three-cornered hat and shoes were made of a gold lamé fabric. The costume was expensive, the equivalent of one hundred and fifty dollars, but I saw it as an investment for the school because it could be used for future productions in palace scenes.

I couldn't understand how parents could afford to pay so much for Carnival costumes. I had seen a similar footman costume in the Piovesana toy shop in Conegliano, but it was dark green, the fabric was cheap, and it had very little detail. It looked like an inexpensive copy of the one I'd bought in Venice, but the costume was double the price. At the school, I chose the child who could fit into the costume so the mothers couldn't claim that I had a preference. They spoke among each other about the similar footman costume in the Piovesana toy shop, and a couple of mothers said they had ordered it for their child. Others mentioned buying costumes in the toy store window that were even more costly. The same mothers who had complained about twenty-dollar tutus for the theater spent hundreds of dollars for costumes to wear in the street! I was furious, but I kept my sentiments inside—that Thursday I doubled the amount of Baci chocolates to sooth my nerves. By the time my train arrived in Venice, I wanted to throw up.

***

I continued to look for an apartment *in vendita,* or for sale, but in Conegliano. I had no car, so I could only look at what was offered in town, within walking distance of my school. There was a mini-apartment listed at ninety-five million lire, or about forty-five thousand dollars, by Tinto's agency, so I called him and made an appointment to see it. The entrance to the building was on the outside of the medieval wall. It was a short distance from the Monticano Gate, with the famous Carrarese Tower over it. The gate was one of the two main gates leading into the walled town. The other, Rujo, was next to the Calle della Madonna, on the other side of the town.

An antiquated, European-style elevator hauled us slowly to the fourth floor. The building, about thirty years old, was relatively new by Italian standards. We entered the apartment and immediately found ourselves in a tiny hall with a closet, or storage room, to the right. Straight forward, a long, narrow living room became a dining area. Tinto explained that two women owned the apartment as a rental investment, so for this reason, it was furnished.

"Non ho mobili." I explained. (I don't have furniture.)

Tinto told me I could have the furniture if I decided to buy the place. A door from the dining area led to the long, narrow kitchen that was parallel to the living and dining room. There was another door at the end, leading back to the entrance hall. A small foyer to the left of the hall took us to the bedroom and bath. Again, there were more doors! In my mind, I was already removing all the doors, except for the bathroom and storage. The place was compact and cozy.

I walked through the mini-apartment again with Tinto. The window shutters that Italians used to keep out sun or thieves were all closed in the apartment. When I arrived at the shuttered kitchen door, I asked Tinto what was on the other side.

"C'é un posto per stendere il bucato," he said. (There is a place to hang wash.)

"Posso vedere?" (Could I see it?) As the shutters went up, I gasped. A wall, named the Rocchetta di Monticano, had been built to the height of a garage, and beyond that, a green hill continued to climb up in the direction of the castle. I would discover later that sheep grazed here, as they had for hundreds of years. The scene was breathtaking! We walked out onto a fairly good-sized terrace, and Tinto pointed out the clotheslines hanging from the railing. I commented about the beauty of the view, but he shrugged it off as insignificant. He asked if I was interested in buying the apartment, and though I tried desperately to contain my enthusiasm, I said yes.

"Posso offrirle il pranzo? Parliamo dell'appartamento." (Can I offer you lunch? We can talk about the apartment.) I accepted, and he took me to the most expensive restaurant in town, Salisà.

Most restaurants in Italy serve small portions, but the famous, high-priced ones gave even less. I could order a forty-dollar plate of ravioli in such a gastronomic temple and receive only two or three! No one complains because it is considered bad manners to do so, but one time I did. One summer, Ovidio had taken me to Cipriani restaurant on the island of Torcello. My parents, who were visiting, were with us. We sat outside under a covered terrace where there was a strong odor of cat urine. Dozens of cats called Cipriani home—my father was fascinated by them—and with the pungent smell above us, we ate lunch.

"We'll have to come back here and enjoy this great experience again," he said with his usual sarcastic tone.

When the food came, I couldn't believe my eyes. I had ordered *spaghetti all vongole,* or clams. On the plate were three *vongole* and three strands of spaghetti. At sixty-five dollars a plate, each spaghetti strand and one clam was worth a little more than twenty dollars! I asked the waitress to call the manager. Ovidio was excited and agreed that this was ridiculous, but in Italy no one speaks about these things. Italians don't want to be called *maleducato,* or badly educated, so they prefer to pretend everything is okay and not call attention to the problem. They just accept it. The manager agreed that the portion was small, so they doubled the spaghetti strands to six. Ovidio pleaded with me to say no more.

Now, as Tinto studied the three scallops in a *cucchiaio,* or spoonful of cream sauce, he carefully constructed what he would say.

"Mi piacciono le piccole porzioni che danno, perché cosi posso mantenermi in forma." (I like the tiny portions they give, because I can maintain my weight.) But at that moment, I didn't care about the wonderful food or the small portions. I could only think about the apartment and how badly I wanted it. When I was approved for a mortgage and bought the apartment, I took a friend to celebrate at the same restaurant. I placed the keys of my school and my apartment on the table.

"Now I have both: a business and a home."

***

Having a telephone at home was not an easy matter. For the average Italian citizen back then, it took weeks to have one installed. So I went to the telephone company in Conegliano to put my request in, with the anticipated long, patient wait ahead. However, I didn't imagine then that it would be the beginning of a nightmarish odyssey.

"Lei è un'extracomunitaria, cosi non puo avere un telefono," said a sour, thin, unpleasant woman with thick glasses. (You are not from the European community, so you can't have a phone.)

I left the office perplexed. *A non-citizen can't have a phone?* Friends said this was ridiculous and suggested I wait until I had my resident papers in hand. So I went to the City Hall in Conegliano to fill out the papers for residency. Unfortunately, it was more complicated than I expected because I was still legally married. It was necessary for me to bring a copy of my separation papers. Also, Ovidio had to come with me and sign permission that I would be residing alone. Once the papers were signed, a *vigile,* or city policeman, would visit me unannounced at home several times to confirm that I actually lived there. If he didn't find me after a couple of visits, I would automatically lose residence there and be declared an illegal resident. I had the ballet school, so it was difficult for me to stay home and wait for the policeman to show up.

The City Hall was open on Saturday morning until twelve-thirty, so Ovidio went with me to Conegliano. We arrived at the offices after twelve-thirty, but the doors were open and people were still working at their desks. The woman at the *anagrafe*, or registry office window, told us they were closed.

"Non è possibile, perchè in Venezia il commune è aperto fino all'una," Ovidio excitedly told her. (That's not possible, because in Venice the City Hall is open until one.)

"Voglio parlare con il direttore," he said. (I want to speak to the director.) A stout woman with short gray hair, dressed in a blue suit, came forward. She curtly informed Ovidio that the office would reopen Monday morning. That's when he totally lost his temper. He began yelling that he wanted the office opened immediately to take care of the business we had come for. The director was snarling as she called the guard to escort us out of the building. I was mortified! As we were about to exit, Ovidio turned back and made a Venetian hex sign at the director. He was attempting to put a curse on her, and then he said,

"Sono un donatore di organi, e se lei un giorno avra bisogno dei miei organi, non glieli daro!" (I'm an organ donor, and if one day you need my organs, I won't give them to you!)

I recall the director shouting something at him, and then a few obscenities escaped. *What was he thinking?* As the guard led us out, he kept repeating that the offices were open until one o'clock in Venice, so it just wasn't possible that they would close at twelve-thirty.

"Il tuo ex-marito ha fatto casino," said Tinto. (Your ex-husband made a hell of a mess.) He explained that now the director of anagrafe would insist on sending the vigile several times to my apartment before approving my resident request. The requirements would be stricter now, and there was a greater probability of denial.

A friend, Lucia, was the aunt of one of my students and had been close to me during this period of transition to Conegliano.

She had I gone to school with Franca, the director of the registry, so she spoke to her. Later she told me she assured Franca that I was a very nice person but my husband was a monster, and for this reason, I was divorcing him.

"Ho detto che non è colpa tua." (I told her it wasn't your fault.) She added that Franca understood after meeting Ovidio and promised to send the vigile only one time. Whenever I ran into Franca in Conegliano, we would look at each other and laugh, recollecting Ovidio's antics in City Hall that day.

Now, equipped with my residence papers, I went back to the phone company. The same unpleasant woman sat at the front desk. She looked up with a disgusted expression as I presented my resident papers. After glancing over the papers, she repeated that as an extra-communitaria, I could not have a phone. This time I left the office angry, but I didn't know what to do next. There was no phone in the school because it was a public space. Posters had to be printed, advertising registration and the opening of the school in September. They had to be ordered in July because the printer was closed in August, so I would have to have a phone number by then. Prior to that time, I had used my home phone in Venice for information. The family of a student offered to let me use their phone number on the *locandine,* or posters, for any inquiries, so this was at least a temporary solution.

The last days in the apartment in Venice were happy and sad. One happy recollection was of the salotto filled with Degas-style tutus in every pastel color imaginable for *Cinderella.* With the terrace door open, the cool air of April mingled with the breezy tulle. The Paris-style park sang with the colors of spring flowers. It was a kaleidoscope fantasy that could bring joy even at the saddest moment. The beauty of the room and the park beyond would bring balance to all the unhappiness I had known there.

***

The ballet *Cinderella* was an enormous success. The school sold even more tickets than the *Nutcracker,* and this helped me to start my new, single life. Without a family and not a penny from my marriage, this money was a blessing. I had refused to take any alimony from Ovidio, because every month I would be reminded of him when I saw the check. I wanted to make it on my own and forget him. But the ballet was not only a financial success; the dancers now were much stronger and had made great progress.

The only thing that didn't go as well as planned was the entrance of Cinderella's carriage. As the Fairy Godmother, I gently pushed the coach from the wings on a cloud of fog. The footman opened the door, and Cinderella ran to the coach with a long, flowing, pink tulle cape trailing behind her, held by two small children in white tutus. She sat in her chair inside the carriage and waved goodbye. However, all of this was barely seen by the public because the stage curtain closed too fast. But we would have another chance to repeat this scene and get the timing correct. We had a request for an encore performance, this time as a benefit to raise funds for battling leukemia. This began a new chapter—presenting ballets to help cancer victims and the research for a cure. *Cinderella* would go to battle against cancer.

The Fairy Godmother in Cinderella

CHAPTER 11

The Rooster and the Swan

"Nothing is absolute. Everything changes,
everything moves, everything revolves,
everything flies and goes away."
Frida Kahlo

The *gallo* shouted his wakeup call in the morning. It was real—not a dream—as I discovered when I opened my eyes. *How did I get here?* What events had preceded my awakening to the sound of a rooster in a small medieval town in Italy? Then I remembered the divorce. *Where do I go from here?* This was the same question I had asked myself in the piazza facing the abandoned church in Venice four years ago. The rooster made his final wake-up call that morning and I cried, alone in my new home.

June arrived quickly. I gave a two-week summer ballet intensive and then closed the school for the long, three-month vacation.

"Get out of Conegliano in the summer. It's like a ghost town here," advised a Canadian acquaintance who owned an accessory shop in town.

"Everyone goes to the mountains and the sea," she said. Only one supermarket had to stay open, by law, for the few residents who were unfortunate enough to remain in town. I was going to New York in July, and afterward, I would stay another two weeks at my father's house in New Jersey. August, I would have to reckon with.

When the time came to part for New York, I was still heartbroken about my divorce, but for the first time in my life as a struggling artist, I experienced a sense of financial security. I could attribute this to the growing success of the school and the ballet productions. I checked into the hotel on Broadway and from there I walked over to the Metropolitan Opera House where the Kirov Ballet was performing. The New York City Ballet performed long seasons at the State Theater next to the Met, and I remember that as a young dance student, I had gone often to see Balanchine's ballets. We had bought the cheapest tickets for one dollar and watched the orchestra seats below to see which ones were empty. The ushers had let us have the better seats when no one claimed them. They had known we were poor dance students and wanted to help. However, with visiting companies, it was different. I had never been able to see the Kirov Ballet at the Met because I couldn't afford a ticket; it was often impossible even to get one. They were sold out for weeks, sometimes months, in advance. So I had never seen this great company.

I walked up to the box office with the slim hope of finding a ticket for a performance.

"We are all sold out," said the man at the box office.

"I have wanted all my life to see this company perform," I said with disappointment. As I started to walk away, the man called me back.

"If you are willing to pay the price, the best box in the Grand Tier is available tonight."

"How much is it?"

"Two hundred and ten dollars," he replied.

"I'll take it." *Why not? I've worked so hard and this is my gift to me.* The man handed me a gold ticket to the ballet *Swan Lake.* I went back to the hotel, unpacked, and ate dinner. Then I returned to the Met and walked up the winding stairway to the Grand Tier. Each box had an usher who unlocked the door to an anteroom. Beyond this room were the red velvet seats, the best in the theater, and I was alone in the box. *What luxury!* The chandeliers disappeared into the ceilings, and I was reminded of when, as a student, I had performed there with the Stuttgart Ballet in *Romeo and Juliet,* and with the Royal Ballet in *Sleeping Beauty.* The orchestra began the overture of *Swan Lake,* and suddenly it happened—my eyelids became heavy and I was falling asleep! The jet lag had finally caught up with me.

I fought to keep my eyes open. Seeing the Kirov Ballet perform had long been an aspiration of mine, and I had the best seat in the theater—I couldn't sleep now! During intermission I drank tons of coffee, so I managed to stay alert and enjoy an evening of dancing that I will never forget.

***

The last days of July, I returned to Conegliano and found half the population had fled the city for vacation. But on the first day of August, I was reminded of a horror film where all the inhabitants disappeared because of some supernatural phenomenon. All cars were gone and there wasn't a soul on the streets. I walked the streets like the lone survivor of some disaster, desperately searching for life. It seemed like a miracle when I found Firmino Pasticceria open. The café was well-known for its excellent bakery in the front. I received a cold, hostile stare from Firmino. A month before, I had stood on the terrace of the Metropolitan Opera House, looking at the majestic fountain and the stars in the sky, and now I was in a stifling, hot, gloomy, unfriendly café in an unheard-of town. The contrast was depressing.

"Cosa volete?" Firmino asked. (What do you want?) Though it was hot, I ordered a cappuccino and read the newspaper. I was the only customer in the café. Firmino returned with the cappuccino and shoved the beverage onto the table. He gave me a hard look and then quickly removed the newspaper, just in case I was thinking about reading and lingering. I stared into space, feeling like an unwanted outsider, not knowing what to do or where to go. Firmino hovered over me until I drank the last drop of cappuccino, then he grabbed the cup and pulled it away. His look said, "Please leave now." I didn't want to go into the harsh, empty world, so I ordered a vanilla gelato with amaretto liquor on top.

The signora who owned the *profumeria* a few doors down entered the café. It lifted my spirits to see another human being, not counting the cold presence of Firmino. She was happy and surprised to see me and came to my table. We knew each other from the orders I had made for transparent hairnets and red lipstick for the ballets. The gelato arrived, and she drank an espresso. I explained that I had recently moved to Conegliano from Venice, the circumstances, and my divorce. But with each word I spoke, I suffered the loss of Ovidio and the pain struck me deeply. I didn't weep or sob, but a single tear ran down my face and into the gelato. My tears kept falling into the gelato as I continued to eat and talk. The shopowner's reaction was almost comical. She was uncomfortable watching me eat my sorrows and looked frightened. I had the impression that she wanted to run away! Then she made an excuse to abandon me but paid for my gelato on the way out. Firmino roughly took away the espresso cup and gelato dish. His look said, "Now you are done, so go." On the street, I experienced a desolation of the soul that I had never known before. I ran home to the security of my little apartment and counted the days until September. It seemed like a prison sentence, but my incarceration would soon be over.

Before my self-imposed prison time was up, I had a strange visitor. A Franciscan priest came to bless my apartment. I had never had my home blessed, but then I hadn't ever had a home. The priest got off the elevator with his bike in tow. I guess he was afraid of someone stealing it if he left it downstairs. He was dressed in a long brown robe and wore sandals. Priests in Italy always dressed for their role, whereas American priests often dressed like normal citizens.

I had once met an American cardinal from Philadelphia while touring Florence. We were both staying at the same hotel, and in the evening we would meet for a brandy together in the hotel bar. One evening he confessed that he was a cardinal and was on his way to live in the Vatican. I wanted to run or fall on my knees and confess all my sins! He said he dressed normally so that people would not be intimidated by him.

I was uncomfortable with the Franciscan priest who did not hide who he was. The fear of religion would always be a part of my life. He looked at me, perplexed, and said,

"Dove è nata lei?" (Where were you born?) I told him New York, specifically the Bronx. He pondered heavily this fact before asking curiously,

"Come è arrivata a Conegliano?" (How did you arrive in Conegliano?)

It was an odd story—how an Irish American from a tough Bronx ghetto had moved to a small town in Italy. I gave my account, leaving out the more gruesome details. He became very interested when he heard that I had married a Venetian in Venice.

"Lei si è sposata in chiesa?" (Did you marry in the church?) I told him it was a civil marriage, and I thought he would damn my soul for this sin. He seemed relieved and told me that the marriage didn't count in the eyes of God, so I was free to marry. My marriage had never existed, according to Catholicism. I wished that it was so easy to cancel the past, but Italian law did not agree with the church.

"Io le auguro di sposare presto un uomo in Chiesa." (I wish that you marry a man very soon in the Church.) "Preghiamo." (Let us pray.)

***

My apartment was sunny and on a higher floor, so the heat was insufferable without air conditioning. The town was at the base of the hills rather than on water, like Venice, so at least it was less humid. I had lived close to the sea all my life, so the hills seemed oppressive to me. I had to create a routine in the summer months so that I didn't go crazy. Every day, I walked Via Cavalotti towards the outskirts of town where Il Gelato, the best gelateria in town, was open in August. They were closed from twelve-thirty until two o'clock, and sometimes I waited on the bench outside for the store to open. Rain, shine, or unbearable heat, I trekked there every day. The owner, Adriana, was passionate about making gelato. We often exchanged long conversations because at that hour of the day, especially in August, there were no other clients. I always ordered *cinque palline,* or five scoops, two chocolates and three vanillas. Over the years, she would dish out the scoops when she saw me coming, and Il Gelato became our faithful sponsor for many ballets.

On the way back, I would sometimes stop at a little chapel that was a few meters from the entrance to my apartment. The chapel was only as big as a tiny room, with an altar to the Virgin Mary. It was always cool inside, and there was a faint smell of incense. I would light a candle for my mother, as I did in every place I traveled in this world. At that time, the door was always open, welcoming believers, and my soul was at peace there.

***

The castle on the hill would once again mark an important event in my life. August 15, or *Ferragosto,* was over, and the population slowly trickled back to town. Signs saying *Chiuso Per Ferie* came down, but it was still too early for the children to go back to school. The day was another scorcher, and I was cleaning my apartment. I remember hating the world that day. I hated the heat, the cleaning, my ex-husband, and the small, medieval village where I lived in exile. My life outside of the school and theater was very lonely. As a foreigner, I wasn't accepted by many of the people in the community. It reminded me of when I danced with the Stadttheater of Klagenfurt in Austria. The dancers were all foreigners, loved by our audiences, but outside the theater, we were not wanted. The environment was not hospitable. It was the same in Conegliano, but I couldn't abandon my school and my dream now that I held them in my hands. If it meant I would suffer, then so be it. I would do anything for my art because it was my life.

I decided the only medicine for my bad mood was a big gelato at café Darling, but I didn't feel like changing my clothes or bathing, which almost stopped me from going. I was sweaty, grimy, and wearing a faded black T-shirt tucked into a short denim mini-skirt. *Who cares? No one will see me. Probably I will be the only customer there, so I will go as I am.* I sat outside in the café and ate a cinque palline gelato. But I wasn't the only customer in the café. There was a handsome young man with long, curly, black hair and a prominent chin. He was dressed in jeans and a white shirt with rolled-up sleeves. There was an old, red, classic Alfa Romeo parked in front of the café, and I assumed it was his. Everything about him spelled "playboy," except for the large, black-framed glasses that he wore. They made him appear more intellectual and less of a gigolo. I hoped he wouldn't talk to me because I knew I would reply sharply. My divorce had turned me off men, and I was in no mood to waste time with small talk or flirtations. But, as I had predicted, he spoke to me. I can't remember his words, but they were innocent and totally unexpected, so I didn't respond coldly.

The conversation continued, and it was like a simple exchange of words between friends. He introduced himself as Gianni, and he told me he was a native of Treviso but he had his own bar/café in the next town, San Vendemiano. After a while, he asked if I would like to go to the castle with him.

"Andiamo," I said. (Let's go.) I walked to his car. He was as surprised by my quick acceptance as I was. But I felt propelled forward by some mysterious force inside me. I could have been accepting a ride from a serial killer, but the anger I had inside made me fearless that day. On the hill, Gianni gave me a tour of the castle. I had toured the castle with a guidebook in hand, but it was more interesting to hear the story from him. He was sincere, unaffected, and comfortable to be with, especially because he could see beyond my messy appearance. After the tour, he said he had to return to work at his café, so he drove me to my apartment. Then he asked for my phone number, and I told him I didn't have a telephone. He gave me his number and asked me to call him, but I didn't want to see any man at that time. I was very mistrustful after the recent breakup of my marriage, and besides, Gianni was much too young for me.

The school registration began to mark the end of a month of sufferance. The last day and hour of registration, Gianni walked in. He said he called the number on my school registration poster, and the mother who had offered to help with the telephone inquiries had told him where I was. We went out for a gelato and decided to meet one night for dinner, but I wasn't sure it was the right thing to do. At that time, I had started to see a therapist to work through my divorce because I didn't want to repeat my mistakes. *Why hadn't I seen the problems right away with Ovidio?* My therapist listened in shock as I recounted the stories of my marriage, his trance broken only by his wife who had the nerve-racking habit of calling constantly during our visits. I asked him what he thought about my seeing Gianni, someone obviously much younger.

"Perché no? L'eta non è niente," he said. (Why not? Age is nothing.) So I went to a pizzeria in Conegliano with Gianni one night. While we were eating, he told me he was twenty-seven and I almost choked. I hadn't considered that he could be under thirty, and I was almost forty-one! There were thirteen years between us. I wanted to stand up and walk out, but I stayed to be polite. However, I kept seeing him because I enjoyed being with him. I looked forward to our time together, and memories of my bad marriage began to fade into the background.

One day my therapist told me it would be our last visit—he had discovered the cure for me. I expected some sort of advice about future relationships; instead, he told me to lie down on his sofa and he shut off the lights. *This isn't good!* I thought he might jump on me, but instead he played a recording of the sound of waves in the sea and left the room. A half hour later he came back and announced that I was cured. I thought it was some kind of a joke, but it was called *therapy:* just another strange adventure in Italy!

***

After the performance of *Cinderella* back in June, I was introduced to the president of AIL, the Italian Association against Leukemia. Teresa Pelos, the president for the Veneto chapter, was a strong, kind, religious woman who had made it her mission to fight cancer. She had lost her only son, who was sixteen, to leukemia. Her presence had the aura of a saint—speaking to her was almost a spiritual experience. Teresa had seen *Cinderella* at Teatro Accademia. Her proposal was to bring the ballet to a theater in a nearby city at Christmas, with the money from the performance going to leukemia victims and their families.

I accepted this project immediately. My goal was to repeat every ballet we did for charity, particularly for cancer and research for a cure. Already, Teresa had a venue in the city of Oderzo, close to Conegliano. The mayor of Oderzo had been personally touched by cancer and was committed to Teresa's cause. The city of Oderzo offered the elegant Teatro Cristallo free for the performance. The theater had been recently restored and, like

Teatro Accademia, it was used as a cinema on weekends. A printer, also sympathetic to the cause, offered to sponsor the posters. The Bottega Veneziana allowed us to use their scenery without charge when they heard that the project was for AIL. In addition, Teresa found other sponsors for smaller expenses. New students were added to the cast, and I quickly ordered costumes for them. As with the *Nutcracker* in Teatro Goldoni, *Cinderella* was easier the second time around.

***

I had been without a phone for months. When I needed to call someone, I went to the hotel Canon d'Oro in the old city, which was close to where I lived. My friend Lucia, whom I saw quite often, accepted my incoming calls. After registration, I had an idea about how to get a telephone. The Italian Yellow Pages advertised local businesses. By advertising my school in the Yellow Pages, I might be able to get a phone through them. I called the company and spoke to their advertising representative, Leonardo, and he assured me I could advertise the ballet school in the phone book.

"Dammi il tuo numero." (Give me your number.) I explained that I couldn't have a phone at the school but asked if I could use a home phone.

"Certamente. Dammi il tuo numero di casa." (Certainly. Give me your home phone number.)

"That's the problem," I said. "The phone company won't give me a phone!"

"Cosa?" (What?) "Perché (Why?) I explained that I owned my own apartment and business. However, because I am American, or extra-communataria, the phone company wouldn't give me a telephone. Leonardo said he would go with me to the office and insist that they give me a phone because there was no reason that the company should deny me one. We made an appointment to meet at a bar/café near the offices of Telecom. A tall, robust, bearded man walked up to me. I was usually recognizable, even to strangers, because I didn't look Italian—I look more Nordic—and I didn't follow *la moda* in clothing.

After introductions he repeated incredulously,

"Non capisco perché non le danno un telefono." (I don't understand why they don't give you a phone.)

When we walked into the office, the same morose woman sat at her desk. With confidence, Leonardo confronted her.

"Questa signora è una straniera e lei ha bisogno di un telefono." (This woman is a foreigner and she needs a telephone.) Without hesitation, she took the request forms, asked me a few questions, and then had me sign the form.

"Lei avra un telefono la prossima settimana." (You will have a telephone next week.)

At long last, I had a phone! After this experience, I understood that survival in a small Italian town depended entirely on whom you know.

***

Finally, in early December, the performance day of *Cinderella* came. It was a very cold day, and when we arrived in the theater, there was no heat. I spoke with the custodian, and he promised that there would be heat coming up right away. Hours passed as we prepared the stage with scenery and a dance floor that we had rented. Then the lighting company arrived, but there was still no heat. My breath froze when I spoke. I complained again to the custodian.

"Il riscaldamento è guasto." (The heating system is broken.) He assured me it would be fixed and said a repairman was on the way. I told him it was essential that there be heat for the dress rehearsal scheduled for three o'clock. However, by the time the rehearsal started, there was still no heat, so I told everyone to wear heavy sweaters over their costumes. After the rehearsal, the dancers went out to eat and stay warm somewhere. Night came and the theater was getting colder. It was painful. *What would the dancers do tonight?* Also, the audience would never stay in a theater without heat.

Something about the whole story didn't smell right. The heating should have been fixed by then, unless it had been purposely shut off. That's when I figured out that it was the latter. Angrily, I went to the custodian, who had probably been told to shut off the heat to save money. I advised him that I was closing down the show because I refused to permit my students to perform in a theater without heat. I wasn't bluffing: no heat, no show! Within a matter of minutes, the place began to warm up. Very few theatrical productions were done in Italy in the wintertime because heating a theater was just too expensive. In contrast, the theaters were closed in July and August because there was no air conditioning. The city of Oderzo was generous in donating the theater for the benefit, but they obviously didn't want to spend extra money on heating.

I had invited Gianni to the ballet and somehow the word had gotten around that he was my new boyfriend. The parents were all curious about him, and I hoped that they wouldn't notice that he was much younger than I. The performance went beautifully, and this time, the arrival of Cinderella's carriage was coordinated perfectly, so the audience had time to appreciate the impact of the scene. But most of all, the evening was a financial triumph for AIL. *Cinderella* raised the equivalent of three thousand dollars. Unfortunately, many students came down with the flu from exposure to the cold at dress rehearsal; I also contracted the flu, which later developed into a debilitating case of bronchitis.

***

Ironically, the most unlikely person in Conegliano became the friendliest. The president of the local SIAE, Signor Bertolini, was a feared enemy who later became a friend. After I had sold his seat at the first *Nutcracker*, he had become a determined opponent. *I would pay for my mistake!* A couple of days after that show, I had gone to pay the tribute demanded for the musical copyrights. He had told me I was one day late and would have to pay a hefty fine in additional to the music rights. I was being penalized heavily for both; then he waved the program at me.

"Tu devi pagare per tutti questi sponsors," he had declared. (You must pay for these sponsors.) I told him my accountant had said that I didn't have to pay because the sponsors were not sponsors—they were businesses that had bought space for publicity in the program. My accountant

Giovanni suggested that Signor Bertolini call him. However, after that, every time I saw Signor Bertolini walking in Conegliano, he angrily stated that he wanted money for my sponsors.

"Il tuo commercialista non mi ha mai richiamato!" (Your accountant never returned my calls!) I shrugged my shoulders and hurried off. For *Cinderella,* I was lucky because he was in Rome. His wife had taken care of the tribute payments when he was away, so I could breathe a sigh of relief. When I saw him in the street, I hid somewhere or changed direction. But one day he saw me and I couldn't avoid him. To my surprise, he was very friendly and shook my hand. As he saluted me and walked away, I wondered what my accountant had said to him that had changed everything.

***

When spring arrived, we were invited by a dance school from Santa Lucia, a little village in the countryside near Conegliano, to perform as guests for a show in Teatro Accademia. The performance was to benefit leukemia, organized again by Teresa Pelos and her organization. Two schools performing together would guarantee more tickets sold and more money for the beneficence. I choreographed *Sinfonia,* which I had done before, and participated briefly with my dancers. We also contributed solos from the repertory of well-known classical ballets. One of my students, Cinzia, was giving her last performance. She was marrying a local man who had a winery in the hills near Conegliano. I decided to teach her the role of the Dying Swan. Because she was small, pale, delicate, and had gorgeous feet, I felt she would be absolutely perfect for the role. We worked for hours on perfecting her *bourrées* and I coached her for expression. She was a hard-working and diligent pupil who gave a superb performance. The whole show went very well and raised a lot of money for the leukemia association.

I received an invitation to Cinzia's wedding in June. It was to take place in a romantic little church right next to her future husband's winery in an area known as Carpesica. Cinzia had told me that she had a surprise for me in the church ceremony, but I couldn't begin to imagine what that could be. The wedding day was sunny, a rare gift in the month of June. Inside the church, a violinist had been chosen to play the music. It was a fairytale wedding, almost a Cinderella story. At one point during the ceremony, the violinist began to play the "Dying Swan." Though it was a strange piece for a wedding, it was very moving. At the altar, Cinzia turned around and smiled at me. I understood that this was her way of saying thank you to me for making her last performance on stage special. The shrill song of the rooster that had made me cry not long ago was transformed that day into the soft violin strains of a swan.

Gianni in Venice

The church in Carpesica

CHAPTER 12

An Injured Firebird

"Our greatest glory is not in never falling,
but in rising every time we fall."
Confucious

L *a fortuna in amore,* or luck in love, had arrived when I met Gianni.
Less than a year after we met, he moved in with me. But at the
same time, bad luck had started to plague me professionally. It
started with a shakeup in the academic school system. A new law was
introduced that ordered children to attend school three afternoons a week.
Before this, students had attended school only until one o'clock, or lunch time.
Their afternoons had been free, so we had begun classes around four o'clock.
Now it was necessary to start at five o'clock. Some students had to use dance
class time for homework, so many dropped out.

Their quality of dancing was now at a higher level. I was proud of my
students and how far they had come in four years. I decided that the
moment was perfect to produce *Firebird* and *Petrouchka,* an evening of
Stravinsky ballets. While they had made great progress, none of them was
ready to dance the role of the Firebird. I had dreamed of dancing the part
since I had seen it for the first time at age nine. A birthday present, it was
the first ballet I had ever seen performed by the New York City Ballet at
City Center. Years later, I had danced the role of the Tsarevna in Richard
Holden's version of the *Firebird* with the New York Dance Ensemble.
From the wings, I had longed to dance the role of the Firebird. Now it was
my chance—the last one I would have. I could envision Sara, an advanced

student, as the beautiful Tsarevna. Roberto, who was now a seasoned partner, would be the prince. Also, his acting experience was perfect for the role of the clown Petrouchka. The acting company would participate again, mostly in the ballet *Petrouchka*. The tall actor, Gianni, who had portrayed Mother Ginger in the *Nutcracker*, would be the wizard Kostchei in *Firebird*.

The *Firebird* scenery would consist of two backdrops. One was a tulle forest that could disappear before the eyes of the audience. The following scene appeared without closing the curtain to make the change of lowering one backdrop in front of the other. This was done through the use of special lighting, and Willi from the Bottega Veneziana assured me that it could be executed. The second backdrop for the production was a palace garden that resembled an exotic oriental scene. The ballet would begin in the forest amidst a fog and slowly fade to the palace for the wedding. Even though the performance was months away, in my mind, I could hear the gasps and applause of the audience when they would see this magical effect!

On the other hand, *Petrouchka* required that an entire set be built. I made the designs for the Russian carnival and puppet stage. Again I designed all the pieces to be flat for storage and easy to assemble. The Bottega Veneziana approved the design and quoted a price. The project was expensive, so I knew I would have to double the number of sponsors in the program in order to pay all the expenses. I wanted to copy every detail of the original Ballets Russes production for both ballets. My idea for a program cover was to make it a replica of a Russian lacquer box, with a design that represented the story of the Firebird. I had bought the box on a trip to Moscow almost twenty years earlier. The program would open like a box, containing the names of the dancers and sponsors.

***

I continued to learn about the absurdities of life in Italy. A letter arrived from the *Finanza*, or the Italian Internal Revenue. They said I owed the equivalent of two hundred dollars in business taxes, so I called my accountant to see why I had to pay this.

"Non c'è ragione. Paghi." (There is no reason. Pay it.) He explained that the government would create a new tax and declare it to have been in effect months earlier. That way they could hit people with a penalty on top of the tax and make more money. Now it was my turn to pay because I had been one of those picked at random. Italians were reconciled to paying taxes that were extraordinarily unfair. I rode two buses to the office that was outside Treviso, in the middle of nowhere. A crowd had formed outside the office, which was still closed for lunch. An employee was waiting for the doors to open to return to work. She was bombarded with questions from the unfortunates who were stuck with paying the tax.

"Perché dobbiamo pagare questa tassa?" someone in the angry crowd inquired. (Why must we pay this tax?) She replied with a laugh. The government wanted money, and this time we were called on to contribute. The next time, other businesses would have to contribute involuntarily. When the doors opened, everyone piled into the office and formed lines at the payment windows. Some continued to protest the injustice, but in the end, we all paid. We had no choice.

I'll never forget an old man who stood in line at the window beside mine. He wore his best jacket, brown, worn-out and frayed at the cuffs, but still used for important occasions. His tired eyes had cataracts and his mummified skin looked baked from the sun. The old man was anxious about the whole matter and stiffly walked to the window.

"Ho solo sei galline che fanno uova. Perché devo pagare questa tassa?" (I have only six chickens that produce eggs. Why do I have to pay this tax?) He was desperate because he didn't have the money and was afraid that they would confiscate his chickens. I remember the man crying, but the Italian government had no pity.

On top of having to pay the business tax, it was time to renew my *permesso di soggiorno,* or green card. I was only separated, not yet divorced, so I could continue to live and work in Italy. However, when the three years' separation was over, followed by two years for a divorce, my future in Italy would be questionable. I didn't have to go to the foreigner's office in Venice but the one in Treviso. At least Il Diavolo wasn't there!

As in Venice, the office was part of the *questura,* or police station. Long, seemingly endless lines of men from Africa waited outside the questura, sometimes for hours. Gianni said he knew the chief of the foreigner's office because they had gone to school together. He made an appointment with him so that I wouldn't have to wait in the long lines. But when the day came, I was told I must wait in a line, even with an appointment. While waiting my turn, a couple of surly Moroccans pushed ahead of me. Their abusive, sexist behavior was infuriating, but I had to swallow my pride and let them go ahead of me. They gave me sly, arrogant smiles. Moroccans were famous for carrying knives and slashing anyone, even the police, who got in their way. They would think nothing of cutting a woman who tried to defend her position in line. The Italian government wouldn't even arrest them if they hurt me, and if they killed me, they would be back on the street in a few days. This is Italian law. It protects delinquents and punishes the innocent.

After I waited a couple of hours on the street, my turn came, and a tall, fat policeman opened the door. He looked me up and down flirtatiously, as though beyond that door, sexual favors would be required. Quickly I entered and said that I had an appointment. Before he could protest, I ran as fast as I could up the flight of stairs where I knew the offices were. The guard couldn't leave the door unattended, so he had to let me go.

The chief carefully examined my documents, asked a few questions, and then sent me down to the floor below. As I walked by the offices, I looked in one and froze in terror. There at the desk sat Il Diavolo, as though he had followed me to Treviso! He didn't see me, and I quickened my step, but I hoped I wouldn't have to deal with him. *What was he doing there?* Probably he had been transferred, as Venice was only half an hour away. I had had enough nightmares about him deporting me.

Downstairs, at the green card window, an attractive, sullen office worker in a police uniform was about to stamp my visa for another two years. She looked at the clock and realized it was time for her break, so she handed the papers to her colleague. It was the best thing that ever happened! The office worker, who was dressed in regular clothes, examined my papers more carefully.

"Sei stata sposata cinque anni con un Italiano?" she inquired. (Were you married to an Italian for five years?) I answered yes, and she congratulated me because I had qualified for a permanent green card. The other woman hadn't cared that I was eligible for a permanent permesso di soggiorno. If the officer in uniform hadn't gone on a coffee break, I would have continued to live in a precarious situation. I would never again have to live through the nightmare of the questura lines—I would never have to see the face of Il Diavolo again!

***

The year of *Firebird* and *Petrouchka*, I decided to buy the costumes and keep them for future productions. Almost all the costumes over the years could be crossed over from one ballet to another, and I would rent them, which would eliminate a lot of time and work. Everyone would pay an equal fee so that no one could complain. This time, except for a couple of tutus, a dressmaker would make the costumes. A couple I knew in Venice had a school in Belluno and was selling some French-made tutus. They were on the train from Venice to Belluno, and as it stopped in Conegliano, we did our exchange. From the train window, they threw me plastic bags of tutus and I handed them an envelope with money! Then the train continued its journey.

The Tsarevna's wedding dress was the most detailed, so I commissioned Adriana for this masterpiece. In addition, she made the costumes for Petrouchka, the doll, and the Moor. From photos and designs of the original Ballets Russes production, she created identical copies. They were expensive to reproduce and were made with the highest quality of fabric. However, I needed a dressmaker who could make the Cossack shirts, gypsy skirts, and matryoshka capes in quantity. One mother recommended a dressmaker named Carla, who was inexpensive and did excellent work. I called for an appointment.

"Chi è?" asked the voice of an elderly woman. (Who is it?) It was more of an angry statement than a question. When I began to respond, she hung up. I reported this to the friend who had recommended Carla. She explained that Carla would never hang up and that probably it was her mother who had answered the phone.

"Chiama nel pomeriggio," suggested the mother. (Call in the afternoon.) I did, and this time I spoke with Carla. She spoke a mixture of Italian and the local dialect in a younger, cheerful voice, and we made an appointment.

Carla was short, sturdy, broad-shouldered, and wore a perpetual smile. She was an optimist whose philosophy was that nothing was worth worrying about. Everything would fall into place in due time. Carla wore a white coat like a doctor, and her operating room was a chaos of sewing projects and material. She cleared some space on a large table, and we talked about the designs. After we discussed numbers and approximate sizes, she totaled up the amount of material and recommended a discount fabric store on the outskirts of town where her cousin Gianfranco worked. I asked how much her work would cost, and she quoted a ridiculously low price.

"Quand'è lo spettacolo?" she asked. (When is the show?) I told her the date.

"Ah, c'è tempo." (There is time.) She waved away the notion of any problem. Unlike Carla, I believe in getting things done sooner, rather than later.

Over the next few months before the ballet, I called Carla once a week to ask how the work was progressing. She asked me again and again when I needed the costumes. When I told her the date, she repeated that there was time. However, as the date came closer, I wondered when she would begin sewing the costumes and became increasingly worried.

***

Preparations were moving along for the ballet, which would be performed in Teatro Accademia at the end of May. A few months before the date, I hurt my back. It was an old injury from my circus days and that had flared up during rehearsals. I was forty-two years old and not in the same condition I had been when I danced the role of the Sugar Plum Fairy. I wasn't teaching aerobic classes, which had kept me in shape. Gianni had heard of a therapist from the hospital who worked wonders. The therapist, Luciano, accepted private patients at his home, so I made an appointment. Luciano was blind, so he had a great deal of sensitivity in his touch. He knew immediately where and how much the body had been damaged. The treatment was a combination of massage and a therapy machine, similar to the one used by the hospital in Venice for my Achilles tendon. Rest was also recommended, when possible. Gradually, this gifted young man eliminated my back pain, and soon I was dancing again.

My second injury was more serious and happened two months before the ballet. It didn't happen in rehearsal but in a stupid experiment. One day Gianni asked how long I could hold my leg in the air. I said I didn't know, so I decided to take the challenge. I lifted my leg high to the side without a warmup and held it there. It remained up there a long time before I lowered it. At that moment, I suffered a hip muscle cramp and was in excruciating pain. I couldn't sit, stand, or lie down, only scream in agony. *What was I thinking?* The pain didn't go away or even lessen, so Gianni drove me to the hospital emergency room where the doctor ascertained that I hadn't broken anything and diagnosed a pulled muscle. A nurse gave me a muscle relaxant injection in my hip, and the pain disappeared. However, while I was aware that the pain was gone, my leg was paralyzed from the hip to the knee! After a few days, the feeling hadn't come back, so I went to see Luciano.

"Mio Dio, Il tuo nervo sciatico è stato danneggiato severamente!" (My God, your sciatic nerve was severely damaged!) That was the bad news. The good news was that the needle from the shot in the hospital had not permanently damaged my leg. Just a fraction higher and the injection would have left my leg irreversibly paralyzed.

"Tre mesi e la sensibilita ritornera," Luciano reassured me. (The nerve sensibility will return in three months.)

***

Under the arches of the old buildings in town, a small *antiquariato,* or antique store, stood next to Firmino's café. The shop window always displayed rare, magnificent antiques that were hundreds of years old. I would stop and admire the contents of the window display, like I was making a brief excursion to a museum. I could never imagine owning such priceless things. My mother and I had been poor, and I had grown up surrounded by cheap, broken furniture that even charity organizations had refused to take. I wanted to walk inside the store, but I always felt unworthy and inferior. I had always possessed confidence in my work, but my humble beginnings made me feel insecure in certain situations. However, one day I opened the door to this fantastic museum of the past and toured the showroom.

The shop was owned by Enrica, the mother of one of my students. Enrica had introduced herself when I had first started teaching at my school. She had shook my hand and said, "Chiamami se hai bisogno di qualsiasi cosa." (Call me if you need anything.) She totally accepted me, whereas the other parents seemed uncertain because I hadn't earned their trust yet. That day, when I walked into her world of art and antiques, an important friendship began. She welcomed me into her shop and called Firmino, next-door, to order a *caffè macchiato* and a cappuccino for us. We talked about her daughter Camilla's progress, and she told me the stories of old paintings and furniture that were there. When Firmino arrived with the order, he looked surprised and stared at me, sitting in front of Enrica. From that day on, he was always extremely polite and respectful to me when I entered his café. He saw me now as a respectable *signora* instead of an undesirable foreigner.

I was guided through a stimulating course of art history from Enrica's infinite knowledge of the subject. She was my teacher. Later, I began to frequent the store often, and we got to know each other on a more personal level. We understood the irony of life in a small town, and we would look at each other and laugh because we shared the absurdity of living in a place like Conegliano. It wasn't like anywhere else. The town had its own hierarchy, bigotry, and outdated codes from medieval times. Enrica loved ballet as much as art and antiques, so she became an ardent supporter and was an important sponsor for the *Firebird* program.

***

We were down to one month before the evening of Stravinsky ballets. Though I couldn't feel my leg from the hip to the knee, I only had to change one step in the pas de deux. I was particularly happy with the monster scene in *Firebird.* The right interpretation meant staying within a delicate line between the monsters looking funny or scary. I wanted them to look frightening, as the rats had in the *Nutcracker.* Moreno was again with us for the ballet. He performed a solo as the most deadly monster in Kostchei's army. This scene combined ballet, pointe, jazz, contemporary, and wushu kung fu in the choreography.

The basic costume for all the monsters was a black, turtleneck, long-sleeved jumpsuit. The ballet soloists on pointe had brown jumpsuits, and one wore green. They had feathered masks that matched the color of their costumes, but I wanted the other dancers in makeup. Their hair would be teased in wild masses, but I couldn't figure out how the makeup should look. Then I remembered *Indiana Jones and the Temple of Doom.* The attendants in the temple had black and white, skull-like faces. We tried it on the dancers, and it produced the horror effect I was looking for. But for Moreno, I had to do something different. The first ballet was *Petrouchka,* and he had the role of the Moor. I had a tube of dark greasepaint that had sat in my red makeup case for thirty-five years, as a souvenir from when I had played the role of a nine-year-old Arab boy in the *Nutcracker's* Arabian Dance. Now it was useful for Moreno as the Moor; however, he had only enough time to wash off the makeup during the intermission of the two ballets. There was no time to make him up as a monster. A mask was impossible for him to use because of the intricate movements he performed. So we decided on a black gauze band over his eyes, which made him look like a blind Ninja.

The costumes that Carla would make all needed decorative borders. It seemed inconceivable that I couldn't find these trimmings anywhere, but costume decorations were non-existent. Perhaps in big cities, like Rome and Milan, they could be found. Back then, it was difficult to have supplies sent from abroad because Italy had a bad record for this kind of thing. Items were stolen so often in customs that most countries refused to do business with Italy. A large quantity of ribbon would have been sufficient, but ribbons were usually sold in small amounts. Gianni had heard of a factory near Conegliano that made ribbon, so we decided to go there.

Outside the iron gate, we spoke through the intercom. The person who spoke couldn't figure out what we wanted, but invited us inside anyway. We had just parked the car and were walking toward the building when an enormous German Shepherd came charging at us. Our first instinct was to run, but at that moment, an older woman came out of the office and commanded the dog to halt. She yelled at us,

"Non fate gesti strani!" (Don't make strange moves!) We were both too frightened to move.

"Lupo!" A man who walked with a limp came outside and called to the dog. Lupo, which means wolf, was the name of the dog. Lupo ran to his owner who cheerfully invited us to enter his office. He assured us that Lupo was a good dog but repeated what his wife said: "Non fate gesti strani."

The man sat at a desk in the office and calmly lit a pipe. Gianni and I sat in two chairs in front of the desk. The older woman was presented as the man's wife. A young man and woman entered, and they were introduced as the son and daughter. It was a family business. All the time, Lupo guarded his owner. He seemed to fill the entire room.

"Dunque, che cosa posso fare per voi?" (Well, what can I do for you?)

I tried to explain what I needed, but it didn't make sense to anyone. They didn't make that kind of ribbon or bordering. We couldn't figure out what they made and they couldn't understand what we were looking for. So the meeting ended and they wished us luck. The entire family smiled and waved goodbye as we walked to the car. Then Lupo ran out of the building and came charging at us.

"Non fate gesti strani!" they yelled, but we didn't listen. We got in the car as fast as we could. My skirt got caught in the car door, and I thought he would tear it with his teeth. Instead, he jumped on the hood of the car and snarled at us. It was like a scene out of the film *Cujo*. The family lovingly watched his antics, and I could almost hear them say, "Isn't he cute?" Gianni and I were in too much shock to care about the ribbon anymore!

***

A week before the first dress rehearsal, I called Carla for the costumes.

"Quando ne hai bisogno?" (When do you need them?)

I desperately explained that in one week we would have the dress rehearsal. She told me that they would be ready in two days. I was skeptical, but two days later I went to her house. Twelve Cossack shirts and twenty matryoshka capes were sewn and stacked in a neat pile, ready to go. The amazing thing was that each shirt and cape was finished with a border! Carla had creatively improvised fancy bordering with strips of fabric. I was stunned by her work and the low price she asked for her effort. Carla would be our dressmaker for many years. Despite my fears that the costumes wouldn't be ready in time for the ballets, she never let us down.

***

The day of the Stravinsky ballet evening arrived. The sets were hung for *Firebird*, though it was the second ballet. We had to do everything in one day, so every minute was important. I would always rehearse so that the last scene would be the first one presented at the performance. This way, a scene was mounted only once and the procedure saved time. The scenery could not be changed electronically. Everything was done the old-fashioned way—by hand. Bepi, the head stage technician, waxed the cords that pulled up the backdrops and kept them from fraying. Then, with strong hands, he manipulated the scenes, and Gianni helped him.

Hours passed, and the lighting company had not arrived. They had been late for *Cinderella*, but the excuse then was that their truck had broken down. Now they were even later, and again they claimed the breakdown of the truck as the reason. This simply couldn't happen twice. The lighting director, Franco, finally arrived with his crew, and they hustled to mount the lights quickly. But while the men were unloading the truck, Franco asked me for a disproportionate cash fee *in nero*, or under the table, without any receipt. Franco sat in the audience like a grand artist and directed his men, but he never lifted a finger himself. When it came time for the transparent forest backdrop, I was told it was impossible. I was devastated! It was clear that Franco wanted to work as little as possible, but how could he ruin our ballet? There was nothing I could do but accept mediocre lighting. I would never call Franco again, but it was too late to pull out then. So the curtain had to be closed between the forest and palace scenes.

At nine o'clock, the ballet commenced, and *Petrouchka* went very well. The catastrophe came with *Firebird*. It was very dark, and the stage was filled with fog. One of Franco's crew was in charge of the curtain. He didn't wait for my cue; instead, he panicked and opened the curtain when the music introduction started. Bepi was finishing a last-minute detail. He was startled when he found himself in the middle of the stage, the curtain open and the audience staring. He ran off quickly, but the audience laughed and applauded his performance. Roberto entered, hunting with his crossbow. It looked like Bepi was being hunted by Roberto, and someone in the audience yelled *bracconiere,* which means poacher! I couldn't help laughing even though it ruined the beginning, but I was feeling worse about the transparent forest that couldn't fade. Poor Bepi! Every time we saw him, he apologized for what happened, but it wasn't his fault. We would always laugh about the *bracconiere!*

I made it through the pas de deux, even with a semi-paralyzed leg. Dancing the *Firebird* meant so much to me, but I would have preferred to dance the role feeling my whole leg. At one point I was performing a promenade on the injured leg in a backbend. My foot had found a hole in the stage floor so deep that the dance floor on top couldn't cover it. It was a strange sensation, my foot turning in a deep hole, the same leg dead from the knee to the hip, and looking at the room turning upside-down. I couldn't imagine a more peculiar set of obstacles in performing the pas de deux.

After the ballet, I was told that a journalist and critic from the paper *Il Gazzettino* had come to see the performance. I was still down about the things that had gone wrong. The next day, I bought the paper and saw in the Arts and Performance section the headline "Applause for Firebird." The title alone moved me to tears, and the article got better and better as it praised the Stravinsky ballets.

***

In July, I relaxed on the bench in front of Il Gelato and enjoyed a five-scoop gelato in the heat. When I finished the sweet, my right hand rested on my thigh and I could feel my leg! Just as Luciano had said, three months had gone by. The injured Firebird was whole again. Now I could pick myself up and once more fly to my dreams.

The Firebird pas de deux

CHAPTER 13

A Prayer Bench

"Whatever it is you are seeking,
won't come in the form you're expecting."
Haruki Murakami

The strange antique kept calling me to look at it again, as I became enchanted by the odd piece of furniture. It was a small jewel and seemed to say, "Take me home." I sat in front of Enrica's desk while she spoke to a client on the phone, and the tiny *inginocchiatoio,* or prayer bench, was on my right side. When Enrica hung up the phone, I asked her about the piece and she told me its history.

"È un piccolo bel gioiello!" she said with animation. (It is a lovely little jewel!) There were three compartments. One opened from the top, and the prayer books were kept there. The front compartment opened outward like a cabinet. The bottom, where the one praying knelt, had a place to store things and opened upward. Centuries ago, nobles kept an inginocchiatoio for praying at home. It was part of the large villa of a well-known noble, titled Italian family, and the heirs were selling off their inheritance. I asked the price, and Enrica looked at me like "You can't afford it." But she respectfully told me the price anyway.

"Lo prendo." (I'll take it.) Enrica was shocked, but the deal was done and I brought the cash the next day.

Most of the furniture in my apartment was cheap and modern, left there by the women who sold me the place. I had two, identical, old wooden chairs from Venice that were copies of those from the eighteenth century.

The chair reproductions were one hundred years old—Ovidio had found them one day on the border of a canal, near a pile of garbage. They had probably fallen into the canal at some point because they had a faint odor of the sea. The sea smell always reminded me of Venice. Ovidio didn't want them, so I had taken them when we separated.

When the prayer bench was delivered, I placed it in the small hall outside the bedroom. This old, elegant object brought out many strange emotions in me. The inginocchiatoio was the tangible of success. It validated my success in a material rather than spiritual way. The antique also brought out my insecurities and made me confront them. The prayer bench now belonged to an Irish American from the Bronx. It would no longer be part of a private room in a villa veneta, where it had stood proudly for centuries, but would come to rest in my humble abode. I felt guilty, unworthy, sad; and I wanted to apologize to the bench for its new home.

***

The misfortunes of the *Firebird* seemed to mark the beginning of a dark period for me and for the school. Thankfully, I had Gianni always by my side during this time. The school director retired that year, and a young, pretty, but hostile-looking woman with glasses came to be the new director.

"What is this ballet school doing in an academic institution?" she inquired the first day of her new tenure. I feared my days were numbered with the changing of the guard.

The first thing that had to go was my scenery, neatly and unobtrusively stored in the back of metal lockers and storage closets. I had designed everything to be one-dimensional, so that sets for different ballets could be placed back-to-back, robbing only a couple of inches from the wall. I was notified in a very formal, official letter that the scenery was a safety hazard. Of course this was absurd, because the heavy lockers and storage closets would have to fall over first before the light plywood scenery could hurt someone. Relentlessly, she attacked me to a point at which every day when

I saw the school, nausea would overcome me.

She eventually won the war. The problem was where to take the scenery for storage. If worse came to worst, I would have to put it in my tiny apartment. However, the mother of a student, Paola, offered a temporary solution. Her parents lived in a big old house in the hills, and because of their age, they only used the first floor. They agreed to let me park the scenery on the abandoned top floor of the house. It was an enormous favor, and I was very grateful to them.

It was quite an undertaking to move the scenery there. The truck was filled with Cinderella's carriage, the *Petrouchka* circus and theater, the *Nutcracker* clock and tree, and boxes of costumes. The big truck twisted and turned with difficulty up steep hills to the final destination. Once we arrived, it was parked at the bottom of another hill, which we had to climb to get to the house. I helped guide Gianni and his brother-in-law Dante, who carried each piece laboriously up to the front door. The next obstacle was maneuvering the large, flat pieces on the tight staircases all the way up to the top floor. In the end, I felt like we had delivered the scenery to heaven! I would dream about the scenery alone in that room in the house on the hill. But I slept well knowing it was safe and that I wouldn't find it dumped in the street, along with an eviction notice, in front of the school.

***

I was innocently introduced by Enrica to a woman named Maria Angela Filetto, who had seen *Firebird* and *Petrouchka* at Teatro Accademia. Enrica said that she was very impressed by the ballets and would like to meet me and that she would like to promote them for the benefit of hospitals and cancer research. I thought of Teresa Pelos and how we were able to raise a lot of money for leukemia with *Cinderella*. The first show covered expenses, but for the encore performance, I wanted to dedicate to a worthwhile cause. So I agreed to meet Filetto at the school.

"Non ho mai visto balletti cosi belli a Conegliano," she praised. (I've never seen ballets so beautiful here in Conegliano.)

Filetto was middle-aged, small, and stout, with an untamed mass of wild hair framing her face. Her skin was olive-colored and her eyes were a light green. People had named her *La Zingara*, or gypsy, because of her physiognomy and the long, colorful skirts she wore. The image of the artist was one she desperately tried to pull off, unsuccessfully. Nevertheless, she was the rich wife of an important bank director and had power and connections in Conegliano. She had decided that her calling was an impresario of *danza*, though she knew nothing about the art. However, my first impression of her had been different when we had met at my school. She had simply struck me as a person who loved ballet and wanted to help raise money for a worthy beneficence. We discussed repeating the Stravinsky ballets at Christmastime for the Comitato Panizza, the committee for the cancer researcher Panizza at the Padua Hospital. I was teaching at the ballet school when she came to meet me, and I agreed to the project immediately. We decided to meet again at a later date.

One day another visitor surprised me at the ballet school: Tinto. He opened the door of the studio and asked if he could speak to me. I thought his visit had something to do with documents for my apartment. The Italian bureaucracy was intricate, and I was worried something was amiss. We went to an empty classroom to speak. Tinto asked me if I would like to move my school into the health club he owned with other partners outside of town. During that period, health clubs were offering ballet classes for children in order to bring in more money. He wanted me to bring the entire school to his club, and he would pay me the equivalent of seven dollars and fifty cents an hour to work for him. It was an absurd offer! I told him I was perfectly happy where I was. Then his tone changed and he became aggressive, insisting that I work for him. I didn't like the direction that the conversation was going, so I repeated that I wasn't interested and had to get back to teaching.

Then he blurted out, "Sei legale in Italia? Hai il diritto di rimanere qua?" (Are you legal? Do you have the right to remain in Italy?) I was stunned at his question, or rather accusation! I informed him that I had a permanent green card and repeated that I had to return to my class. He left the school angry and I was shaken. Later, I confessed to Gianni that I was afraid that the meeting would have repercussions. But my permesso di soggiorno was in order, so what could he do? Still, I was uncomfortable.

Within a couple of weeks, a vigile presented himself at my apartment. I was away that day, but Gianni was at home when he came. The policeman said that he had an order to inspect my apartment because I was an extra-communitaria. He told Gianni that he wanted to be sure I had a toilet and could bathe somewhere, because the extra-communitari did not have good sanitary habits. When Gianni told me what happened, I was livid. There was also a summons for me to appear at the local *Carabinieri* station, the Italian national police force. I was ordered to make an appointment and to bring academic diplomas and certifications to teach ballet; and I would be tested to see if my Italian was sufficient. This confirmed that Tinto had sought vindication.

When I met with the marshall of the Carabinieri, he complimented my Italian. He looked at my high school diploma and was impressed that I finished school. In Italy, many people my age were dropouts. It was the first time my high school diploma had ever been useful! Then he studied my Dance Masters Certificate. All of this was crazy because none of the teachers there had a certification to teach. Most of them had no experience teaching and had never danced professionally. They improvised. A short time after this, Tinto found a teacher and offered ballet classes at his club. The experience was the first of many attacks that would follow from others like Tinto. I had introduced an art to Conegliano, one that produced envy.

***

Maria Angela Filetto made an appointment with me to discuss the ballet at Christmas, and we met at Firmino's outdoor café. At the appointment, I was surprised to meet another dance teacher, Mirella Bellano from Mestre. Two years before, she had bought Carmela's school, the oldest in Conegliano, on the other side of town. Carmela's school was in decline, and she decided to sell it before she was forced to close. I didn't see Mirella as a competitor because she had mostly jazz classes, while I specialized in ballet.

Filetto presented Mirella and turned the discussion over to her. The plan for the Stravinsky evening was scrapped, and it became two local schools partnering in a show. It was suggested that I bring one of the two ballets, and the second half would be Mirella's recital. I didn't like the idea, but I couldn't think of a valid reason for not accepting the proposal. Also, I had promised to do this for beneficence, and it would be wrong of me to pull out. Between both Stravinsky ballets, *Petrouchka* was the one with more dancers, so I was told to bring this one. The idea was that the more dancers who participated would mean more tickets sold and more money collected for cancer research. Filetto said she would call me as soon as a date was confirmed in Teatro Accademia, and both women left the café, in different directions. I wasn't happy about the entire meeting with these two women. They were both authoritative, with an air of superiority.

We began rehearsing for *Petrouchka*. The dancer who had played the doll had graduated and gone off to college. She had continuously missed rehearsals the season before, and I was always standing in for her, so as her substitute, I was well prepared to dance her part. Besides, I had had fun working with Roberto and Moreno together in the ballet. Filetto notified me of the date, but I hadn't expected that the show would be in the morning. This would mean a poor turnout, but Teatro Accademia couldn't offer another time. A few weeks before the performance, Filetto asked Gianni to distribute the posters, and Conegliano became wall-to-wall publicity for the performance. She always acted like a superior rich woman, expecting everyone to take her orders. I was told to sell as many tickets as possible, and I did—but not for her. I did it for the benefit of cancer research. Without the work of Gianni and me, the theater would have been empty that morning. We were never told how much money was raised by the performance for cancer research that day.

***

Over the years, the austere weather conditions of the Regione Veneto seemed to produce excellent, committed dancers. I was hungry to take them beyond the confines of a small town and introduce them to a big-city dance world. The first opportunity presented itself with an invitation from the Royal Academy. The academy was presenting a *Rassegna di Danza*, or Dance Festival, in Turin at the beautiful Teatro Alfieri, and they invited us to participate. It was to be presented the last weekend of April. I thought this would be a wonderful chance for my unrivaled students, Sara and Elena, to dance outside of Conegliano. Solos were not allowed, the maximum time was three minutes, and the minimum was three dancers in a piece. I asked Mara, a talented young woman who taught the pre-ballet classes for me, to be the third dancer. The music I chose was Bach's violin piece, *Senza Definizione*, or translated in English, Without Definition. The choreography describes the uniqueness of each dancer. They started together, then moved in separate directions and were reunited in the finale. We rehearsed with a tape, but one day I heard a violin in the next room that sounded like Bach's work. A school of music had begun to share space with us, and the artistic director, Alberto, was an accomplished violinist. The four of us ran to hear him play and listened with awe to the real thing! It was quite different to hear every string on the violin. I begged him to play the music while the girls danced, but he was timid and embarrassed, so he refused.

Along with the performance invitation, an announcement arrived for the scholarship auditions for Vignale Danza. Sponsored by Teatro Nuovo, the auditions were held at the same time as the Dance Festival. The minimum age was thirteen, so Sara could try out, but unfortunately, Elena was only twelve and therefore too young. I had made a reservation in one of the numerous hotels that offered discounts to the Rassegna and scholarship participants, teachers, and their families. The one I selected was near Teatro Alfieri, where we would be spending most of our time. An old guide book gave it a high rating. After a four-hour train trip, we arrived in Turin and took a taxi to our hotel. The grand lobby, with various *salotti*, or small parlors, was impressive in dark mahogany and beige marble. Everything was pre-war and illuminated by an enormous crystal chandelier in the main entrance. Heavy, turn-of-the-century furniture graced the high-ceiling rooms. *I made the right choice!* However, the beauty faded away as we climbed the stairway to the top floor, which was like an attic. The walls and carpet became old and dingy. It was obvious that this part of the hotel had never been renovated since the war and was desperately in need of restoration.

We had reserved two rooms. I bunked with Sara and Mara, and Elena stayed with her mother who had accompanied her to Turin. All of us looked at one another in disbelief when we saw our rooms. *Was this a joke or something?* The wallpaper and curtains were torn, yellow with age, and filthy. The carpet was stained with cigarette burns, and the smell of stale smoke permeated the air. Nevertheless, our spirits were high with the excitement of performing in an acclaimed theater in an important Italian city. Tolerance of any inconvenience was only a small price to pay for this great experience and adventure. The hotel was to be our home for four days, so we would make the best of it.

We unpacked and went out to dinner. It rained constantly and it was unusually cold for April, so we huddled together under two umbrellas. The hotel recommended a simple trattoria, so we ate there. The schedule for the scholarship auditions, rehearsals, and performance had been sent to me, so after dinner, we studied the program for the next four days. We had a rehearsal late the following morning. The day after, we would have the scholarship auditions at Teatro Nuovo, and on the last day, we were back in Teatro Alfieri for the performance.

It was late when we got back to the hotel. We waited for an elevator that never came. It seemed like they shut it down after a certain hour, so we trudged up the stairs. I gave Sara the key to the room, but when she turned the doorknob, it fell off in her hand. We were too tired to laugh. I called the desk from Elena's room and explained the situation and was told a handyman would come and fix it. The hotel handyman was a towering man with big hands and feet and an enormous head with a high, protruding forehead. His clothes were old and tattered. He was a perfect double for Frankenstein's monster, and we were frightened when we saw him climb the stairs. He stumbled as though he was drunk, and with an unsteady hand, he fixed the doorknob. When the door opened suddenly, he fell into the room. He adjusted himself and left the room without a word. None of us slept well that night because somehow we felt we were being watched. The decrepit hotel and creepy handyman fed our imaginations like a horror film.

All of us managed to survive the night and wake up the next morning. However, we woke up to another surprise: there was no hot water for a shower. Our phone didn't work so I knocked on the door of Elena's room. They didn't have hot water either, so I called the desk from their room.

"Stiamo facendo la riparazione, Signora. Sara sistemata piu tardi," the manager said. (We are making repairs and it will be working later.) Later didn't help us at that moment, but the shock of cold water sharpened our senses and reflexes. After this torture, we were greeted downstairs with a breakfast I will never forget. Tantalizing pastries were displayed on antique silver and white linen. Turin is famous for its pastries, and they had everything for a continental breakfast fit for a king. It was a total contradiction to everything else in the hotel. The breakfast kept us going all day, until dinner.

The five of us jumped into a taxi to go to the theater. Teatro Alfieri was sumptuous! The stage was large and not so slanted or raked as those in other Italian theaters. Spectators could enjoy the beautiful, gilded masterpiece of the interior before seeing the performance. It was like a museum. Dancers wore colorful costumes and practiced while waiting for their limited time to rehearse on stage. Our time came, and the girls danced very well. After they rehearsed, we stayed in the theater to watch the other dancers. The rain continued to fall, so we remained there all day. We went back to the hotel when we were conscious of hunger pains. There was still no hot water in the shower, but we were assured that there would be the following morning. It was never repaired, so we had only cold water all four days in Turin. It reminded me of when we had no heat in Teatro Cristallo at the performance of *Cinderella*. Most likely, they had turned off the hot water to make up the loss of money on the discount they had given us.

The second day, we went to Teatro Nuovo for the scholarship audition.

When we arrived, I discovered that the minimum age had been lowered to twelve, maybe because of the lack of participants. Only those who had sent a request to audition before the deadline could participate. Elena was dying to try out, so I quickly thought about how I could get her into the audition. A large, corpulent, distinguished, older man with a moustache and a goatee came down the school stairs. The man was the school representative for Teatro Nuovo, and he called the names of the dancers auditioning in her age group. I went to the man and lied, telling him that I had made the request before the deadline. The representative looked worried as he combed the list and finally asked me to spell Elena's name as he wrote it down. Elena's mother took a taxi back to the hotel to get her dance bag, and I prepared her hair in a bun.

Sara and Elena auditioned at different times. They said the class went well and they were confident that their performances were good. It would be hours before they read the names of the scholarship winners. Because Teatro Nuovo was surrounded by a large park and the rain continued to pour down, there was no place to go. We paced the floor of the theater lobby like everyone else. Finally, the representative descended the stairs with envelopes containing the results. The maximum awarded was five weeks, the entire Vignale summer course. The lesser award was two weeks. First, Sara's name was announced, followed by Elena's—they both had won! They opened the envelopes to find that they had received the maximum five-week awards. They were my first students to win important scholarships, and they had honored their hometown of Conegliano. I was proud and excited for them. Later, we went out to a pizzeria and celebrated their success.

The last day was the Rassegna performance at the Teatro Alfieri, which would last several hours. The various schools that were dancing rotated dressing rooms. After they performed, they changed and took all their things with them. Most of them watched the rest of the Rassegna from the audience. The performance went beautifully, and at the end of the evening, a special award was given to one school. The announcer declared the winner, and the school that won was proudly taking home two scholarships, both for *two* weeks, not the two *five-week* scholarships our school had won. There is a big difference between four and ten weeks, so I had to wonder how they had gotten this honor. Along with joy, there was the disillusion of unfairness, which often comes in the dance world. Nevertheless, Sara and Elena had each received the highest award, and no one or nothing could take away that happiness. Back in Conegliano, I wrote an article for the *Tribuna* and *Gazzettino,* recognizing the accomplishments of the two girls. The Vignale scholarship auditions in Turin every spring became a tradition in the school, one that lasted ten years.

When the summer arrived, Sara was ready for the course in Vignale, but Elena decided not to go. I was shocked!

"Perché?" (Why?) How is it possible that anyone could throw away such a great opportunity? Elena and her family maintained that she was too young for such an experience. That decision would cause her future in dance to decline. A lifetime ago, my teacher Madame Maria Swoboda at the Ballets Russes School referred to me as "little one," because I was the youngest in her class. One day you are too young, it seems, and the next day, too old.

***

We had a demonstration at the end of the school year, with all the students. Parents, families, and friends came to watch, and I served Italian prosecco afterward. The parents and students presented me with a tremendous chest of flowers. Gianni was working, and no one could give me a passage home. Alone in the school, I looked at the leftover prosecco bottles and the flower chest. *I can carry this home.* Though my apartment wasn't far from the school, I stopped often to rest. There was a slight tearing in my left shoulder, but I ignored the pain. That foolish decision would cost me. But I had other problems to deal with at that moment, so my shoulder pain was put on hold.

CHAPTER 14

Fifth of Treviso

"Life is not a question of how to survive the storm,
but how to dance in the rain."
Khalil Gibran

The drop in enrollment continued after the first impact from the afternoon *rientro* in school. The economy was not good in Italy, and many schools had already closed. But the other factor was the opening of an indoor swimming pool in Conegliano, on the edge of town. Pediatricians began telling parents that ballet was bad for their children. The doctors said the best exercise for children was swimming. It seemed like the doctors were being paid to endorse the pool.

The interest in classical ballet had also abated, and in order for a school to survive, other dance courses had to be introduced into the program. Right before the end of the school year, Mirella called me for a meeting. She said she wanted to close her school and asked if I would like to incorporate her jazz courses into mine. Her jazz teacher and thirty-five students needed a place to go. In two years, I had lost two-thirds of my students, but I was still open for business. Other schools in Conegliano had closed. I had only thirty-five students of ballet, so the extra students would be an advantage. Two schools could be combined into one. Mirella wanted the equivalent of nine thousand dollars for this merger, with payments that could be spread out in the ten-month scholastic year. I didn't believe it was worth that much. However, I had to do something to keep my school open, so I spoke to my accountant Giovanni.

"Stai lontana da quest'affare!" (Don't touch this deal!) It was too risky, he said. But he had an idea for me to propose to Mirella, if she was convinced her school produced at least this much money monthly. It was simple: I would use the jazz students' total monthly tuition to pay the teacher and the hourly rent. The leftover money would go to Mirella for one year. I wouldn't make any money the first year, but I wouldn't lose any either. Mirella agreed. In September, we started the jazz courses, along with classical. Right away, it was evident that Mirella's students were not bringing in the money she had declared, but she was content with anything that came into her pocket.

***

In September, I decided to repeat the *Nutcracker*. Six years had flown by, and the little children in the first ballet were now young women and accomplished dancers. Elena had been one of the children under Mother Ginger's skirt. Now she would dance the role of the Snow Queen and Dewdrop in Waltz of the Flowers. Sara would dance the Sugar Plum Fairy with Roberto, and I would be Madame Silberhaus, Clara's mother. Sara had improved tremendously after her intensive summer training at Vignale Danza. She had become an amazing dancer! The *Nutcracker* was much easier this time because we had every single prop and many of the costumes.

In October, Filetto announced another Christmas show for the benefit of the Comitato Panizza for cancer research. Despite closing her school, Mirella was involved as the artistic director. I was ambivalent about doing business with her, even after Giovanni had prepared an infallible deal, but I didn't want to refuse the invitation to participate in the benefit. The previous Christmas benefit performance had been an unpleasant experience. I consoled myself with the thought that the show was for a good cause. This year would be different because many schools were invited to perform, bringing in more money for the beneficence. Each group could have up to five minutes maximum on stage, and choreography for a large number of dancers was encouraged. I decided to bring the finale of the *Nutcracker* to the show, with thirty-five students, and I would choreograph this before the rest of the ballet.

December arrived and it was time for the performance at Teatro Accademia. A couple of weeks before the show, Filetto brought a roll of tickets to my school.

"Vendi biglietti," she commanded. (Sell tickets.) With such a large group of dancers performing, I was able to sell many tickets.

We were well-prepared, and the *Nutcracker* finale went superbly, but other than the five minutes on stage, the evening was awful. The show began at nine-thirty instead of nine o'clock, with the hope of last-minute tickets that were never bought. Most of the tickets that night were the ones I had sold. The performance finished at one o'clock in the morning. Some of the schools had two dancers who were on stage for twenty minutes because they were friends of Mirella. My students danced in the beginning, so we had hours of waiting in the dressing room before the finale of the show. Students from the other schools smoked and cursed—and while we were on stage, they even robbed us! Once again, my desire to help the benefit for cancer research had blinded me to all the negatives of working with Mirella and Filetto.

***

After Christmas, Gianni decided to sell his part of his bar/café. Once it was sold, he wanted to go back to Treviso. His family lived five miles outside this small town where he had an apartment. At first it seemed like he wanted to go back home by himself, without the baggage of an older woman. I had met his brother, three sisters, and his parents. One sister was vehemently opposed to our relationship and made it known. His parents were unhappy about the situation, but they avoided any confrontation with their son. An objection might push him away, and they loved him too much to let that happen. *But did he love me?* I wasn't sure.

With so few students, my income went way down. I had increased tuition over the years, which helped a bit. My mortgage was variable, and the interest was at twenty-two percent! When Italy became part of the

European community, this loan-shark rate was considered illegal, so it went down to eighteen percent, which was the border of legality in the European community. But even with the high interest rate, it was the same cost as renting an apartment, so it was better to own. Gianni had asked me to come and live with him in Treviso, but I didn't know if he felt sorry for me or if he couldn't live without me. I hoped it was the latter. After my bad marriage, I was in no hurry to tie the knot again. The only thing I wanted was a child, but at forty-four the chances were slim. Gianni didn't want children, and I was probably too old to have them, so we were compatible in this respect. We decided to begin a new life together in Treviso, and I would rent my apartment.

My accountant Giovanni warned me that it was risky to rent because Italians would often stop paying and continue to live in a place for years. At the time, Chinese families were flocking to Italy, and many were opening restaurants. The food was good and cheap, so they were especially successful in tourist cities like Venice. A Chinese restaurant opened below the palazzo where I lived, and the family sent their two daughters to study ballet with me. They were extra-communitari like me, and I trusted them. I asked them if they knew a person that needed to rent an apartment, and they said they would ask around. A few days later, I received a phone call to come to the restaurant. When I arrived, I was presented to a fiftyish, friendly Chinese man named Paolo. Of course Paolo wasn't his real name, but no one seemed to know his Chinese name. I knew Paolo already, and everyone was acquainted with him because he had once owned the first Chinese restaurant in Conegliano. But Paolo was notorious for another reason: he was the head of the Chinese mafia in Veneto. He was always laughing, especially when he appeared on the front page of a newspaper in Veneto, handcuffed by the Carabinieri for criminal activity. I guess he laughed because he knew the Italian law was a revolving door. Paolo and I shook hands like old friends and he laughed. I explained that I wanted to rent the apartment and what I was asking. He said the rent didn't matter— he was willing to pay whatever I wanted. But the strangest thing he said was that no one would be living in the apartment. *He only needed the address.* Immediately, I understood why he wanted or needed my apartment. He had a racket going for immigration. The Chinese would have his guarantee for a job and a place to live for Italian immigration, and he was paid an enormous sum of money for making the arrangements. This form of trafficking was common in Italy and all over Europe. I decided I wanted no part of his offer, but I told Paolo I would think about it.

I went to a real estate agent to find a tenant, and after two months, he found a young Sicilian couple that had come to Veneto for work. Cousins of the couple lived in Conegliano and took care of negotiations and the deposit. They bargained down the price, so the mortgage I had was not completely covered, but they guaranteed for the couple. In case the couple didn't meet their obligations, they would pay the rent. Except for my inginocchiatoio, Venetian chairs, and TV, I would leave the furniture I had found there when I moved in. The Galitti couple from Sicily moved in and I went to live with Gianni in Treviso.

***

Treviso is a quiet medieval town surrounded by a wall. Unlike Conegliano, the area is flat and there is no picturesque castle. However, the center is a maze of narrow streets that are too small for a car to enter. There are many canals with bridges that remind visitors of the town's proximity to Venice. But there is no congestion from crowds of tourists like in its famous neighbor. The shadow of Venice obscured the city and protected it from being commercialized. Gianni and I enjoyed lovely walks there together. He had grown up in Treviso and knew everyone, so he introduced me to his friends. In the spring, I admired the flowers everywhere. Even the smallest street or piazza was a burst of color and perfume. Unfortunately, we didn't live in Treviso but a place called *Quinto di Treviso*, or the Fifth of Treviso, because it was five kilometers outside the city.

The place was known for the artist Ciardi, who had lived there and painted the *campagna,* or countryside, during the impressionist period. His imposing villa stood in the center of town and was perfectly preserved. However, the landscape around the Ciardi villa had changed drastically since the painter had lived in Quinto. An unnecessary but busy airport had been planted in the open country fields where it polluted the surrounding nature, including the important river Sile. The heavily trafficked street, the *Noale*, cut the area in half. The narrow road was a popular truck route, and the fumes from the engines made the air hard to breathe. People knew they were in Quinto because everything was made of concrete and asphalt. Gianni had nicknamed the place "Concrete" instead of Quinto. But among all the concrete, asphalt, and polluted air, there remained a small field of red poppies that could have been the subject for Ciardi paintings. In the car, I would ask Gianni to take a detour on the way home, just to see the poppy field. It was like a breath of fresh air among all the concrete, but unfortunately, one day it too would be cemented over by progress.

***

Before spring, it was announced that a dance festival would be presented for the Comitato Panizza. This time it would be a three-night production, and schools from all over Italy would be invited. The Christmas show had had only schools from the province of Treviso. The bitter experience of that benefit had left me uncertain, so I left the decision of whether or not to participate up to the students and parents. I pointed out to them that it was a chance to rehearse the snow scene for our *Nutcracker* on stage. The benefit reason was hard to sell. We were never told how much money had been raised from the other performances. Judging by the past and the expenses they accumulated, they had probably lost money. The girls decided that they wanted to do it, but the parents didn't want them to stay beyond midnight because of school the next day.

The three-day marathon would take place one week before the *Nutcracker*. This meant a significant loss of spectators for our ballet. With a small number of students, I depended on the school's reputation to bring in outsiders to see the performance. There was no reason why the dance festival had to be so close; even one month before would have been sufficient to give us breathing space. I asked Filetto why she had chosen a date so close to the *Nutcracker* and explained the problem of selling tickets. She became furious that I would question her decision and accused me of being against the benefit for cancer. I had always sold more tickets for her show in the past than any other dance school, so the accusation was absurd.

The night of the performance, Filetto didn't even say hello. The Waltz of the Snowflakes was flawless. From that day on, she began a relentless war against me.

***

After living one month in Quinto di Treviso, Gianni and I recognized we had made a terrible mistake moving there. But we couldn't retrace our steps because my apartment had been rented for one year. So we tried to make the best of a bad situation and hope that things would somehow improve over time. They didn't. Now that Gianni lived within walking distance of his parents, everything changed. The family didn't see me as a threat anymore because he had come home to them. They just totally ignored me, hoping I would disappear. I was alone in Concrete and wasn't invited to family gatherings. Their rejection was based on three reasons—my age, my being American, and my being a ballet dancer. The order of these three reasons depended on which family member you spoke with. One thing was certain—I was miserable there. I tried to put my happiness aside for the moment and focus on the positive. For example, Treviso was closer to Venice. Living in another town was an escape from work. Also, renting my apartment was a temporary solution to the financial problems due to the decline in school enrollment. I didn't live in constant fear of losing everything. It was with pride that I still held the keys to my apartment and school. I hadn't lost either. Yet.

***

My shoulder got worse over the months, and I began to wear a sling to keep it immobile. I promised myself that I would see a doctor after the *Nutcracker*. The second production was much more professional. The dancers were far better, but the lack of them was noteworthy. I had a small number of Snowflakes in the snow scene. Elena, as the Snow Queen, was such a talented dancer that she filled the emptiness on stage. In the Waltz of the Flowers, she did the same with her dancing in the Dew Drop solo. I hadn't used soloists in these two dances in the first *Nutcracker.* The two dances contributed by the jazz courses were separated into a second part of the program. It was lopsided because the *Nutcracker,* in the first part of the program, was one hour and forty-five minutes long, and the second part was not even ten minutes long. I didn't like putting both of them together in one evening; they seemed to clash.

The relationship I had with Manuela, the jazz teacher, was very unpleasant because there was a complete lack of respect from her and her students. It seemed that they were only interested in a temporary space to take classes and practice, not to be a part of our school. Manuela wanted money to come to the performance the night of the show, which is unheard of, but I paid so that her students wouldn't feel abandoned. I had my doubts about her future with our school, but her students loved her. After the performance, however, my only thought was to see a doctor for my shoulder. I had plenty of enemies to fight and I needed to be strong for the battle.

***

I was still technically a resident of Conegliano, not Quinto di Treviso. With socialized medicine, people had to choose a doctor in the town where they resided. The doctor would write a request for an exam, based on the client's symptoms or problems. The patient would take this to the hospital and make an appointment. People could wait months, or even up to a year, for a visit. Specialists at the hospital would often have private offices for those who wanted to get an appointment sooner. I went to see an orthopedic specialist privately, and he diagnosed the injured shoulder as a torn rotary cuff. He recommended immediate laser treatments and rehabilitation at the hospital. I never understood why people of reasonable means in Italy were indignant about paying a small amount of money to go privately. They would stubbornly wait months and complain just to have a free visit with a specialist. The same people would think nothing of spending half their monthly salary on clothes, jewelry, and beauty spas.

***

The worst part of living in Quinto di Treviso was transportation. The train from Treviso to Conegliano took only half an hour, but the infrequent buses from Quinto to Treviso made the trip both long and inconvenient. Some buses never came or arrived late, causing me to miss the train to Conegliano. It would take an entire day for me to travel back and forth to have the treatment at the hospital. Also, I felt vulnerable waiting for the bus after a particularly humiliating incident. While I was waiting one day, an Arab man walked by and suddenly turned to me. He grabbed my breasts and squeezed them, then continued walking. It happened so fast that I was in shock! After that, I dreaded waiting at the Quinto bus stop.

With all that was happening in my life, I began to suffer from panic attacks. The worst ones were on the train. I sensed that there was no escape when the train was moving and had difficulty breathing. I needed to keep moving, so I walked restlessly from car to car. When the doors opened at each stop, I wanted to jump out, but I didn't. I would breathe the air of freedom until the doors shut and I began to pace up and down again. If I sat down, I would break out in cold sweats. One night, on my way back to Quinto from work, the train stopped before a town called Spresiano. It was black outside, as the train moved slowly to the station. There were police all over the tracks, searching for something with flashlights. I anxiously paced up and down as usual and then stopped to look out at the scene. I watched the activity on the tracks, then looked down under the window. The headless body of a small man, wearing jeans and a red plaid shirt, was lying there. I fell backward in shock, caught my balance, and started walking again so I wouldn't faint or vomit. There was only one other passenger in the train car. A disinterested woman sat in the corner, looking out at the darkness and facing the opposite direction of the scene. She looked at me and I alerted her to what I had seen outside the train. She said she had imagined something horrible when she saw the police on the tracks, so she had decided not to look. Later, the newspaper recounted that an old man on a bicycle was killed when he tried to cross the train tracks. I kept seeing the tiny, headless body on the tracks and thinking how life can be over in an instant. A train had severed the head full of memories from the body that had lived them. The anxiety attacks stopped the day Gianni and I decided to move back to Conegliano.

***

September came quickly, and with the new dance year, I would automatically double the number of students at the school—or so I thought. I had finished paying Mirella, and the amount of money was far less than what she had originally asked for. The jazz courses would now bring in extra money for the school. But one week before the classes were to begin, Manuela pulled a surprise on me. She called and told me she was quitting. The bad part was that she did it at the last minute so I wouldn't have time to substitute her. By the time I could have found someone, the students would have gone somewhere else. Later I discovered that she had told all her students in June that she had no intention of returning in the fall. Fortunately, I had listened to my accountant when it came to doing business with Mirella. I didn't lose any money, but I was right back where I had started, with thirty-five students. One day I looked at Gianni and told him that I must sell my apartment. It was an agonizing decision.

I went to the realtor Gandolfo and put my apartment up for sale. He had found the Galitti couple and had written the contract for the rental. I was careful not to appear desperate when I met with Gandolfo, so I fabricated a story about buying a house in Florida for retirement. Gandolfo was known for being shrewd. Gianni and I went to speak to the Galittis to explain that I was selling the apartment. The agency would call them to make appointments for potential buyers to see the place.

We were walking to the entrance of the apartment building when we spotted a vigile looking for someone. Gianni and I looked at each other, and he walked over to the vigile and asked him if he was looking for Barbara File.

"No. Sto cercando Vito Guarone." (No. I'm looking for Vito Guarone.) We were surprised and looked at each other again. *Who was Vito Guarone?* The vigile gave us my apartment number, and I told him that was my apartment. Satisfied with this answer, he shrugged his shoulders and left. We went upstairs to speak with the Galittis. As soon as we walked in, we saw extra beds in the living room. Gianni was furious. I asked if Vito Guarone was living with them, and they admitted that he and his wife were living with them temporarily. It was obvious that they were subletting from Galitti because of the residency request. I was an extra-communitaria in Italy, so this situation could have serious consequences for me. If Guarone had a criminal past or present, it could affect my permission to stay in Italy. Besides, it violated the contract they had made with me. We told the Galittis that Guarone and his wife had to leave or we would have to report them living illegally in my apartment.

"Barbara, tu sei come una sorella per me," Galitti said. (Barbara, you are like a sister for me.)

"Beviamo un caffé insieme." (Let's drink a caffé together.)

"Niente caffé," said Gianni coldly, and we left.

After several months, Gandolfo hadn't sent anyone to see the apartment, claiming that no one had been interested, which seemed very odd. The contract ended, and the Galittis were moving out. A week later, Gandolfo called me for a meeting with this possible buyer. The man, a crude *contadino,* or farmer, said he would pay in cash but much less than what I was asking. I said I would think about it, but I knew what the apartment was worth.

I had a feeling Gandolfo was helping this contadino rather than working in my favor. So I planned to test him to see if my hunch was right. I told Gandolfo I would sell to the man, and he said he would relate this to him. I waited two weeks for an answer before Gandolfo called me. He said that the man had changed his mind and decided to offer even less. Gandolfo would eventually claim that no one else was interested in buying, so I would be forced to sell for nothing, out of desperation, while he would be paid well by the contadino. I told him, "No, thank you," and he angrily told me that I was stupid to turn down the offer. Gianni and I had decided to move back to my apartment so we would sell it ourselves.

"Ben tornata!" (Welcome home!) This was the warm greeting from all my neighbors. These were the same neighbors who had been unfriendly when I had first moved there years ago. No one had ever said hello to me before. *What had changed in one year?* Gradually, the story was revealed. The Galittis had constantly knocked on doors to sell olive oil that they somehow were bottling in my apartment. Four people and an olive business had been residing at my address! The olive oil was stuck to my kitchen walls and was a nightmare to clean, but I had had no idea they were making it there. Others told me how Vito Guarone had threatened to kill people and how, once, there were even gunshots. So the American was a better neighbor after all!

In a month, I sold the apartment for the price I wanted to a couple who were getting married. The young woman fell in love with the view, as I had. Her father was buying it for her as a wedding gift. When Gandolfo heard that I had sold the place myself, he wanted a percentage of the sale. I refused, and he threatened to sue me. I had added another enemy on my growing list.

When the apartment was sold, I felt like a failure—it was sad to hand over the keys to the new owner. I still had the keys to my school, which consoled me. However, what seemed like a tragedy at the time would actually save me later on.

Gianni with me in Cansiglio.

CHAPTER 15

The Power of Enemies

"If you wait by the river long enough,
You will see your enemies float by."
Sun Tzu

A short time after I sold my apartment, we moved into an old townhouse in Viale Gorizia, *Parco Rocco,* considered an exclusive area in Conegliano. The entrance hall of the house was majestic, with high ceilings and a long marble stairway to the second floor. The square, box-like rooms were all connected to this hall, and the ceilings were higher than the width of the rooms. On the ground floor was a living room and separate dining room, with a chimney chute for a stove-like fireplace. The kitchen was the size of a closet, with a very low ceiling, disproportionate to the rest of the house. The back door led down two steps, shaded by an enormous fig tree, and into a garden. Another large, old tree divided the property from the townhouse that was attached to ours. There was a moldy garage with a shed and storage room attached. A narrow river had once flowed behind these buildings but was later covered. The land had been filled in to the height of the roof of the garage, and parking spaces had been placed over the covered river. The second floor held three bedrooms. One tiny bedroom had a small balcony that looked onto the street. The most incredible thing about the house was that red roses grew randomly all over the front fence, and they never asked for care. They seemed to grow simply from our admiration. A passerby would often stop to admire their beauty.

The house adjacent to us faced the angle of Viale Gorizia and another street. Once a picturesque, three-story, brick mansion, it had been neglected and was now rundown, which gave it the look of a haunted house. In contrast, gorgeous gardens surrounded the villa. White, pebble-stone pathways encircled the house and roses grew everywhere. There was a huge pine tree in the garden, which had been planted as a small Christmas tree years before and had exploded into something magnificent. A couple of times, at Christmas, the pine was covered with snow, nature's own adornment. The windows on the side of our house, in particular our bedroom window on the first floor, had the best view of it.

The owners didn't live in the house but rented it out. It was divided into two separate apartments, one upstairs and one down. The occupants were three women, a teacher on the ground floor and two sisters living together on the top floor. One of the sisters, Nadia, suffered from agoraphobia and never left the perimeter of the house. Sometimes she walked within the confines of the garden, but she never ventured outside the high iron fence that enclosed the house. She was a beautiful woman in her early fifties, with thick, shoulder-length, burgundy-red hair.

The first time we met, we were both outside in our gardens when she came to the fence and introduced herself. Her voice was friendly, but raspy because she was a heavy cigarette smoker.

"Ciao, mi chiamo Nadia." (Hi, my name is Nadia.)

"Io sono Barbara." (I'm Barbara.)

I liked her immediately, but at one point in our conversation, something strange happened.

"You know, Dorothy," she said in Italian.

"Well, Dorothy, it was wonderful meeting you."

A chill touched me and ran up the back of my neck when she called me by my mother's name a second time.

"Piacere di conoscere lei," I responded. (It was a pleasure to meet you.)

"Per favore, Dorothy, dammi del tu." (Please, Dorothy, give me the familiar you.)

This meeting left me with so many unanswered questions. *Why had she called me my mother's name, over and over?* It's not an easy mistake to make and it couldn't be a coincidence. She always called me Barbara after that. My interest intensified when I heard rumors that Nadia read the tarot cards, had visions, and could see things that others didn't. Her kitchen window faced my bedroom window, so we waved or exchanged a few words together after that first introduction. But I wanted to speak with her and ask her why she had called me Dorothy that day.

It was a long time before the right moment presented itself. Again, we met in the gardens separated by the fence. After discussing the flowers in bloom, I asked her the question:

"The first day we met, you kept calling me Dorothy. That is my mother's name, but you didn't know that then."

"That day I didn't see you, but an older woman," she said, and she went on to describe my mother.

"I never met you until later. I kept calling her Dorothy because that was the name she gave me. I saw Dorothy that day, but I never saw her again."

This was the first time someone other than I had seen my mother, and I broke down and wept. Nadia explained that she never told people what she could see unless they believed in such powers and wanted to know. I told her I believed that special people could see things that others couldn't, and I asked her to please tell me anything that she saw in my present, future, or past. She then warned me to be very careful because I had a powerful enemy, a woman, who was trying to destroy me. Maria Angela Filetto came to my mind, so this warning didn't surprise me. However, the description of the woman she saw was not the description of my archenemy.

"I see a tiny, very plump, pretty woman, with short, curly blonde hair and blue eyes," said Nadia.

"Are you sure?" I asked. "The enemy I've been fighting doesn't fit your description at all." But Nadia said she was absolutely certain: she could see this woman very clearly.

I discovered through the parents of my students that a woman had been determined to close the ballet school and was working to shut it down. She believed that the after-school program, which her son attended, should have the dance studio. A dance school was an unnecessary waste of space, she had stated at the parent/teacher meetings. A new principal had replaced the hostile one. The new director believed that the ballet school gave the elementary school prestige and had refused to close it. Nadia had been right! The woman was exactly as Nadia had described her and had been working behind my back for months. Shortly after this, the woman moved to Bologna.

***

Almost every summer, I went back to the U.S. to visit my father. My stepmother would make my visits more and more impossible. As the years passed, she became the domineering, demanding wife who also acted like a capricious child. She refused to recognize me as my father's daughter because it would establish the fact that he had been married before and had had a life with my mother. In the strange relationship they had together, she had become his daughter. Then one day, she legally changed her name to mine. *She had stolen my identity!* It was weird that we both had the same name.

I would escape the craziness of their house in New Jersey and go into New York. There I attended classes to learn new methods in teaching. On the pleasure side, I would see ballets and Broadway shows and dine in fine restaurants. A small pizza in Italy was the same price as a lobster dinner in New York. I particularly enjoyed shopping in the Garment District where I could buy rhinestone crowns and sequined applique for practically nothing. My credit card joyously ticked away every summer and went on a sabbatical the rest of the year in Italy. I shopped for everything from music to aspirin. In Italy, a box of aspirin would cost around ten dollars for five pills! An eyebrow pencil that sold for a dollar in Walmart would be a hefty twenty dollars in Italy.

How did Italians manage to live when their average pay was nine hundred dollars a month? For one thing, they had socialized medicine and a free university education. The keys to an apartment, given by the family, meant no burden of a down payment or mortgage. Italians would visit family and eat together, so their small paychecks were used for the little extras in life. Wealth was usually inherited and rarely created. In Italy, you are what your family has managed to build for you.

I began to understand that there was no future for me in Italy. The small amount of money that was left after the sale of my apartment wouldn't even buy a closet in some remote village, and my school was always on the brink of extinction. Also, I would always be an outsider in the country. I asked myself one day, "Is it worth all this just to live in Italy?"

While shopping at a supermarket in New Jersey one summer, I picked up a brochure of homes in Florida. I couldn't believe the prices, and for the first time, I could hope to own my own home. Kitchens, bathrooms, electric appliances—even a swimming pool—were included! In Italy, you bought an empty, box-like space, and everything had to be installed. So from that day on, I began mentally preparing my eventual return to the United States.

***

It was time to take inventory of my battle wounds. I had survived several injuries, but luckily none of them had done permanent damage. Unfortunately, my rotary cuff hadn't healed the way I hoped it would. After the therapy was finished at the hospital, I still couldn't lift my arm beyond a certain height. In socialized medicine, a certain number of therapy hours are alloted for a particular injury. The doctors won't go beyond that number of hours—in the end, you are either cured or not. This is one of the system's disadvantages.

"Purtroppo, la spalla non sara piu come prima," the therapist, Giuliana, informed me. (Unfortunately, your shoulder will never be the same as before.) However, I refused to give up and accept that my arm would have reduced mobility, so I devised my own exercise program and followed it until my shoulder became flexible again. A year later, I ran into Giuliana outside the hospital.

"Come va la spalla?" She asked how my shoulder was and I told her it was back to normal. She looked at me quizzically. I told her I had created my own exercise program and the mobility had gradually come back. I wanted the full capacity of my body to return. *After all, I needed to be whole on the battlefield!*

Over the years, the *sala gialla,* or dance studio, had become colder and colder. In the early years, there was almost too much heat radiating from the enormous, old heaters under the windows that made up one wall of the room. The price of gas and oil had increased tremendously, so to save money, the schools had begun to shut the heat off early in the afternoon. By evening, the giant radiators were frigid. We would roll down the massive shutters as soon as it became dark out to try and keep the warmth in. Sometimes we worked on Sunday mornings because in Italy, the children went to school on Saturdays. Sundays were a sufferance. We could see the frost in the air with each breath, and I doubted whether even the Russians had worked under these conditions in Siberia!

At night I would look forward to going home, but it wasn't much better there either. There was no heat in the entrance hall or all the way up the icy marble stairway to the second floor. Only the master bedroom had heating. Because there was no heat in the other two bedrooms, we never used them. The one bathroom at the top of the first flight of stairs was so small that a heater couldn't fit into it. When the house had been built, the bathroom had been in another building, probably the storage room outside. The routine I followed was to put my jacket, gloves, and boots on when I needed to go to the bedroom or bathroom upstairs. The hallway was colder than the outdoors, and again I would exhale frost. Finally I became creative, or I just learned to improvise, and I bought a tiny electric, portable heater. I went from room to room and connected the device, keeping it close to me. Of course I had to disconnect it every time I moved through the hall, but I was able to endure the cold long enough to get to another room. I would race up the stairs, holding the heater, and plug it in as fast as possible. It heated the bathroom quickly, so I could eventually undress. This way of life became normal for me. The cold and dampness were my worst enemies in Italy because they wreaked havoc with my health.

***

The enemy-turned friend, Signor Bertolini of the SIAE, was a mystery to me. As I mentioned earlier, at every performance, there was a menu of all the high officials who were to be invited to come to Teatro Accademia. Their seats were reserved and no one else could sit there, even if the invited guests didn't come. The number of seats was around fifty, all in the best positions. This represented a sizeable loss of ticket money, so I always complained. My complaints resonated with one mother. After an absence of a few years, Signor Bertolini decided to come and see one of our ballets. Enthusiastically, he took his reserved seat in the theater. The sympathetic mother came down the aisle and confronted him.

"Disgraziato! Come ti permetti di portare via cinquanta biglietti!" she said. (How dare you take all those seats for yourself!) He was confused and tried to explain that he had taken only one seat. The mother came and told me the whole story, and I said it was true: the SIAE only had one place. She had thought I had complained in the past that he had taken all fifty seats! We both looked at each other because we thought he would be furious and retaliate in some terrible way. Instead, he just laughed about the whole thing when I went to pay him.

"Mi è piaciuto lo spettacolo," he said. (I liked the show.) All I could think was: *Which one?*

Before another show, Gianni had driven the scenery truck and had hit Signor Bertolini's car. The entrance to the scenery loading dock was on a steep, narrow street, directly across from the Conegliano SIAE office. The accident was unavoidable. Signor Bertolini ran out of the office but was very nice to Gianni. He took the name of our insurance company. Then we waited for the bad news about the cost of damages. I had visions of all the money from the ballet performance going to pay for the repairs. But the phone call never came. He never asked for anything. I kept wondering what my accountant had said to him after our first show years before that had made him change his behavior toward me.

***

One morning, I ran into Giorgio Fabris on my way to the main post office.

"Hai sentito che Carmela Rigoletto è morta ieri sera?" (Did you hear that Carmela Rigoletto died last night?) I was shocked! He explained that she had caught the flu and had gotten a very high fever that had led to a coma. She was only thirty-nine years old. There had never been any love lost between us, but I was still sad to hear of her death. After selling her school to Mirella Bellano, she had married a wealthy man from the elite profession of notary. In Italy, everything had to be notarized, and it could cost thousands of dollars just for one document. As part of the wealthy class, she had become involved in volunteer work. This was all I knew about her because we hadn't traveled in the same circles.

A reporter from *La Tribuna* called me to ask if I had anything to say about Carmela for her newspaper obituary. I said I hadn't known her well but had heard she was a good person. The following day, Gianni brought home a copy of the newspaper, with her obituary on the front page. I began reading the story that someone had dictated to the journalist. After the information that I more or less knew about Carmela, the story took a twist. I couldn't believe the words that followed. Apparently, Carmela had opened a ballet school inside an expensive, private Catholic academy in Conegliano. The Collegio Immacolata was only a couple of blocks from where I had my ballet school! The obituary said that her studio had the best barres, mirrors, and a high-quality wooden floor, all paid for by her rich husband. The best part was that she offered ballet classes free! Ambitious parents who couldn't afford the Catholic academy could now send their children to mingle with the wealthy in ballet classes. It was open to everyone.

Then the obituary began to read like a marketing campaign. The person dictating the article glorified Carmela for giving free lessons. It said that Carmela's motto was that no child should ever have to pay for ballet lessons. *Students had paid double the price of other schools for lessons in her first school!* Then it became a hate campaign. The reporter claimed that a foreigner had opened a ballet school in 1990 and had "dirtied the art of dance by asking money for lessons." Everyone knew who the foreign teacher was, without the reporter using my name. I was certain that the person who gave the information for the article was Filetto, who wanted to defame me in the newspaper but couldn't use my name. Carmela was her close friend and later she would dedicate every ballet to her memory.

Carmela had been generous on the one hand, but with the other, she would have closed my school if she had lived to continue her work. No school could compete with free lessons! She had married a rich man, so she didn't need to earn a living. But I needed to support myself teaching ballet. Lack of money would always be my Achilles heel, and rich competitors knew my weakness. My school would have slowly died, but instead, she had died. I was struck with the frightening thought that some powerful force had killed an enemy before she could hurt me.

I was angry with the journalist who had written the trash that I had "dirtied the art of ballet by asking money for lessons" so I called to complain. Signor Basso, the journalist, responded with disdain and claimed that he only wrote the words that were told to him by a woman that he refused to name. I explained that anyone could print lies about others in the newspaper if the reporter agreed to write them. Accusations should be ascertained to be true first, before using them to defame the reputation of another. His reply to this was that he found it disgusting that I would discuss what was written in the obituary of such a beloved citizen of Conegliano.

"Io perdono la tua maleducazione perché sei solo uno straniero," he pompously declared. (I pardon your bad manners because you are only a foreigner.) Then he hung up. Gianni went to his office in Conegliano and spoke with him. In the end, he unwillingly apologized and promised to write a piece for our upcoming ballet.

I was living my life and accomplishing many of my dreams, but the only thing Filetto seemed to be living for was to get rid of me. Life is so short. I could never understand how anyone could throw away their precious time trying to hurt someone else. But this was what she had chosen to do.

"Someday I will drive you out of Conegliano," she announced one day. But I would leave voluntarily before she could accomplish this. In the meantime, I followed the newspapers every day, expecting more slander to be written about me.

CHAPTER 16

On Your Toes: Musical Madness!

"First they ignore you, then they laugh at you,
then they fight you, then you win."
Gandhi

In addition to the performances we offered in Teatro Accademia and other important theaters, we were also invited to dance at smaller-scale functions. We danced in two shows that remain outstanding in my memory, if only for the sheer absurdity of them. Sometime after our first successful benefit for AIL, organizers called me for Via Natale. The well-known oncology center in Aviano, near Pordenone, had decided to build a housing complex for families of cancer patients who came there for treatments. The project would be named Via Natale, the name of the street where the apartments would be built.

The organization decided on a show to raise the necessary funds for this objective. They asked me to bring only a few soloists, because the highlights of the show were a singer and musicians. They told me that the concert would take place at the sport stadium in town. I informed them that we didn't perform on grass, but they assured me that a portable stage would be mounted in the center of the stadium. An elaborate lighting system and special effects would be installed. I prepared three of my best dancers with repertory variations. On the night of the performance, we were in for a surprise. The stage was a small, square, portable wooden floor, and around this space was a high steel fence. The classical orchestra and opera singer that I had imagined turned out to be a famous, local hard-rock group. Only the lighting, special effects, and fog machines lived up to expectations.

More and more people poured into the stadium. The crowds became overwhelming, as throngs of people pushed against the steel fence rather than view the show from their seats. The audience became wild and rowdy with their alcoholic beverages, mostly beer, and glass bottles could be heard breaking as the occasional whiff of marijuana drifted through the air. The heat and humidity hung heavily that night, and everyone was dripping with perspiration. The musicians' costumes, old jeans and dirty, white undershirts, were soaked. The wooden floor became wet from sweat. The body odors were nauseating but were diluted by the dry, artificial fog and the smell of marijuana.

The group decided to take a break, so it was our turn to take the stage in this hard-rock nightmare. The dancers appeared in elegant, classical tutus. The stunned crowd was confused and fell silent. The ethereal dancers performed beautifully on pointe to recorded classical music, but there was no applause. The quiet mob seemed spellbound, as if they were wondering how much they had drunk or smoked to cause them to see what they were seeing. For a few minutes, a wild rock concert had become a refined performance. Then the musicians returned to the stage and the spectators went back to their frenzy. Though the solos went very well, we were embarrassed to be there. It was awkward and uncomfortable, so we slipped away as quickly as possible. However, the evening was a huge success for Via Natale, as they raised enough money from the show to achieve the housing project, something that gave us great satisfaction.

The other memorable performance took place in a top restaurant in Vittorio Veneto, the town north of Conegliano. For this engagement, my students danced for their supper! We were invited to perform for a group of pharmacists that met together monthly at one of the best restaurants in the area. Gianni knew the president of the organization, Rocco, who was acquainted with the work of my ballet school. Rocco decided to give the dinner party a touch of class and asked us to dance for the small, private event. He offered to pay five hundred euro, so I jumped at the invitation. The school desperately needed two new portable barres, and this was my chance to raise the money to buy them. We had always performed for beneficence—this time we would be the receivers of a benefit. But before accepting, I wanted to visit the restaurant and see the banquet room where we would be dancing. I wasn't certain that it would be possible to work there until I evaluated the space.

This show reminded me of vaudeville in the late nineteenth and early twentieth centuries. Restaurants would hire entertainers to perform on a small stage while diners ate. A vaudeville show might include a ventriloquist, magician, opera singer, contortionists, and even classical ballet dancers. Shows changed frequently to cater to regular customers. The performers were paid very little, but the pay was steady and a hot meal was included. For some, it was their only meal of the day. I admired these artists of the past because their commitment had to have been total to accept such hardships. The year I toured with the circus was close to the vaudeville experience, though we shared the stage with exotic animals. The animals performed for their supper, but we paid for ours because there were hundreds of us in the show. Now, having my students dance for their dinner would give them a taste of the vaudeville experience.

The banquet room had a small space for the dancers to work. A large window was the backdrop, and it overlooked Vittoria Veneto. Two unfriendly pillars would chop up the dances, but with minor changes in spacing, the choreography could be left untouched. The biggest obstacle was the tile floor, which was hard, slippery, and with seams that could easily trip a dancer. Gianni suggested that thin linoleum spread over the floor would eliminate this problem. So I accepted the work. However, by the time we totaled the cost of all the materials for the floor, the five hundred euro was eaten up. I would have flooring that I would never use again instead of new portable barres.

The three dancers rehearsed the afternoon of the banquet. I brought three solos from the *Nutcracker*, and the dancers would change costumes to perform two variations from *Sleeping Beauty*. Elena would perform the Black Swan variation. The dancers prepared for the performance as the pharmacists arrived at the restaurant. We didn't know when the dancers would go on stage, but we were told it would be between one dinner course and another. We waited an eternity and watched with anticipation, as the empty plates came out after every course. *Do we perform now?* Then the next course appeared with more bottles of wine. It was clear that the owner of the restaurant wanted the waiters to finish up quickly, because if the evening dragged out too long, with a show in the middle, he would have to pay them overtime. So when the dinner was finished, the dancers were called to perform. They danced beautifully, especially with all the obstacles, but unfortunately, the dinner guests couldn't appreciate it. They were all drunk from the different wines they had had with every course. Most of the guests were lost, bewildered, and barely acknowledged our presence. After the show, in another smaller dining room, we were served a feast. We could order anything on the menu we wanted, thanks to our gracious hosts.

"Well, girls, tonight you danced for your supper," I said. They laughed and ate voraciously.

***

The year I sold my apartment marked my tenth anniversary in Italy. The move into Viale Gorizia signaled the end of a dark chapter for the ballet school and the beginning of the best years. Enrollment went up and I felt like celebrating, so I decided to produce a musical in my eleventh year. It was a dream I had had on the back burner for a while, and it sat there motionless until I could resolve some of my problems. Now I was free financially, without a mortgage strangling me, and I had nothing to lose. The first possibility was the musical *Can-Can,* which I had danced in at the Stadttheater of Klagenfurt. However, I had many children enrolled that year, so I couldn't quite picture their roles in the musical. Though I had never danced in the musical *On Your Toes,* I had seen it two times and loved the show. One act of the show is the scene of a hypothetical oriental ballet, which gave me an idea. I could substitute this with one act of the oriental classical ballet *La Bayadère.* The advanced students could perform the traditional solos, and a *corps de ballet* of children could participate as small temple dancers. The project was massive, so I began preparations immediately, starting in September.

Before I started the choreography, I needed to be certain that I had the vocal cast. I asked Diana Tarantelli, the director of our neighboring music school, if she knew of three leading professional singers who could work with us. I needed a young male and female to play the starring roles of the couple that fall in love. Also, an older man with a bass voice was needed to play the ballet impresario. Diana found the couple right away, and our impresario was a seventy-year-old professional opera singer who lived in Conegliano. The chorus of singers was a group of voice students at the school, directed by Alberto Pollisel, the violinist who had briefly played for the dancers in Bach's *Senza Definizione*. A pianist named Giorgio, who worked with the maestro Pollisel, was perfect for the role as the composer/choreographer. So I had my cast of singers and a musician.

Gianni enjoyed bartering furniture as a hobby. He had negotiated, at a very good price, three barber chairs from a barber who was retiring. One day he took two of the chairs to Milan and came back with two beaten-up, long church benches from the late eighteen hundreds. The door was open on the first floor balcony, and I looked down as the old Fiat pulled up. The two benches were tied to the roof.

"Cosa hai fatto?" (What did you do?)

I nearly cried when I shouted this question from the balcony. *Where will we put them?*

Gianni was disheartened because I didn't like them. The benches lined the long entrance hallway in the house. They became a source of displeasure, but soon they would find their calling in the *On Your Toes* production.

Nino, the father of a student, worked at the hospital in Conegliano, and he arranged a meeting with a respected doctor of oncology who was devoted to helping cancer patients at the hospital. The *primario,* or head, of the cancer ward was a handsome, distinguished man who seemed both reluctant and annoyed at the meeting. He had formed a non-profit association, *L'Associazione Contro Cancro*, or the Association Against

Cancer. We discussed *On Your Toes* and the idea of dedicating the performance to raise money for his association. He told me that he knew a printer who would give a half-price discount on the program, which would be a great help. I knew that we would sell out the theater with the musical. Between the schools of dance and music, we had a colossal cast, which meant big ticket sales. The doctor promised to sell at least one hundred tickets in the hospital, as he half-smiled for the first time. So I agreed to dedicate the show to his beneficence.

***

Early in the year, Roberto announced that he was hanging up his dance shoes permanently. He had married and had two children since the beginning of his journey in dance, starting with our first *Nutcracker*. I didn't know what I would do without him. He was the most dependable partner and person.

"Mio fratello vuole studiare danza." (My brother wants to learn how to dance.) His brother Flavio came to work with us, and I could see he would be a perfect partner for Elena, who was just beginning to learn the art of pas de deux. I planned to teach them the *Bayadère* pas de deux. Flavio and Elena were both small; he was timid and she was very confident. Together they were very compatible and extremely hardworking. We could work for hours and they never tired. In addition to Flavio, I had two other young men, Davide and Elvis. Both of them were interested in partnering, though they weren't able to commit as much time to practice. They would have smaller roles in the production.

With most of the cast in place, I went to the Bottega Veneziana to choose and rent the appropriate scenery for the musical. Nothing had to be built, so this would save money, which was especially important since I would have to pay the three professional singers. The windows from *La Sonnambula* were perfect for the conservatory scenes. For *La Bayadère*, there was the oriental palace that I had used in *Firebird*, and the plain blue backdrop was a simple solution for the modern ballet. All were backdrops, so a normal-sized van, rather than a big truck, would be more than adequate. However, the piano from the music school would need spacious transportation, so renting a truck again was inevitable. There was a problem with chairs for the conservatory. I had many singers and dancers in this scene, which had to look like a classroom. Here is where the church pews Gianni had bought became useful. The two long benches were perfect! There wasn't enough sitting space for everyone, but the taller singers could stand behind them. Gianni was thrilled.

"Lo sapevo che sarebbero tornate utili!" he announced with pride. (I always knew that they would be useful!)

As for costumes, I ordered six tutus from Fantechi in Florence, three in burgundy red and three in emerald green. When the costumes were ready, Gianni and I made a trip to Florence for the day. We arrived by car at noon and ate lunch in a local trattoria. After lunch, we walked by the gigolo gelateria, and I gave him the history of the place. We shared a gelato at the empty café. *Where had all the gigolos gone?* Sitting in the café, I could feel that times had changed here. We walked through the Piazza dei Signori and into the market in front of the Palazzo Uffizzi. Every stand was selling African statues or umbrellas and porcelain from China. *Where was the leather market?* Florence was famous for its crafted leather and was once the site of the biggest leather market in Italy. Years before, on a trip to Florence, I had bought a leather chess set with brass figurines representing the city. I can't play chess but I cherish its beauty and the memory of Florence. It sits on the Venetian chair, where the perfume of leather mingles with the scent of the Venetian waters.

Before leaving the city, we went to pick up the cumbersome bags of costumes. Fantechi had moved their company. Now it was located in a shabby neighborhood and a rundown building. As we walked up the narrow stairway, the inviting smell of ethnic cooking came from different apartments. The large, elegant showroom they had once had in a pricey neighborhood had been reduced to a small, crowded, squalid space. *How much had changed over the years!* Before leaving Florence, we went to the famous square that overlooks the city. The only thing that hadn't changed was the incredible view that Michelangelo had gazed upon with nostalgia every time he returned home.

Carla would make the skirts for the temple dancers and the three slaves in *La Bayadère*.

"Quando è lo spettacolo?" (When is the show?) She would always ask this over and over. Now I knew what to expect: in the end, she would deliver good costumes on time. This would be her third show with us.

"Stai attenta." (Listen carefully.) She opened all discussions with this warning. We spoke about meeting on Saturday. Then she explained that if it was a nice day, she would be killing chickens. If the day was bad, she would stay home.

"Passa sabato, e se non sono a casa, sai che sto uccidendo I polli." (Come by Saturday, and if I'm not at home, you know I'm killing chickens.) In the country, or *compagna*, everyone had chickens and rabbits that were part of the Veneto diet. In Via Cavalotti where I had had my apartment, an old lady lived across the street in a tiny house, with chickens in her front yard. A part of the past was sandwiched between two modern buildings. The only chickens I had ever seen in New York were hanging headless and featherless in a butcher store.

The other costumes came from everywhere. The *Bayadère* protagonist would wear the Arabian ensemble from the *Nutcracker* and the Indian Prince the Moor outfit from *Petrouchka*. For the jazz ballet, I wanted all the dancers in black, with top hats and tuxedo jackets. The black unitards that the rats had worn in the *Nutcracker* were the perfect base. I ordered the top hats from England, but the tuxedos were a dilemma. Paola, the mother who had saved our scenery in her parents' house, came to the rescue again. She was talented with a needle and thread. Now I asked her for another favor—the tuxedo jackets. They would be made from the same pattern as the jackets used for *Holidays in Hollywood*. Everyone in the first act would wear normal clothing that could be adapted to the fashion of the period, the mid-nineteen thirties.

Since I was the only one who had professional acting and dancing experience, I cast myself in the role of the Russian ballerina, Vera Baronova. Moreno, who was on his way to China, was perfect as her jealous partner Constantin. There wouldn't be much time to practice with him, so I used him as little as possible in the choreography with others. He would portray the Indian prince in *La Bayadère* and perform wushu kung fu. Moreno could use his sword specialty again, as he had done in *Petrouchka*. With this magnificent weapon and prop, he could prepare everything much faster, because he was doing something he already knew. Because he was the lead male dancer in the musical, I wanted him to perform the drunk solo, which utilized his other wushu kung fu specialty. I gave him the music and let him choreograph both pieces while in China.

My favorite rehearsals were the ones with the music and dance schools together. This is the scene where the American tap dancers at the conservatory challenge the visiting Russian ballet. In the beginning, I prepared the tap dancers, who were the more mature students. I gave the tap number lead to Lara, a young woman, and she agreed to play a guy. As a male dancer, she was convincing, wearing pants with suspenders, a man's shirt with a bow tie, and a green cap that hid her long, curly blonde hair. Later, I choreographed a swing dance, with the three male dancers and Lara coupled with four female dancers. The Russian dancers were led by Elena, with her deep-knee character kicks, also dressed as a male dancer in a Cossack costume. When the dancers were ready, we worked with the chorus of singers. Alberto directed the group and Giorgio played the piano. Rehearsals became more and more lively, and by the end of the evening, we were all energized. Afterward, Alberto, Gianni, and I would go to a local pub with some of the dancers and singers, and we would stay until closing time. It reminded me of the after-work parties we had had in the circus train while on tour.

I worked with three partners, Davide, Flavio, and Elvis, in the jazz ballet *Slaughter on Tenth Avenue*. I wore the red fringe costume that I had worn in *Holidays in Hollywood*. It was as though I had turned the clock back ten years, and I had fun dancing the role. At the end of the dance, Moreno was supposed to come in and partner me to the last pose together. I had a premonition that Moreno would somehow miss those last steps of the music. The feeling was so strong that I decided to choreograph the steps so that I could perform them alone, if worse came to worst.

The last month, I was pleased with how the rehearsals were going, and everything was coming together nicely. Or so I thought. When the program proof was ready, I asked Gianni to bring a copy to the doctor.

"Cos'è questo casino?" he snapped. (What is this mess?) Gianni was shocked and asked him what was wrong. He replied that it was a book of publicity. Gianni explained that my programs were made up of many small sponsors. The best part of this was that many local merchants participated in the production, not just one rich, powerful business.

"Lei non è nessuno se non ha un grande sponsor." (She is no one if she doesn't have a big sponsor.) And with that statement, he tossed the program back at Gianni. When I asked Gianni if the doctor had liked the program, he regretfully told me what he had said. We were both baffled and saddened by his behavior.

The performance day was nearing and tickets were on sale, but no one was buying. I thought there would be an avalanche of tickets sold. Everyone said they were waiting to get tickets on the day of the show. *Why not now?* I called the doctor to see how many guest tickets he needed, and I hoped he would keep his promise about selling one hundred tickets at the hospital. He was cold on the phone and asked if a dinner was being offered before the show at the theater. I was dumbfounded by the question and thought he was joking. He went on to tell me that I had to book the Ridotto Sala in Teatro Accademia and offer a catered dinner for about two hundred people—doctors, their friends, and families. This would mean the equivalent of thousands of additional dollars! I told him we didn't have that kind of budget and that the money we raised from the musical should go to the association. *Wasn't this money for the cancer victims?* I was appalled and disgusted at the same time. The doctor threatened that if there was no dinner, he and his friends wouldn't come to the show. I was stunned when he hung up.

Usually we had one day in the theater to prepare everything for the performance at nine o'clock that evening. However, with so many details and such a large, diverse cast, I asked for the theater the day before the performance so we could rehearse. Giorgio Fabris, the owner of Teatro Accademia, helped us on the additional cost because it was for beneficence. The day before the first theater rehearsal, we bought three large pieces of plywood. A hardwood floor was necessary for the tap dancing so the audience could hear the sharp, clear sounds. We painted the wood black and placed it over the black dance floor that muffled sound. The wood was removed after the first act because there was no more tap dancing in the performance.

The backdrops and lights were hung, but the lighting company was not happy about the additional microphones needed for the singers and everyone who had a dialogue to speak.

"Cosa c'entra il canto con la danza?" yelled Luigi, the lighting director. (What does singing have to do with dancing?) This was the question on everyone's mind. Musical theater was not part of the Italian culture. The idea that actors would speak dialogue and then transition into a song and dance was insane. Everyone thought I had lost my mind, mixing it all together. I began hearing their fears in whispers. *The show would be a flop!* I heard the singers say that they hadn't invited anyone because they didn't want to be embarrassed. Then I understood why tickets hadn't been sold!

Ledo Freschi, our bass singer, watched the technical chaos and was upset. He turned to me and said,

"Sai quello che stai facendo?" (Do you know what you're doing?)

"Si," I replied.

"Spero." (I hope so.)

We started the rehearsal, but the cast began to discuss what *they* thought should be done at every move. Everyone wanted to be the captain. No one wanted to be part of the army. Italians don't embrace individuality when it comes to fashion or thinking. They want to be accepted, so they follow what's in style. However, when it is necessary to follow someone who is in charge, they become individuals and self-appointed leaders. This is fatal in war but also constitutes a disaster in any organized effort or project. I knew I had to assert myself and let them know who was in command. I called everyone onto the stage and asked for their complete attention. Then

I explained that they must do exactly what I say, when I say it, and without question. If they did what I told them to do, the show would go smoothly; otherwise it would be chaos. I was their captain, they were my army, and they had to follow my orders!

Gianni had asked his friend, the celebrated DJ from Radio Padua, Barry Mason, to be our emcee, and we were thrilled when Barry accepted. The night of the show, only two things went wrong, but the audience didn't notice either one. The temple dancers had gold-painted shoes, but unfortunately, the paint hadn't dried because of the humidity. They left gold footprints all over the dance floor. The second thing that happened was that my premonition about Moreno came true. Someone distracted him backstage, so I had to perform the last steps alone, but he was there for the last pose.

We performed for a half-empty theater that night. The show was an enormous success, but very few people saw it. The doctor reluctantly came that night because he had been pushed to go by Nino.

"We would have invited people if we had known it would go so well!" This was the comment from most of the cast members.

"We had so much fun!" they said.

They wanted to know when we would repeat it. So many people could have enjoyed a wonderful show that night, and so much money could have been raised for cancer. But, on the one hand there was greed, and on the other hand, obtusity; so the show became a musical madness.

Ledo Freschi in *On Your Toes*

Piazzale Michelangelo, Florence, Italy

CHAPTER 17

Romeo, Juliet, and the Tarot Cards

"When you come out of the storm,
you won't be the same person that walked in."
Haruki Murakami

"**A**h si, Il Dottore. Mi dispiace per te, ma ho avuto la stessa esperienza con lui." (Oh yes, the doctor. I'm sorry that you had the same experience as I did with him.) I was sitting with Diana Tarantelli in her new office in Palazzo Sarcinelli as Minister of Culture for the city of Conegliano. I went to congratulate Diana on her important new appointment and to tell her what had happened to the money for the cancer benefit. Apparently the money from the benefits always went for the doctor's dinner parties. In addition to the lack of tickets sold, the printer went back on his word about a 50 percent discount on the programs and posters. Instead, he doubled the price! Gianni was witness to the discount agreement and Nino was testimony to the doctor's promise of the same.

"Probabilmente ha dimenticato la sua promessa," said Nino, embarrassed. (He probably forgot his promise.)

"Sei un bugiardo!" screamed the doctor! (You are a liar!) I confronted him about the promised discount on the phone, and he hung up. In the end, I barely broke even from the musical.

Diana agreed with me that AIL was a legitimate benefit, but I questioned the legitimacy of some of the other organizations, especially Comitato Panizza. She told me that Filetto came to her office constantly and treated her like a servant. Filetto wanted large amounts of money from the city to sponsor her benefit performances for Comitato Panizza. She never asked her; she ordered her. Diana decided to investigate the benefit and see where the money went in the Padua Hospital. She found that no money had ever arrived there and planned to expose Filetto at City Hall. However, if Filetto could demonstrate that all her spending was necessary, she could justify that there was no money left for the benefit.

A short time after, I heard that Diana had been fired as Minister of Culture and was no longer the director of the music school. I invited her for coffee in a local café, and we talked about what had happened. Filetto had used all her influence to get Diana fired from public service when she found out that she was being investigated. She didn't continue the Comitato Panizza beneficence but closed it and started another project to stop any further investigations. *Amici di Burkino Faso,* or Friends of Burkino Faso, was her new cause. Diana left Conegliano after that and went to Sicily, where she directed a music conservatory.

***

When spring arrived, the tradition of scholarship auditions in Turin nearly always came with it. Each year they lowered the age minimum, which was a sign of the times. The Teatro Nuovo was trying to reach out to young students who would choose a life of classical ballet. After Sara and Elena, my next candidate was a talented student named Giulia who was ten years old.

I went to Turin by train with Giulia and her mother Luciana. We stayed at the Hotel Crimea, which I had booked. This hotel gave a discount to all participants for the scholarship auditions at Teatro Nuovo. It was small, clean, and the only hotel that provided hot water to the Teatro Nuovo guests. All the other hotels turned off the hot water to recover money from the discounts they offered. This hotel became our home in Turin every year that I brought students for the auditions, and we were always welcomed back by the staff. The three of us arrived early because we wanted to go and see the Sacred Shroud, which was on display. The shroud was only shown for a brief time after a determined number of years, so we were lucky to be in Turin at that moment. Whether or not you believe that it is the cloth that covered Christ, the image is powerful. When I brought students to Turin, I would always try to squeeze in a visit to the Egyptian Museum. It was second only to the Cairo museum in Egypt for Egyptian antiquities. I believed it was important for the students to visit the sights in every place where we danced because it made the experience more culturally significant for them.

Giulia auditioned with the youngest group of dancers, and the results were that she received the maximum scholarship for five weeks! The joy on the faces of every student and their parents was worth everything to me. It always reminded me of my first scholarship, which had been awarded to me at age ten by my ballet teacher, Irine Fokine.

***

My ballet teacher, coach, and mentor in New York, Mischa Katcharoff, was a former dancer with the Ballets Russes Company. Like many of their dancers, he had lived through a difficult period in history, so he was not only a great artist and teacher but a very wise man. I will never forget his advice about love.

"After the passion is gone, you become good friends, so choose a man who shares your same interests." I remember feeling shattered by this declaration because, at that time, I believed that passion lived forever in a couple who loved each other. Later in life, I understood what he meant. Gianni and I had become good friends after five years, and our age difference had faded into the background. It no longer mattered. He was more of a husband to me than Ovidio had ever been. But there was one point when I understood how much I loved him and how I couldn't imagine my life without him. This recognition arose from a disaster that took place in Conegliano.

It was June. The rain fell in torrents and never stopped, so walking outside was unthinkable. One of the elementary school custodians saw my predicament and offered to give me a lift on her way home. It was only a few feet from the door of her car to my house, but I was soaked to the bone.

Inside, I heated a kettle to prepare a cup of hot tea and changed out of my wet clothes. The rain pounded the closed shutters of the back door, but at one point the sound changed, as though the water was rising up the back steps. I opened the shutter doors and found the water had risen almost to the top step. The backyard had become a lake! The plastic yard chairs floated, and a tub that contained flowers was now a boat without a navigator. I ran to the first floor and, from the balcony, watched a swift river flowing down the street. Cars were already half underwater, and at that moment, I was sure I was going to die. I thought that soon the house would be swept under by the fast-rising floodwaters.

I called Gianni to tell him to stay where he was, that it was impossible to come home. A part of me needed to speak to the last person on this earth who meant so much to me. It was a goodbye call. How many people have made such a call when death was almost certain? Gianni said he would come right away, but I insisted that he should stay where he was. I couldn't save myself but I wanted to save him. From the balcony, I watched the river of water take over the city. All kinds of objects were rushing by in the current. Twenty minutes later, I saw Gianni at the end of the street, wearing an extremely worried expression. He was holding on to the high iron fences that barricaded every house from the street. It was too dangerous, so I waved for him to go back, but it only made him more determined. At one point, he had to leave the safety of the fence and cross to our side of the street. Finally he made it safely to our house. When I think of my love for him, I see him walking through that swift river to rescue me.

The rain eventually stopped and the river waters went down, but the damage everywhere was stunning. People had to dig out of the mud that was left behind. Tragically, I had moved the scenery down from the hills into our garage a week before, and it was now covered by a thick slime. I put on my thigh-high boots from the Venice Acqua Alta, and all night I worked furiously to save what I could. Most of the pieces just needed a touch of paint on the bottom after they were washed down. The *Nutcracker* tree seemed to be destroyed, but Willi from the Bottega Venziana explained how to fix it. The whole disaster was the result of City Hall not cleaning debris from the river that flowed through the town. The rain had aggravated the situation, causing the banks to overflow.

***

The one good thing that came out of my business deal with Mirella Bellano was inheriting the job of choreographer for the Dama Castellana. This was a local Renaissance festival that took place every October. Mirella had been handed the position when she had bought Carmela's school. The first choreographer for the production was Tiziana, so a full circle had been completed. Most people didn't want the responsibility for more than a year or two because there was no pay, a lot of work, and limited freedom with the choreography. It was coordinated with the *vendemmia,* or grape picking, for the wine and prosecco in the hills. The piazza in front of Teatro Accademia was painted like an enormous chessboard, upon which a game of chess was played between the two winning quartiers from the many around Conegliano. The final game was played with living chess figures dressed in beautiful Renaissance costumes representing the colors of the quartiers. An audition was held each year for the hundreds of participants in costume.

Months before the Dama Castellana, I was called to the committee meeting at the old San Francesco Convent on the hill below the castle. There was no heat in the beautiful, historic convent, but the committee members were numerous, so we kept warm by huddling together in a small conference room. The artistic director, Carmen, introduced me as the new ballet choreographer. The members studied me doubtfully. *What was an American doing in the Dama Castellana?* The reunion was heated by clashing personalities and ideas. I was asked to vote on certain issues after the details of each proposal were explained to me. Committee members fought about problems that, as a first-timer, I couldn't understand, and some people angrily walked out. The ballet had live Renaissance music, and the leader of the musicians promised to bring me a copy of the various pieces that they had taped. I could decide which of the pieces I wanted to use for the ballet. A few days later, he came to my house with the tape but said his musicians wouldn't perform because the organization wouldn't pay.

"Cosa faccio con questa musica?" (What do I do with this music?)

He laughed and told me I could use any piece, but they just wouldn't play live unless they were paid. I tried to select the music that was dynamic, but most of it was rather boring.

"Fai I passi semplici come una danza rinascimentale," said Carmen. (Make the steps simple like a Renaissance dance.)

Between boring music and limited steps, I could see why my predecessors hadn't stayed long. Three young men, Mirko, along with Davide and Elvis, who later performed in *On Your Toes,* had learned the gracious steps over the years. Roberto and Gianni's friend Antonio completed the cast. Each cavalier had two female partners, except for the principal dancers.

There were complaints from those who had seen the Dama Castellana over the years that the ballet had been terribly monotonous. Making matters worse, the ballet costumes were flimsy, faded, and in poor condition. I wanted to do something more dramatic with the choreography to spice things up, so I decided to add small lifts and promenades to make the dance more interesting.

The day of the first Dama that I choreographed was more exciting than I had ever imagined. I had never seen the festival before, so everything was a surprise. The huge procession met at the San Francesco Convent, which was bustling with life and color. Everyone was dressed in Renaissance costumes and I was out of place in modern dress. The performers and *figuranti,* or supernumeraries, formed a snake in the open court. The moment the parade began, I wished everyone *in bocca al lupo,* in the mouth of the wolf, which means good luck in Italian. Then the snake moved quickly, and I used the shortcut down the hill and over to the sound technician, stationed high above one side of the piazza. There was the incredible silence of anticipation hanging over the town. Then I heard them: the drums pounded through the hills as the procession came down the old, winding streets. It was so powerful I experienced chills and goose bumps! It took another hour for them to fill the area in front of Teatro Accademia. It was one of the most spectacular entrances I had ever seen, and I felt honored to be the choreographer of the ballet.

The ballet went well, and the audience appreciated the few simple lifts I had added. But the sensation of the day was Paola's daughter Giulia. One part of the Dama is the reading of the tarot cards to predict the vendemmia for the successive year. A rather plump *maga,* or sorceress, dressed in a magnificent gold brocade costume would make her prediction at the show. The life-size cards are worn by female figuranti. Usually those who play the tarot cards fall short of the height requirement for ladies of the court or nobles. The bulky cards form a circle around the maga, and a jester moves the card that the sorceress calls. The jester is usually chosen with the same criteria as the cards; however, the candidate must be able to perform cartwheels. I had chosen Giulia because she was proficient in acrobatics, but I was criticized for my choice because she was younger than the age requirement and smaller. I guaranteed that she was a serious performer, but Carmen wasn't convinced. At the moment the maga gave her prediction for the future grape crops, she dropped her scepter. Giulia went into motion immediately, and after a series of cartwheels across the piazza, she stooped, picked up the scepter, and handed it to the woman. The applause was thunderous, and she had saved the heavy sorceress from the ungraceful exhibition of bending over to pick it up!

The chess game with figuranti was played until the game was won; then the nobles of the winning team were cheered by the crowds and carried in a simple cart up the hill to the castle. As their prize, they received the keys to the city for one year. Then the entire cast walked up to the castle, where a buffet was offered in the garden. It was a warm, sunny late afternoon of an Indian summer, and there was joy everywhere. My choreography was received with enthusiasm and compliments, and I was welcomed into their committee for the first time. At our meeting a few weeks later, Carmen stood up and applauded the work I had done and admitted that she hadn't believed an American could pull off Renaissance choreography!

The second Dama, I added more dramatic poses and concentrated on the two soloists. It was the first time that Flavio, Roberto's brother, had worked with us. I introduced Elena into the Dama, and she danced with Flavio, which worked out well. However, there was a problem with her costume—it was too long. I explained the problem to Carmen, and she didn't want to cut it, which I understood, so we worked out a solution. The dressmaker shortened the length by tucking the extra material and sewing it into the empire waist bodice. Elena was flat-chested, so it added to her bustline. The stitching could be torn out later and returned to the original, which was meant for someone taller. While the second performance was even better, the weather was not as good. We had a light rain, and it was colder. The buffet was permanently discontinued due to the expense, so everyone went home at the end of the show and things just fizzled out.

By the third year, I decided to be bolder. First, I asked if the dancers could have new costumes. They had shabby, worn-out frocks, while the figuranti were dressed in rich, opulent dresses. The director said there was no money to refurbish the costumes, so that was that. Our *corteo* in the parade was also very bland, and I asked why there were no children used in the production.

"Non abbiamo mai voluto i bambini nello spettacolo," I was told. (We never wanted children in the show.) The reason was that they feared the children would conduct themselves badly and ruin the performance. The wardrobe had smaller tunic shirts for females that had been substituted for male dancers when none could be found for the ballet one year. The four tunics could be altered temporarily for children, so I convinced the organization to include the four children who had won Vignale scholarships in the *sfilata*, or parade. This time, as the *maestra* of the ballet, I asked to be costumed in order to walk with my group of dancers through the city. Giulia, the talented young girl who had won a full scholarship at Turin the previous spring, would accompany me. We were both dressed in beautiful Renaissance gowns—mine was all black and Giulia wore gold. Now the ballet had its own magnificent *corteo!*

I had decided to use the music from Prokofiev's *Romeo and Juliet* for

the piazza ballet. The music could either make me cry or my veins throb
with passion, but it always left me drained from emotion. My body could
feel all the steps, as I remembered them from when I performed in *Romeo
and Juliet* at the Metropolitan Opera. The Dance of the Knights from the
score was one of the most dramatic pieces and was perfect for a
Renaissance dance. I risked criticism and being fired after the show
because of deviating from the traditional. But at least I would end my
Dama tenure with some artistic satisfaction. The dancers loved the piece
as soon as I began the choreography, and the music stimulated their
artistry.

The day of the performance, our corteo walked proudly. Not only had
tickets been sold for the performance, but the sfilata attracted huge crowds
from all over. The experience reminded me of the year I had performed
with the circus, where I could see the faces of the spectators. That had been
my last parade: in Salt Lake City, Utah. There I had sat high on the mighty
shoulders of my elephant Peggy and was protected by her. Now, as I
walked in the Dama Castellana parade in Conegliano, Italy, it seemed like
everyone was critically looking at the American, posing as an Italian. The
four pages, led by Giulia, marched into the piazza to the opening of
Prokofiev's *Romeo and Juliet* reverberating all over the city. Following in
my ostentatious black velvet costume, I slowly turned toward the dancers
when I arrived at the border of the chessboard. This was their cue to enter
and take their positions for the dance. The rain fell lightly, making the
painted chess board slippery, but the dancers worked without a mishap.
After this Dama, the ballet became the talk of the town.

"Non perdere La Dama il prossimo anno, perché il balletto era una cosa
fantastica!" (Don't miss the Dama next year, because the ballet was
something fantastic!) I heard similar praise over and over.

"Sentivo la pelle di oca quando ho visto il balletto!" another declared.
(I felt goose bumps when I saw the ballet!) Instead of firing me, the
organization complimented my work.

The final year with the Dama Castellana, I went even further with the
choreography and fulfilled another dream, which was to produce the

Romeo and Juliet pas de deux. From the steps of Teatro Accademia, the vision became alive. There was a small space in front of both statues at the entrance to the theater. One could be used as Juliet's terrace. Romeo could walk up a few steps, then lift Juliet from this podium. Flavio and Elena, two diligent workers, were perfect as the ill-fated lovers. Classical ballet with a Renaissance theme would be performed on pointe. But I didn't know if the association would agree to this because it was far from traditional.

As soon as the school year finished, we began practicing the pas de deux. I explained to Flavio and Elena that there was no guarantee they would be allowed to perform this at the Dama. However, if it wasn't possible for the Dama Castellana, I would find some way and somewhere for them to perform the piece. I choreographed the pas de deux without pirouettes because of the concrete chessboard pavement, but I substituted the turns for many intricate lifts. When the dance was ready, our next step was to rehearse it in the piazza.

"Che cosa fate?" asked Riccardo, who was the secretary to the mayor and part of the Dama committee. (What are you doing?)

"Stiamo provando," I replied. (We are rehearsing.)

I thought he would send us away with the excuse that dancing in a public place was not legal. But he just smiled and quickly moved on. There was an occasional bystander who stopped to watch, but late afternoon on a hot summer day was not a popular time for the citizens to be outside. Teatro Accademia was closed, so we could peacefully work without any interruption or disturbances. We worked in July and August; then it was ready to present to the organization. Luck was in our favor when a new artistic director was hired. Nicolao, the new director, was the owner of a costume atelier in Venice. Over the years, the Dama had rented their most sumptuous costumes from Atelier Nicolao. I knew him and his workshop because of special costumes we had rented from him in the past.

I arranged for him to see the pas de deux and proposed that it be performed at the *Preludio*. This prelude performance was always held the night before the Dama. The old oil lamps added to the atmosphere of the

Renaissance period. There was a ceremony in which the chess victors from the prior Dama would hand over the keys to the city, which they had held for the year. I could visualize the terrace scene, with the pas de deux danced at night in front of the theater. Nicolao was impressed with the presentation and agreed to have the couple dance at the *Preludio*. There would be an encore the next day at the chess game, right after the dancers repeated the knights' ball from the year before. We were thrilled to have this opportunity.

In addition to the ballet, Nicolao asked me to choreograph movements and formations to music for the tarot cards. They had had limited mobility in all the previous productions, and the effect was stagnant. The huge cards on the front and back of each figure did not offer much freedom of movement. I decided to approach the choreography with the idea of card shuffling, because this way, different moving positions could be formed. We had many long rehearsals, but the tarot cards finally came to life!

With the Saturday night Preludio, I realized another dream. The pas de deux was performed in a real Italian piazza, at night, and from an actual terrace, exactly as it was meant to be. Elena was the perfect Juliet, petite, with long black hair and a tragic expression. I experienced a significant emotion watching my student dance the role, and my eyes filled with tears of joy. I had waited for this moment for many years. The Dama on Sunday went well, though we had a light rainfall, which almost seemed to be a tradition. During the week, an article and review came out in the newspaper. Endless pages and photos were displayed for readers, and the ballet had received raves, both for the night of the Preludio and for the Dama Castellana. However, a surprise came along with applause for the tarot cards. The stiff cards had finally come to life, according to the journalists. But the big question in the news was: Who had prepared the movements for the cards? No one seemed to know. How could the organizers not know that I had done the work? The people didn't connect the ballet choreographer with the movements of the tarot cards, so they didn't give me credit for the preparation. The moving tarot cards remained a mystery.

I couldn't wait to repeat the ballet again the following year, but wheels behind the scenes were already in motion, planning the contrary. The president of the association for the Dama Castellana admitted that the job had been given to the wife of a wealthy sponsor. With the pledge of big bucks for the association came demands and concessions. The woman had no experience, and she turned the production into a fiasco. The organization decided to repeat the show in June, and they paid Carla Fracci to substitute for her. The Dama's reputation had to be repaired after the 2000 disaster, and rumors were that Carla Fracci was paid a fortune to pull up the show.

At least we had had the chance to perform the *Romeo and Juliet* pas de deux once, and it would be talked about for years to come. Now only the mystery of the tarot cards held the future for my ballet school and for me.

The Dama Castellana

Romeo and Juliet

The Tarot Cards

Dancers prepare at the St. Francis Convent

CHAPTER 18

The Bailiff at Midnight

"In every one of us there is another that we don't know."
Carl Gustav Jung

The doorbell at the front gate rang at midnight. Gianni and I, along with Sissi and Andy, two bulldogs we had adopted, were watching television. We looked at each other.

"Chi é?" I asked Gianni. (Who is it?) He had friends who would drop by without notice, but at midnight?

"Vado a vedere," he said. (I'll go and see.) He opened the window of the front door and looked down the short garden path to the gate. A tall young man with glasses, a beard, and a moustache stood outside the iron gate.

"La Signora File è a casa? (Is Mrs. File at home?)

I knew something was very wrong, just by the formality of this total stranger. I didn't move a muscle.

"No, non è a casa," responded Gianni. (She isn't at home.)

"Chi è lei?" (Who are you?)

The man explained that he was the *ufficiale giudiziario,* a bailiff, and that he had been ordered by the judge in Treviso to enter my home. With that declaration, Gianni opened the door and Sissi and Andy ran out, snarling. Gianni repeated that I wasn't at home, and the dogs dared him to force an entry beyond the gate.

We both knew the law: the bailiff could not enter the house without my presence. Gianni told the bailiff he was there to feed the dogs while I was away. *What did he want?* In Italy, when a bill is not paid, a judge will give permission for an officer of the court to enter the debtor's house and claim any possession that can be sold to pay the debt. Only beds and refrigerators are untouchable. This usually happens after it has been determined in a civil case that the person definitely owes this money. However, in my case, the bailiff started knocking on my door long before I had been declared guilty of anything! The officer usually came between nine o'clock and five o'clock, and I never answered the door. Our house always seemed abandoned because I kept the shutters closed all the time. I had no car, so the driveway was free during the day.

The bailiff's midnight arrival threw us. The officer tried to bluff Gianni, threatening to call the Carabinieri if he didn't let him in. He stood his ground and the bailiff called the police. Gianni came back into the house, shut off the lights, and called our dogs back inside. Everything was staged to look like no one was in the house and he was just leaving. As he pulled his Jeep out of the driveway, the Carabinieri arrived.

I was considered a criminal for not having paid a phony bill in a country where a murderer is often set free within a day. *How did I get into this mess?* A corrupt Italian judge had authorized that I be treated like a Mafia boss. Therefore, the house could be raided by the Carabinieri at midnight. Ironically, it was the legalized Mafia of the north that was treating me like a *Mafioso*! This story had all begun years ago, with the ballet *Cinderella.*

***

"Voglio presentare un uomo molto importante in Conegliano," said Fabio. (I want to present an important man in Conegliano.)

More than six months had passed since the production of the *Nutcracker* in Teatro Goldoni. Ovidio and I were separated but still living under the same roof in Venice, and I had continued to see Marina and Fabio at their gelateria. I was preparing the first *Cinderella* when Fabio suggested I meet this man. Gian Luigi Ronzio was a lawyer, former mayor, and president of a sport and cultural association. The association, ICSA, Italian Culture and Sports Association, had its headquarters in Rome. But Fabio also added reluctantly that Ronzio had Mafia connections. When I heard this, I said that I wanted no part in meeting him. Fabio assured me that the Mafia would have nothing to do with a ballet school, and even I believed this was far-fetched. He guaranteed that the association was legitimate and without criminal ties. He insisted that the alliance with Ronzio would bring us to a new level. So I agreed to meet the *avvocato*, or lawyer, Ronzio, as he was called.

Fabio made an appointment and accompanied me to Conegliano. I would propose a full-page ad for ICSA in the *Cinderella* program, which would help sponsor the ballet. Ronzio had a large, modern office with two men present who appeared to be part of the furnishings. One in particular was mean and tough-looking, and his angry eyes gave me an unpleasant welcome. The avvocato was a tall, slim, well-dressed, but odd-looking type. He had a smooth, round, chubby, baby face that was almost innocent—not at all threatening. But his fast, brusque manner indicated that he was accustomed to being in control. Fabio introduced me and recounted a little about the *Nutcracker* at the Goldoni. Ronzio was totally uninterested and wanted to wrap up the meeting fast, so he came out and asked me directly, "What do you want?" I spoke about the new ballet *Cinderella* and how I was selling space in the program to sponsor the show. He agreed immediately to a full page but had one request, which was that the ad would appear on the back cover. This was no problem. Fabio and I were happy when we left the office, especially since avvocato Ronzio had promised to double the price of the page to one thousand dollars.

When it came time to get the program ready, I took the ad designs to the printer Baravelli, who had printed the *Nutcracker* programs and posters. When he saw the ICSA publicity, he asked if it was the organization connected to avvocato Ronzio, and I confirmed that it was. He said that he had never met the man but had heard that he never paid for anything. I told him that I believed he would pay for the ad, and he commented with sarcasm, "Spero per te che lui lo faccia." (I hope for your sake that he does.)

The ballet was only a couple of weeks away, and I started assigning the sponsors tickets and their preferred seats in the theater. I called avvocato Ronzio and asked him where he would like to sit in Teatro Accademia. I gave him four tickets instead of the usual two for a one-page ad. "Only four? I expect at least ten!" he yelled into the phone. I was shocked by his tone but granted his wish. However, each day, his secretary called for additional tickets, until the total of number of seats came to thirty. Then, right before the performance, he called and asked that an enormous, long ICSA banner be placed under the entire stage. I wasn't going to ruin the beauty of the ballet with an ugly sign under the dancer's feet, so I said no. He called again and asked that all the dancers hold the banner in the finale, and I informed him that we weren't a sporting event. If I allowed this, other sponsors would never return or would expect that I do the same for them at the next show. Publicity tacked all over would destroy the aesthetics of our productions, so I stood firm and refused.

After the performance, I met the photographer for the ballet, Da Rios, to order photos. He told me that avvocato Ronzio had called and wanted him to transpose the ICSA banner on some photos of the finale. Da Rios thought this was unusual, but Ronzio had said he needed these photos for the association headquarters in Rome. I had other things to think about. All expenses had been paid except for the printer, Baravelli, but I dreaded going there to discuss the bill.

***

A desperate mother asked "Dové sono I programmi?" (Where are the programs?) She was helping backstage the night of the ballet *Cinderella*. I was numb. The programs had not been delivered as they should have been. Baravelli had finished the *Nutcracker* programs at the last minute but compensated by delivering them. With *Cinderella,* he had been negligent; the delivery wasn't made. The business was closed, so the mother called his home. His wife answered and said he was at a card game. She said she would call someone to open the factory and deliver the programs. By the time this took place, the show was over. On the way out of the theater, I saw that several boxes of programs had arrived and been left at the exit. A few days later, I distributed the programs to annoyed students, families, and sponsors. Luckily, they didn't blame me.

A friend gave me a lift to the Baravelli factory, which was on the outskirts of Conegliano. I had planned to ask for a discount on the programs because they hadn't been delivered in time. Another person would have refused to pay anything for such a catastrophe. When he presented me with the bill, I just stared at it because this wasn't what we had agreed on. When I asked him why the bill was one thousand dollars more than the estimate had been, with a sour expression, he informed me that he had done extra work on the program. I asked him innocently, "What extra work?" He went into a rage. Baravelli stood up and grabbed my arm and pulled me out of his office. When we got to the entrance, he opened the door and threw me into the street. So much for a discount on the programs. I was upset and humiliated—and I had a long walk back to town.

I was shaken by this terrible experience and wasn't sure what to do. Paying full price for programs that weren't delivered in time for the show was ridiculous, but to pay one thousand dollars more was outrageous! There was one sponsor who hadn't paid me yet—avvocato Ronzio. I dropped by his office and was escorted in to see him. The two thugs were sitting in the same place, and Ronzio wasn't happy to see me.

"What do you want?" he demanded. I asked him if he had liked the ballet and he said yes. Then I delicately reminded him of our agreement for the ad.

"Dammi una fattura per venti million." (Give me a receipt for the equivalent of twenty thousand dollars.)

"Cosa?" (What?) I pointed out that he promised one thousand dollars. He then told me if I wanted the thousand dollars, I would have to write him a receipt for twenty thousand. This was more money than all the sponsor payments put together.

"Non posso dare una ricevuta per questi soldi." (I can't give you a receipt for this money.) He insisted that he needed a big *fattura* in order to get money from the headquarters in Rome. This was a common scam in Italy. I was supposed to write a receipt for twenty thousand dollars, and

201

Ronzio would give this to ICSA in Rome, who would then receive the reimbursement from the government. The association would pay Ronzio twenty thousand, and he would give me one thousand. This was how he became rich, like many others in Italy. I wanted nothing to do with this.

He asked, "Hai qualche grossa spesa da pagare come un tipografo?" (Do you have a big bill to pay, like a printer?) I immediately thought of Baravelli, so I told him that the printer needed to be paid. He assured me he would take care of the payment with Baravelli, and I was relieved. Two dishonest men could defraud together. It was done, and I ended any future collaboration with Ronzio and Baravelli. Then, one day, I had an unwelcome visitor at the school. I was just finishing a summer workshop when the thug from Ronzio's office paid me an unfriendly visit. He explained that the avvocato had been pleased with the show and now was the time to organize our inclusion in his association. I listened. He went on to explain that the organization wanted a percentage of the money from the monthly payment of every student. The amount of money they wanted was half of what came into the school!

"Perché devo pagare tutti questi soldi?" I innocently asked. (Why should I pay all of this money?) The man looked at me like I was either sarcastic or stupid. He was angry and frustrated.

"Per protezione!" he replied. (For protection!)

"Protezione? Ho gia un commercialista," I answered. (Protection? I already have an accountant.) In Italy, every business needed a shrewd accountant to keep it from financial disaster. I stupidly thought that this is what he meant and refused his offer. Then he stood up and looked down at me with contempt.

"Un giorno ti pentirai." (You will be sorry one day.) Those were his last words to me. I still didn't understand the significance of the visit until I told Gianni the story.

"La bustarella!" (The bribe!)

It was only a matter of time before they would make me pay. This was not the Mafia that kills people, but a legalized one. You pay them a monthly quota and they leave you alone; otherwise, one day they will destroy you. A phony lawsuit is dropped into your lap out of nowhere, and you are forced to pay a fortune to them in order to break free. They waited a few years, and then they smacked me with the lawsuit. It was time to pay the bribery money I hadn't paid then—and with interest on top.

***

Five years after the incident, the final rehearsals took place for the Dama Castellana. It was an early evening in October, and a man whose face I cannot recall asked to see me. Someone had pointed me out while I was rehearsing the dancers for their part in the Renaissance festival performance. He walked toward me with a determined step and asked;

"Lei è Barbara File?"

"Si."

"Per lei." (This is for you.) He deliberately handed me an envelope, turned, and walked away.

Confused, I stared at the envelope. I had witnessed this scene many times in the movies, but I never had experienced it myself: I had been served with a court subpoena.

What did it mean? My trembling hand opened the envelope, and my troubled times with the Mafia of the north began the instant I opened the letter.

The letter was simple. It ordered me, in one sentence, to pay the printer Baravelli sum upon sum of money and interest fees or face a court trial. The next sentence was a threat by the lawyer, Cristina Dorelli, who wrote the order. She told me I owed her 2,000 euro (around $2,300.00) for writing this one sentence and ordered me to pay her. It was legalized blackmail! I associated the crooked printer immediately with Ronzio because of their partnership in the sponsor scam. Then I remembered the thug who had threatened me with the words "You will regret it later" when I hadn't paid the bribes. Fear and nausea were followed by anger. Five years had gone by since *Cinderella*. If Baravelli hadn't been paid by Ronzio's sponsorship, why had he waited five years to tell me that the bill hadn't been paid? On top of the bill, he had added five years of interest. It was clear that the printer, the lawyer, and Ronzio had decided to make some money at my expense. At that moment, I knew I had to lawyer up.

Gianni had a friend, Riccardo, from childhood, who had joined a law firm in Treviso, and Gianni referred to him as a "mean rugby player." I had met Riccardo before, at a wedding. When we met at his office, I was reminded of his angelic face and youth. *Could he go up against the Mafia sharks?* I recounted the entire story and Riccardo understood it was a scam to make money twice from *Cinderella.* He said the programs had not been delivered in time for the show, so Baravelli hadn't fulfilled his commitment. Therefore, he shouldn't even have been paid to begin with. The opposition couldn't prove that I had ordered the programs after so many years. They operated on the assumption that I feared what they could do to me, so I would pay them whatever they wanted.

"First of all, do you have *beni*?" This refers to the amount of money, number of houses, or other assets belonging to the accused.

"Nothing," I said.

Later, Riccardo contested the 2,000 euro letter sent by Dorelli and the outlandish amount of money that the printer Baravelli had demanded. Dorelli threatened to get a court order to take away my car to pay her and her client if I had no real estate or had hidden my *beni*. They underestimated the fact that not only did I have no assets or car, I didn't even own a bicycle. A successful dance school and wealth don't always go hand in hand.

The next question was, what proof did they have against me.

"Did you sign a receipt?" Riccardo asked.

"No," I replied. However, a few days later, Riccardo called and said that they had a receipt with my signature for the ballet programs, received the night of the performance. I knew I hadn't signed anything, so I wasn't worried, but then I thought that maybe they had forged my signature. The signature turned out to be an illegible straight line, and I was able to prove immediately that it wasn't mine. But that didn't deter the judge, or *giudice*, Manzini, who was Baravelli's tennis partner and a good friend of Ronzio. It would come out that all three were friends and had played the game together. Baravelli had met Ronzio for the first time when they had used my ballet *Cinderella* for their interests. The judge decided to proceed with the case without proof and a signature that wasn't mine. Riccardo was disheartened. He had never seen a case proceed with no evidence.

The first bailiff was an ugly woman who looked like the witch from the *Wizard of Oz* and had a matching personality. She came to my school with an order from the court to pay up immediately or the court would strip me of everything I owned. There hadn't even been a trial yet! All my personal things were to be sold to pay Baravelli. They thought this would frighten me, but I decided to fight. Now I needed the strength of my Irish ancestors. Quickly, I made a plan.

All personal things that could be confiscated I stored in Gianni's garage at Quinto. The money from the school was collected by the mother of a student, so this exchange could not be touched by the bailiff. Then the money would be hidden in the garage. All work-related material, like costumes, scenery, and props, could stay at the house. The idea was that I needed to continue working in order to make money for them. The mandate lasted three months, so I just had to lie low and not answer the doorbell. If, after this date of expiration, the bailiff hadn't found anything to confiscate or had never found me at home, my life would go back to normal. The first authorization came and went, and nothing happened. Gianni and I almost celebrated, but we knew they could arrange another mandate in the future. It was a very expensive process, which Baravelli paid for, but if I lost the trial, I would be expected to reimburse him, along with the other expenses.

Right after this mandate, I ran into a former neighbor from my old apartment in Via Cavalotti. He said that a court officer had been looking for me but he had told him I had moved away. When the officer asked where I went, he had confessed that he didn't know. I contemplated this development and discerned that I would have come close to losing my apartment if I hadn't sold it when I did. So what had seemed like a terrible loss at the time—the necessary sale of my apartment—was actually a blessing in disguise.

I began to understand how a great loss can actually be fortunate and how it can often open a new door to a better opportunity or circumstances for the future. I was reminded of an experience I had had as a young ballet student when the Bolshoi Ballet had come to New York. Because I had been too tall to dance a children's role with the company, I was heartbroken. This had prompted my mother to take me to audition for the School of American Ballet.

"Will you promise to quit if they say that you will never be a professional dancer?" I said yes and she made an appointment with the school. The audition day came and the school accepted me, much to the chagrin of my mother. So without the disappointing loss of the Bolshoi role, the fantastic opportunity at Balanchine's school would never have happened.

***

Months went by; then a couple of years passed. Gianni believed that Baravelli and Ronzio had given up, but I didn't. One Saturday, a nondescript man followed me home. He tried to dodge me, but I could tell he wasn't a stalker. His actions belied a determined purpose. I began to play his game and took him around in circles, but I couldn't shake him. Finally I arrived at the gate to my house, and I was curious as to what the man would do next. He watched from the sidewalk a few yards away, as I opened the gate with my key. His expression said, "Now I know where you live," and he walked away. The bailiff had been looking for me at the old address because apparently the slow bureaucratic system hadn't registered my new residence. For this reason, the first mandate had been unsuccessful, so they decided to have someone follow me to find out exactly where I was living. I knew it was only a matter of time before another court order would come. And it did.

I asked myself what they expected to find in my house. Did they think I rented a shabby, empty house, had no car, and had a Picasso on a moldy wall? I could visualize the bailiff or Carabinieri, paid by Baravelli and ordered by the corrupt judge Manzini, planting drugs somewhere in my house. I would be arrested. This was their ultimate goal. If they couldn't get money out of me, they would get rid of me. They wouldn't kill me, but they would send me to jail. This type of setup had been confirmed by a Roman Carabiniere I had met on vacation with Gianni, so I was determined that the bailiff would never get into our house.

Ultimately, the trial came, and I was asked a few questions, but I could feel that the judge had already decided. A week later, Riccardo sadly gave me the bad news: I was declared guilty. Judge Manzini said that there was no evidence to prove I was guilty, but he *felt* I was. He even mentioned in his declaration that a receipt with a signature had been submitted as evidence but had been proven not to be mine. Years later, in another mandate, he changed his declaration and wrote that I was guilty by the proof of my signature on the receipt! The level of corruption was astounding.

***

The night the Bailiff came at midnight, I sat on the marble stairs in total silence, my body trembling. The quieter I was, the more I would remain invisible to the predators that threatened me outside the iron gate of my house. I was worried that they could hear my body tremble and remained immobile, but my mind was very active. I thought about who I was. *Who was the animal inside me, a frightened mouse or a courageous lion?* In a vivid, unforgettable nightmare I had had many years before, I had changed into a tiger. Another tiger had appeared in the forest clearing where I stood and we had attacked each other. For the first time, I felt the instinct to survive and the determination to live, whatever it cost. I had won the savage encounter with every bloody detail in that grotesque dream. With a start I had awakened from this nightmare, but years later I had never forgotten the horror or the message.

Now I looked inside myself and found the tiger. I knew that if I had to, I would fight to the end and not submit to my predators. The tremors in my body were from my blood boiling with anger, not fear. I had discovered the tiger inside the shell that I inhabited. Barefoot, I slowly climbed the stairway and went to the bedroom to stretch out on my bed. The phone rang incessantly all night, but I didn't dare leave the receiver off the hook because the bailiff would know that someone was inside the house. I couldn't sleep with the phone ringing, but my body rested. At dawn, the sun came through the bedroom window and the phone stopped ringing. The bailiff's night shift was over.

I called Gianni and we quickly worked out a plan. He would come to get Sissi and Andy, who had been close to me all night. The small travel bag I had prepared was ready. If Gianni observed that the street was clear of the police or other authorities, I would run to the Jeep and we would drive away. Once outside the gate, I would be safe. If they stopped me in the street, they couldn't enter the house. The most they could do was strip me of my money or any jewelry I wore, and I had neither. Our plan was successful, and we sped away to the Sporting Club where Gianni worked in Vittorio Veneto. With my escape, I experienced what freedom means to a person who has been hiding. My hideout was only for one night. I couldn't imagine living like this for years.

Sixteen days! Only sixteen days! In sixteen days the mandate would expire, my reclusion would end, and I could return home. The Sporting Club had an empty room upstairs, and we slept on the floor with Sissi and Andy. It was the end of April, and I continued to work on our new show at the school. Ironically, it was our second *Cinderella*. On day sixteen, the four of us happily returned home. The next day, the ballet posters were placed around town to advertise the performance fourteen days later. The night of the show, we were worried that the ticket money could be taken at the box office by the bailiff, because no mandate was required to do this. Fortunately, nothing happened. Again, I had remained unscathed.

An Italian friend of mine once said that you could steal an apple in Italy and go to prison for years but a murderer could be back out on the street the next day. Italian law was a contradiction. I recalled an absurd scene at the Friday market in Conegliano. The place had always been a haven for gypsies, pickpockets, thieves, and legalized begging. A young man played the violin on a corner in the midst of this *follia,* or absurdity. He played beautiful classical music and brought peace to the chaos of the marketplace. Two Carabinieri arrived in their elegant winter uniforms and walked up to the musician. Where was his permission to play music? The SIAE expected him to pay a quota for standing on the corner and playing his music. In the meantime, the criminals went about their business untouched or uninterrupted, but the young musician was forced to stop playing. I felt so angry I wanted to say something to the officers but I stayed silent. I figured I had enough problems with the law.

The frightening experience with the Italian law and Mafia taught me a valuable lesson. All of my books could be taken away, but they couldn't be removed from my mind if I had read them. I came to the understanding that a bailiff couldn't carry away a person's memories. The *Ufficiale Giudiziale* couldn't confiscate experiences. I could travel the world, eat delicious foods, and enjoy the beauty of nature with all my senses, and none of these things could be taken away. But most of all, they couldn't remove my creativity and auction it for money. From that moment on, I understood what was important in life. Money, objects, and things don't define us or our lives. When we leave this world, we take with us all of our memories, but the material baggage we leave behind. So out of something bad had come important life lessons. That night when the bailiff came at midnight, I had discovered many things about myself, but most of all, I had found the *other* that lives inside of me: a tigress who will fight to the end.

CHAPTER 19

The Conegliano Castle

"Sometimes a man searches for treasure in faraway
places, and doesn't realize it is already in his possession."
Kahlil Gibran

"Il mio capitano di ferro!" (My iron captain!) Ledo Freschi saluted me from the Scalinata degli Alpini. His great voice could be heard by everyone around.

He had given me this title of honor after the success of *On Your Toes*. He had even written about the musical experience with immense enthusiasm in his book. Our friendship grew. We often met for a caffè and to exchange stories about our memories in the theater. Ledo and I always met in the street, halfway to the Café Teatro in Piazza Cima where we had our appointment. He would say that after years in the theater, we were disciplined to arrive early—the performance was at a certain time but the performer was there long before that to prepare. So we prepared for our meeting and met on the way.

"La gente di solito è in ritardo," he would comment in his deep baritone voice. (People are usually late.)

In fact, most Italians were always late. It wasn't that they never learned to be on time. Punctuality was simply not la moda, and it could be downright embarrassing to be on time. It was like wearing something unfashionable.

***

210

Elena had made it to the finals of the Padua competition, Sfera, and was nominated as one of thirteen prodigious soloists in Italy. She had auditioned by video with the Black Swan solo, and we continued to perfect it for the finals in Padua's Teatro Verdi. Her turns were flawless, and each time she performed precise double *fouetté* turns, the most difficult in classical ballet. I was often a *Broadway Danny Rose* in the encouragement department for performing students. I believed in them above and beyond anything else, more than they believed in themselves. But Elena believed in herself, and this never wavered when she performed.

Even though Padua was close to Venice, neither of us had ever seen the Scrovegni Church, with the artist Giotto's frescoes, so we went there before the performance. We were wholly absorbed with Giotto's masterpiece, completed around the early fourteenth century. There were no other visitors in the chapel, so we could appreciate it even more. The frescoes presented a series of religious stories, and the background was painted a deep blue. Trompe l'oeil images graced the walls, and between us there was only the deafening silence of awe. We interrupted our visit when it was time to go to the theater and prepare for the performance.

Elena performed magnificently, every pirouette perfect. Her interpretation was cold and calculating, exactly the character of the Black Swan. I don't remember all the other contestants, except one. The dancer performed the Kitri variation from *Don Quixote*. When the dancer made her entrance, she flicked open the fan in her hand. Sounds of cheering roared through the theater and paled the applause for Elena's perfect fouettés. *How is it possible that the flick of a fan merits more approval than double fouetté turns on pointe?* There was nothing outstanding about her performance, especially compared to Elena's. Sometimes I wondered if I was prejudiced when it came to the ability of my students. In the end, the Kitri soloist won. We were disappointed, but as the audience piled out of the theater, a revolt took place. Some people recognized Elena and asked if I was her teacher.

"Lei doveva vincere!" shouted a teacher, referring to Elena. (She should have won!) Others joined and anger mounted.

"Non è giusto!" (It isn't fair!)

Many said that they would write to the organizers, complaining about the results, and others threatened never to return. At least I knew that my judgment was correct and not blinded by my own prejudice. But there was the sad reality of every ballerina. Elena's performance was over in a minute, then gone forever. Unlike Giotto's frescoes that had survived for centuries.

***

The school had now participated in dance festivals, competitions, and scholarship auditions in Italy. We had toured the country, but the next step was to go beyond the borders and travel to other European countries. Elena was one of the most talented classical soloists in Italy, so I was convinced it was time for her to compete with other dance students on the world stage. The Prix de Lausanne was the ultimate international classical ballet competition, and I wanted Elena to particpate. While I knew she couldn't win, the participation itself could help decide her future. It was one thing to be one of the best in Italy but quite another to be one of the best in the world.

The teacher and student could decide on one of five repertory variations to dance for the international jury. We chose Aurora's variation from the wedding scene in *Sleeping Beauty*. In addition, we chose a contemporary variation to perform. It was October 1999, and we worked constantly to get ready. Students and teachers were expected to stay in Lausanne for one week. Several hotels offered discounts for participants, and meals were included. The candidates would study all day until the finals. Our only inconvenience would be a very long trip by train to get there. Flavio surprised us by offering to drive to Lausanne and return to pick us up. The trip was about seven hours by car but double that time by train, so we truly appreciated his offer.

***

The new millennium came upon the world. Gianni had to work at the Sporting Club that night and I went to join the festivities. I don't like partying on New Year's Eve, or any other time, but I wanted to be with Gianni on this important night. The heat was shut down with the hope that so many celebrating bodies would warm the place, but it didn't. It was brutally cold, and I was sick the day after.

***

The Prix de Lausanne officially opened on January 23, 2000, at the Beau-Rivage Palace, where a sumptuous buffet was offered. Elena took class at the Beaulieu Theater every day, and I watched, along with the other teachers. The dressing rooms were divided according to continents, except for the English-speaking people who were kept together. Americans and Australians were right at home with each other. At the theater, students covered themselves with everything they could to keep warm, but Elena was comfortable in a sleeveless leotard, without legwarmers or a pullover. We were amazed at how hot it was inside. Even buses were heavily heated in Switzerland. I began to peel off my sweaters. Snow was everywhere, but there was no humidity. Anything we washed and left in the bathroom overnight was dry the follwing morning. We were astounded! The reality of Italy is so different.

At the Prix de Lausanne, we met a group of Americans and Australians in the hotel lobby. An American teacher from Boston told me that the group was planning to take a cable car up to the top of the mountain in Lausanne.

"Everyone is so excited. There is a real castle on top of the hill!" she exclaimed. Elena and I looked at each other.

"It's very cold up there and the fog is thick at this time of the year, we've heard. But the ruins of the castle are still there."

"Ruins?" I asked.

"Yes, there are big rocks from the old castle," she said with enthusiasm. "Would you like to join us?"

We graciously declined the invitation, citing the cold as an excuse. Later, I said to Elena that we have this beautiful, well-preserved castle in Conegliano and we don't think about it. These people are going out of their way just to visit a few rocks on a miserable, freezing day in Switzerland. Sometimes we don't appreciate what we have in Italy. That was when I decided that the Conegliano castle would be in every poster for every ballet we did from then on.

Elena didn't make it to the finals so she never performed her variations, but we stayed for the winners' award ceremony. There were hundreds of wonderful dancers from all over the world who had come for the chance to compete, but only a few were picked. The grand prize was a scholarship to a professional ballet school with a company. The Asian dancers were unbeatable and swept away the prizes.

The following morning, we left Lausanne, with Flavio at the wheel. The combination of sun and snow on the Swiss Alps was blinding on the return trip back to Italy. At one point, Flavio stopped the car and we got out to look silently at the scene in awe. Before us was a magnificent creation of God, the greatest artist of all time. The powerful, white mountains were like enormous, still clouds, with the sun illuminating them. For a few moments, it seemed like we were in heaven, and I inhaled a deep breath of the cleanest and purest air. We continued our voyage to the Italian border where everything changed. A black powder from the air pollution in Italy dusted the white snow. A rundown house at the border checkpoint had laundry hanging outside to spoil the view. The border officials aggressively took apart our suitcases to see if they could confiscate an expensive Swiss watch. *Ben tornata!* Welcome back to the land of corruption.

***

Cinderella was the ballet I had chosen for our tenth anniversary, but before that, I decided to bring *Senza Definizione* back to the stage as part of our anniversary celebration. We were invited to the Agon Dance Festival at Teatro Nuovo. Flavio drove us this time, and we stayed at the Hotel Crimea. The next day, we were to perform at Teatro Nuovo, and the company was also there, so I asked the director if Elena could take the company class. He said she could and gave me permission to watch. Elena was stronger than many of the other dancers, and I thought about speaking with the director after class. She still had one year left in high school, so I was certain he would suggest that she spend the last year at their school. But before I spoke, I wanted to talk with her. She wanted no part of Teatro Nuovo. For Elena, it was La Scala or nothing, and they had turned her away at an audition because she didn't have the kind of body they wanted. But her body was fine for the Teatro Nuovo dance company.

I wondered what was blocking Elena from grabbing the opportunity to become a professional dancer. Her mother had told me that a friend of the family had discouraged her, suggesting that dance brings heartbreak. "So does love," I replied. "Do we avoid love because it could bring heartbreak?" They reflected on what I said, but nothing changed.

***

I asked Enrica if she had any ideas where I could find an elegant chair that could be used as a throne.

"Io conosco una Signora che ha un vero trono del quattrocento." (I know a woman with a real throne from the fifteenth century.)

I couldn't imagine anyone owning something like this. It belonged in a museum! The thought of using such a precious and priceless antique on stage made me shudder, but Enrica insisted that it would be okay.

"Ma pensi che la signora ci dia permesso?" (Do you think she will give us permission?)

Enrica reassured me after speaking with Signora Casserotto, the owner of the throne, that there would be no problem exhibiting it on stage and that she was happy to help the ballet performance. It was a great honor to have the presence of history in our *Cinderella.* We had a separate van just for the throne, and it arrived the day of the ballet at Teatro Accademia. The van door opened, and the throne stood in the middle, ominously locked down like the serial killer Hannibal Lechter. It was wheeled out with the pomp of royalty but handled carefully and respectfully, as was required for its advanced age. I kept the priceless chair in my temporary office/dressing room, next to the stage. Everyone was warned to keep their distance, not to touch it, or to do the unthinkable: sit on it. When the palace scene was done, it was whisked away in the van and I breathed a sigh of relief. That night, however, the throne was not the only royal presence. An Austrian prince and his family came to see the ballet. I had once danced for Prince Ranier of Monaco, so I appreciated our royal guests for the ballet performance. Elena danced the role of *Cinderella* and was brilliant technically but tragic in her interpretation, even after she had won the prince.

***

The second *Cinderella* was a triumph in many ways. It was our tenth anniversary and the school had made progress and had had many accomplishments. Technically, the students had reached a high level, so it was now one of the foremost private ballet schools in the country. The performance was economically successful, which was important for the future. Also, I felt I had escaped going to jail with the end of the Baravelli mandate. But my archenemy, Maria Angela Filetto, was still working behind the scenes to destroy me.

Three weeks before *Cinderella,* we awakened to see the city of Conegliano plastered with posters advertising the ballet *Coppelia,* to be performed by the professional ballet company of the Arena di Verona. Elephantine banners were placed across the main streets downtown. I had never seen such wall-to-wall advertising for an event anywhere. Then the stomach-turning moment came when I saw the date of the ballet. It was scheduled a few days before our *Cinderella.* With two ballet performances in one week, most people with average paychecks would have to choose one or the other, and a professional company would win the contest. The beneficiary was Amici di Burkino Faso. Filetto was behind the whole thing, and this time she had made sure the beneficiary was far away in Africa, so no one could investigate where the money went. Her goal was to make a significant dent in my ticket sales, not to help Burkino Faso.

"Cosa fara la prossima volta; chiamera il Bolshoi?" asked Gianni with irony. (What will she do next; call the Bolshoi?) His extravagant prediction almost came true a year later.

***

Two traditions had become a part of each performance, commencing with the year of the musical *On Your Toes*. One was before the show and the other was after. The first was the participation in a benefit show for the *universita degli anziani,* or the school for the elderly. A thirty-five-year-old was considered senior or elderly because at one time in Italy, a person at this age had retired. The benefit for this group of Italians was held in Santa Lucia, a small village near Conegliano. We would bring variations and a pas de deux, usually from the performance we were about to present in Teatro Accademia. The little theater in Santa Lucia was part of the *parrocchia,* or church parish. The tiny stage was made smaller by a grand piano downstage. A permanent trompe l'oeil backdrop had been painted onto the stage walls, giving the stage the image of a southern Italian terrace. Beyond that was a collage of the Conegliano hills, mixed with a fantasy of impressions, including the Egyptian pyramids. This miniature place of dreams was difficult for dancing, but we looked forward to it every year, and the publicity we received served as an announcement for our ballet at Teatro Accademia.

The other ritual was carried out the day after the ballet, with a tranquil lunch at the Jin Don Chinese restaurant. I usually slept late; then I would go to the eatery, which was right around the corner from us. Americans often seek McDonald's in foreign countries in order to feel at home, but I always chose a Chinese restaurant for this same reason. My recollections went back to my grandfather who had introduced me to Chinese cuisine when I was nine. After a period of working as a mounted policeman in New York City, he had become a detective in Chinatown. He enjoyed Chinese food and took me to his favorite restaurant in Chinatown. The owner knew him well and taught me how to use chopsticks. Years later, while dancing at the Stadttheater of Klagenfurt, I would dine every Sunday at the one and only Chinese restaurant there. I was the only customer there and the only one at Jin Don. I didn't have to do anything or respond to the millions of questions people would ask about the show, so I was at total peace with myself. The family who owned the restaurant spoke Italian, so we became good friends. Sometimes they invited Gianni and me to join them for dinner at the restaurant.

***

Ballet preparations became easier and smoother with each year that passed, so I decided to challenge the school with a new production, *Sleeping Beauty*. Elena had already prepared the Aurora variation from the wedding scene for the Prix de Lausanne and was the strongest candidate for this role. The scenery and costumes that I had collected from each ballet were interchangeable. Only one or two small pieces of scenery were needed to complete the production. With our second *Cinderella,* City Hall had shown their appreciation of my volunteer work in the Dama Castellana by sponsoring the theater rental for the ballets. The one-thousand-dollar rental had grown over the years to three thousand dollars, so we welcomed this help. They continued to do this every year, with every show we did.

I wanted to create an outreach program in the community so that children could see a ballet. I went to speak with the new Minister of Culture, Loris Balliana, who was the former director for the Dama Castellana. The project would bring local elementary students by bus to the theater in the morning to observe our dress rehearsal. Loris was enthusiastic about the proposal. However, I would need permission to have the theater the day before the rehearsal and performance so that the floor, lights, and scenery could be installed, and I would need the owner of the theater, Giorgio Fabris, to approve this.

Giorgio met with me, and I explained that I needed the day before for setup so that we could do the rehearsal in the morning, when the local children could come from school as a field trip. Giorgio liked the idea of the children visiting the theater and agreed to give us the day before. His little daughter Giorgia studied with me and would be participating in *Sleeping Beauty*. She also studied piano. He wanted me to give her time on stage to perform a piano solo, but there was no place for a child playing a piano in the full-length ballet.

Then the solution began to come to me. *Sleeping Beauty* is a long ballet, with four pauses between acts. The kids would get restless during this time, so I thought that it would be interesting for them to watch the work on stage rather than stare at a velvet curtain. With this new perspective, I could see Giorgia playing the piano during the pause. Giorgio loved this plan and suggested putting a portable ballet barre with two or three of Giorgia's classmates practicing. In the end, it was a lovely, short vignette with a ballet barre, grand piano, and four little girls dressed in white tutus. In the background, the men worked to change the scenery for the next act. The teachers appreciated it because it kept the children in their seats, watching all the action on stage.

Everyone was happy and the project was a huge success. Many of the students wrote letters to the school, telling us how much they enjoyed the ballet. Unfortunately, there were protests that this was unfair to other schools, which considered the outreach program as a way for me to get publicity, so we were never allowed to repeat it. Schoolteachers requested this program to introduce children to the arts, but the power of my enemies wouldn't allow it.

The night performance for the public was also successful. I decorated Cinderella's coach with black and purple tulle for the entrance of Carabosse at the palace. The carriage was unrecognizable and was accompanied by two coachmen dressed in rat costumes and masks from the *Nutcracker*, but they wore long black capes and three-cornered hats. Gianni had found a bamboo baby crib that had been thrown in the garbage, and we painted it gold and covered the top with white tulle for Aurora's christening. The boat that I used as the Lilac Fairy in the third act was problematic. We couldn't afford an electronic or battery-operated boat, so we had to be creative and imaginative. I decided to use the Cinderella carriage base on wheels and a one-dimensional silhouette of a boat attached on one side. The boat could be pulled slowly from one side of the stage to the next, with the fog machines making a soft mist on the imaginary water. One had to imagine the passage of time with Tchaikovsky's score. Bepi, our stage manager, installed a wheel-like lever on both sides that would ensure a smooth sail for Flavio, the prince, and me. With Gianni and Bepi on the floor, each on opposite sides, they slowly worked the lever. We balanced ourselves with an oar, and as passengers on this small vessel we made it across the water.

One outstanding thing I remember about that night was the thunderstorm. At the end of the second act, a loud clap of thunder cut off the lights in the theater, when Carabosse puts her curse on Aurora. The cast fell asleep as the lights went out with the curse. The curtain closed because it was still operated manually. The audience didn't move during the pause, and the lights came on again just before the intermission was finished. A grand applause resonated in the theater when the lights came back on.

***

I continued to take students to Turin every year in the spring for the Vignale summer scholarships. The age limitation kept falling until it reached the point at which a six-or seven-year-old could audition. To spare unnecessary disappointment, I presented only the students that I was absolutely certain would be awarded scholarships. Unfortunately, the majority of scholarships were never used. Parents were happy to see their child in a newspaper photo, but in the end, they went somewhere else in the summer.

Most of the time, parents blocked their children from a dance career, a sad reminder of my own parents who had done everything to stop me, even though ballet was the oxygen that kept me alive. It was futile to work so hard for nothing, but every spring I had high hopes that one student would take the path to becoming a professional ballet dancer. Over the years, my students were awarded thirty scholarships, which was rewarding and frustrating at the same time.

***

That summer I went to the Dance Masters convention in New York, and to my surprise, Raoul Gelabert was a speaker there. When I was ten years old, he had been a guest at a party given by my first ballet teacher, Irine Fokine. The party had been for the winners of the scholarship that Fokine awarded once a year. Judges from the dance world would pick the best student at each level for the award. To the dismay of my parents, I won that year. *How was it possible that so many years had gone by?* I was almost fifty, so I didn't think Mr. Gelabert would still be alive. He had written many books on dance injuries and rehabilitation therapy and was quite distinguished. His conference was packed with teachers. I was startled when I saw him—he looked the same as he did almost forty years ago! This slight, calm little man with big, round eyes possessed a charisma that mesmerized the audience.

His quiet voice had a powerful message, and his advice revealed the truth of an unanswered question, helping me to understand something for the first time. He explained that a student with talent, but the misfortune of having a bad teacher, will often find his or her way to becoming a professional. The bad teacher will gain a wonderful reputation from the good fortune of having had a talented student who became a professional. However, an excellent teacher may have the bad luck of teaching dancers who are not interested in a performing career or who have no talent. They are unjustly recognized as bad teachers because they are seen as not being capable of producing a ballerina. In the end, it is luck that will make us or break us. For the first time, my frustration was explained. The lack of interest of my students to become professional dancers was not my fault. I couldn't be blamed for the fact that they chose to do something else with their lives. Tears streamed down my face. I remembered the words of my friend Hundertwasser. "You can't live in the dreams of others." I couldn't make my students live in the dreams I had for them.

CHAPTER 20

David Meets Goliath

"The most terrible of the sensations,
is the sensation to have lost hope."
Federico Garcia Lorca

In the year 2001, the darkness descended—nothing would ever be the same. A black cloth fell over everything like a woman covered in a veil, and only the eyes could see the horror all around. A long night had fallen on the world, but even as the sun came up, we knew it wasn't over. A seemingly endless war had begun. Everyone will remember that day forever and how it touched their lives. The evil of 9/11 will never be forgotten. We remember where we were that day and the moment when the devastating news was relayed to us.

It was the first day of registration at the ballet school and I was anxiously waiting for parents to enroll their children. The first to arrive was a tall, odd-looking Russian woman whom I had never seen before. She came to register her ten-year-old daughter Maria. Her face was very sad and she said she was so sorry to hear about the terrible thing that happened in New York.

"What terrible thing?" I asked her.

Then she recounted the story, which sounded like a science-fiction film on TV. I didn't believe her narrative of two planes attacking the Twin Towers and the fall of the buildings. It was too outrageous to consider. How could I believe this strange woman I had never met before, who looked like a tall Betty Boop and told me this crazy tale? I dismissed the whole thing when she left and decided she had probably seen a film that seemed so realistic she believed it was true. Nevertheless, the whole thing was disquieting. The next parent who walked through the door was someone I had known for many years, so I asked her if she had heard something about a terrorist attack. As far as she knew, nothing had happened. A teacher from the elementary school emerged from an office, and we asked if she had any information. Without emotion, she told us the truth: the worst attack on the United States in its history had just taken place. For a time, I woke up every morning hoping that it was just a bad dream, but nothing changed.

***

I had never given up the dream of performing the *Nutcracker* at Christmas. It was the fourth production of the ballet. The last one had left some bitter memories: my injured shoulder, the lack of students, and the unpleasant union of Mirella's jazz school to our ballet program.

We had to relocate our performance that year because of the restoration of Teatro Accademia. The electrical system had to be substituted, by law, after the Teatro La Fenice had burned to the ground in Venice. However, there were other things that needed to be restored in Accademia, as well. The humidity over the hundred-some-odd years had rotted the floor. After *On Your Toes*, we had left the wood tap floor sheets at the theater. The next day, when we had gone to pick them up, we had found that they were warped and destroyed by the dampness inside—just in one day! *But where would we go now?* The nearest theater was Teatro Verdi in neighboring Vittorio Veneto. The theater had already been restored and, like Accademia, was used as a cinema on weekends. I made a reservation for June so that we could premiere the ballet there.

I had begun restoring the *Nutcracker* Christmas tree that had been nearly destroyed after the flood. The mud was scraped and washed off in the backyard and the canvas tree hung to dry under the sun. This process had to be repeated several times. It was faded and blurry after all the washing, so now it was ready for painting. The tree was around fifteen feet high when it was fully extended. When I tied the top wooden star to the second-floor railing, the bottom of the tree touched the first floor of our house. The only time I could paint was in warm weather because there was no heat in the hallway. My body was warm with layers of clothes, but my hands were stiff from the cold. Gloves would protect my hands but wouldn't give me much mobility. I worked on a ladder, and the whole project took a few years, due to the interruptions. However, in the end, the tree was more vibrant with color and looked better than it had before the flood damage. I was proud of my work and happy to have saved this important piece of scenery.

My problem with performing at Teatro Verdi in Vittoro Veneto was finding sponsors. The school would have to pay for the theater rental, which added a substantial cost to the production. Teatro Accademia was reopening in December, so I decided to propose performing the *Nutcracker* there for Christmas.

"Non fa parte della nostra tradizione," the Cultural Minister Balliana said. (It isn't part of our tradition.) The church choir's *Concerto di Natale* was a ritual in Italy, not the ballet.

"Nessuno andra." (No one will go.)

But I insisted that we give it a chance. What was wrong with a ballet *and* a concert at Christmas? One was different from the other. So we confirmed a date, along with the assurance of sponsoring the theater rental fee for Accademia. With this assurance, I could ask sponsors in Conegliano to buy program ads for the ballet, which would premier in Vittorio Veneto in June but would open in the restored Teatro Accademia at Christmas. Some sponsors liked the idea of having publicity in Vittorio Veneto to enlarge their client base. I recognized that I wouldn't make a profit for the first performance in Teatro Verdi because of the theater rental cost, but I would in Accademia with the ticket sales and no rental fee.

The ballet had some new players in the cast. The Sugar Plum Fairy would be performed by a small, pretty girl named Francesca, who was a good student and dancer but who was also insecure. Flavio began partnering her, and they had an excellent relationship from the start. Moreno was in China, so I had no Rat King for the first time. I changed the gender of the character and created a Rat Queen, a role I decided would be fun for me to dance. The role of the Nutcracker now went to Flavio. We worked on a duel together, which was very effective because I was much taller, especially on pointe, so I appeared more aggressive. A Russian company that I had seen in Venice had used a Rat Queen in their production, so it wasn't unusual. In addition, I felt physically strong and in shape, so I also danced a modified version of the Dew Drop solo in Waltz of the Flowers. The ballet was victorious at the Teatro Verdi in Vittorio Veneto, but the excitement over our success was short-lived when I received a notice of eviction from the Kennedy elementary school.

***

The moment I had dreaded for years had come at a time when it wasn't on my mind. It was June, and I had the summer to find another place for the school. The reason they had given me was that a lunchroom was to be installed in the space. I went to speak with the mayor, and he suggested I move some place out of town, which at the time didn't make any sense to me, though later it did. We had our usual end-of-the-year party at the school, which was more like a farewell to the home our ballet company had had for many years. We had worked there for more than ten years— another ten with Tiziana. The hallway at home temporarily housed the barres and mirrors, and my life seemed to be packed away in this tiny area. *Would I ever work again?* First I had had to give up the keys to my apartment, now the keys to the school. I felt like I had lost everything. But the school was more than four walls in a building. As the teacher, I was the school, and it would go wherever I went.

A space turned up in a pre-war elementary school, Marconi, near home. Inside, there was an old gym with a moldy, black wall on one side.

"Possiamo dipingerla," said Franca from the City Hall. (We can paint it.) Franca was now in charge of city space to rent instead of the office of Anagrafe. She helped me to find this place for the ballet school. However, she warned me that there was one big problem, which was why no one wanted to rent it: the heating system. The old heater that rattled so loudly when turned on that it was impossible to hear anything.

"Lo prendo," I said. (I'll take it.) She stared at me. *It was better than nothing.*

I remembered the ratty dance studios where I had studied in my youth. Most had been demolished by now and replaced by high-rise buildings. They had lacked heat in the winter and air conditioning in the summer. The roaches had fallen from the holes in the walls and the wooden floors had been well-worn and consumed by decades of dancers' sweat. Usually there had been a big window at the end of the studio, and the sound and smells of the New York streets had filtered through while a pianist would pour his passion and soul into the class music. But the most important thing was the teacher. We had accepted every obstacle and unpleasant place just to study with a particular teacher. Today it seems that high-tech studios are more important than knowledgable teachers. Somehow we would make the space work, I thought. And we did.

We started rehearsing for the Christmas *Nutcracker* in our new home. I missed the sun on the buildings outside the Kennedy school, sun that had reflected the seasons of life. But the red sky at sunset could be seen from one of the massive windows and the afternoon sun shone like a spotlight from another. I understood later that every studio where I had taught had had its own particular light that represented a chapter in my life. As the winter came on, the gym turned icy without heat, but we kept working toward our goal.

***

The December *Dance Magazine* arrived punctually. In it, there was an article about Irine Fokine, my first ballet teacher, and her *Nutcracker,* which was about to celebrate its fifthtieth anniversary. The article brought back memories, especially of my first *Nutcracker* with Fokine forty-two years before. I had been nine years old at the time and, as usual, I had portrayed a boy. As a tall, long-legged, and awkward kid, I had been chosen as one of the three Arab boys who brought gifts to Clara in the

Arabian Dance. The costume had been purple satin harem pants with a pink lamé vest—I had no breasts yet, so I had a boy's chest—and a turban that matched the vest. Pale and freckled, I had had to cover my exposed body with dark greasepaint. I still have a tube of this in my red makeup case, the same tube Moreno had used as the Moor in *Petrouchka.* I wrote a letter to *Dance Magazine,* recounting my experience with the Fokine Ballet *Nutcracker* back then and how I would be repeating this tradition in a small Italian town for the first time. A year later, in December 2003, to my surprise, the letter was published in *Dance Magazine.*

***

Finally, my dream of a *Nutcracker* at Christmas became a reality. The ballet was filmed by TeleNordest TV and played over and over at Christmastime. Contrary to Balliana's prediction, the theater was packed. However, according to the number of tickets sold, the theater was half empty. I had hoped to make enough money to buy new portable barres, which we desperately needed, but that wasn't going to be. *How had this happened?* I was determined to get to the bottom of it, and with the help of a couple of parents, we discovered that people had crashed through a side entrance of the theater where the door was unguarded. It disgusted me that people would steal from the school just to save a few dollars. From that time on, I had to request guards for every performance in order to prevent people from sneaking into the theater. Unfortunately, this cast a shadow over the first *Nutcracker* at Christmastime in Conegliano.

***

Months later, I was on the train to Venice when I met the teacher from the Kennedy school who had unemotionally given me the terrible news of 9/11. She greeted me on the train and we chatted. The conversation came around to the lunchroom that had replaced my ballet school.

"Non hanno mai fatto il progetto e la stanza è rimasta vuota," she casually mentioned. (The project was never done and the room remained empty.)

"Cosa?" (What?) I could feel my lunch come up into my throat! Apparently, the space wasn't used for anything and no one had been granted permission to use it. *Why had it been taken away from the ballet school?* It didn't take me long to uncover the culprits responsible for the eviction: Filetto and the good sisters of the Immacolata. They hadn't been able to suffocate the school by offering free lessons, so they had had us evicted! The mayor had become more religious after surviving stomach cancer, so everything the nuns or the church wanted was granted. God had saved him with their prayers, so he owed them his life. I remembered how he had tried to subtly convince me that it was better to leave town and set up my school somewhere else. The lack of recognition for the contributions I had made to the community was a hard slap in the face. *Where was the loyalty after all these years in this town?*

Everything to do with the nuns had always been a curse for me, and my history with them as a child was rather ambiguous. Now they had returned to haunt me. *We will ask God to save you from cancer if you drive Barbara File out of town.* The Sisters of Charity were master dealmakers. It took me back to my school years, where I had been under the thumb of the nuns.

***

"I will give you excellent grades in math if you agree to make murals for the classroom bulletin board." This offer came from Sister Maureen who was young and pretty but who had a severe manner. I was thirteen years old and surprised by the dishonest proposal, but she quickly reminded me that I was failing in math, so I had no choice but to accept her deal. Every month, I decorated her bulletin board with a new mural, based on the season and the theme of education. While other students studied math, I designed, drew, and painted murals. This was how I passed mathematics with flying colors.

Our principal was Sister Catherine Daniel, a big nun who was built like a football quarterback and was definitely more Daniel than Catherine. She loved the girls but hated the boys in the school. According to Sister Catherine, boys were responsible for all the sins in the world. A large paddle accompanied her on all her disciplinary missions to drive the devil out of the sinful minds of young boys. While she was the principal, she was also our teacher, along with Sister Maureen for math. A scooter transported her rapidly from office to classroom. Her black veils breezed through the air as she flew by, reminding me of an immense witch on a broom. Luckily, I was the pride and joy of Sister Catherine Daniel.

When the parish did a fundraiser, I was called to perform a ballet solo. It didn't seem to matter that the Catholic Church frowned on tutus. I could wear any costume as long as tickets were sold. Another time I was ordered to participate in a local art contest in the name of Our Lady of Good Council.

"We have to beat the public school," she would say. If I had any doubts about participating, her strong, masculine voice would make things very clear. I didn't have a choice: it was an order. When I won first place, Sister Catherine Daniel was like a proud mother.

Most of the time, my classmates were left alone while our teacher took care of her duties as principal. We were left unattended for hours, with nothing to do but create havoc. The battle of the sexes began, with boys insulting girls and their insults disrespectfully bouncing back at them. Anger prompted erasers, pencils, and notebooks to become weapons, as the fighting went to new levels. I sat in the middle of all this and wanted to be anywhere but there. One time, an antagonistic boy attacked my commitment to ballet with constant, nagging harassment.

What am I doing in this mental asylum? That's it! I rose from my desk and walked out of the school. Ironically, I exited through the emergency door at the back of the classroom. This exit led to an open area bordering the woods, which was very muddy from melted snow. As I began to run to my freedom, fear of the consequences from this decision made me run faster. Suddenly, I realized I had lost my shoe in the mud. After turning back to find it, I stooped down to pick it up, and a tall black figure loomed over me. It was Sister Catherine, staring down at me without compassion. All hope of escaping the nuns and religious oppression was gone when I lost that shoe. I knelt in the mud and cried. Many times in my life I have remembered that day and that feeling of hopelessness.

***

Up until that time, I had been too busy writing my own destiny to research the lives of my ancestors. Then one day I was browsing through a bookstore in Mestre when I found a book on Irish history, written in Italian. It was a small paperback—very expensive like all the books sold in Italy. I read quickly through the pages to see if there was something interesting and found the name Bourke. The book explained that the Bourke family had castles in Ireland, which had been awarded for their bravery in war. There, written in Italian, were practically the same words my grandmother had spoken! Until I read those passages, I had wondered if it was all her fantasy. The book said that a few of the Bourke castles still existed. This confirmed what she had said. *But how had she known this?* It wasn't the kind of information you find easily—she just seemed to know it. The information must have been passed down through the generations. This book was destined to fall into my hands and give me the push I needed to go forward. The moment that I saw the family name on paper in a printed work it became real.

The historical book said that the original name was French, de Burgh, and that it went all the way back to Normandy. Our roots were French. When had the Bourke name begun in my family tree? Nanne was Mary Monihan, and before that, Mary Barrett. Where would I begin? Genealogists say the best place to begin is with your family. Ask them what they might know about the past. I thought my father might know something, so I called him.

"Nanne was one of three orphaned sisters from Ireland," he told me. "They came from Ireland during the Great Famine." He added that Nanne's birth certificate had been lost in a fire in Ireland. I was able to confirm that a terrible fire had destroyed important public records in Dublin at the turn of the century. Birth, marriage, and death certificates had been lost, though they could still be found in the archives of the church. However, there was a discrepancy with the Great Famine, which was between the years 1840 and 1845, before Nanne had been born. There had been another famine, which had come later in history, so this was probably the one he referred to.

From there I took my first step backward in time in order to go forward with the research. I started with Nan, who was born in 1898, and I requested a copy of her birth certificate in the archives of the state of New York. Six weeks later, the certificate arrived—it was an eye opener! There were so many things I didn't know about my family. My great-grandparents were married in New York in 1897. I discovered that my grandmother had been born at Four Hundred West Sixteenth Street where the Monihan family lived. The shock came when I read in the certificate that both my great-grandparents had been born in Lost Creek, Pennsylvania. Nanne was not born in Ireland, but in America! *How could that be?* My father was mistaken. Then I read that Nanne's mother was Bridget Bourke, born in Ireland. The story of three orphan sisters from Ireland belonged to my great-*great* grandmother. This would place her in the Great Famine period when she had emigrated to the United States. The next step would take me to Lost Creek, in Schuylkill County, Pennsylvania. Unfortunately, the research had to be put temporarily on hold.

***

When the tragedy of 9/11 took place, there was fear and uncertainty all over the world. This resulted in a freefall in the stockmarket, and fortunes were wiped out. After I sold my apartment, I had had my savings and pension invested with the Banca Nazionale di Lavoro, one of the biggest banks in Italy. Gianni's brother Luigi had introduced us to his financial planner, Serafino, who worked for the bank. Luigi was a prudent man who guaranteed the trustworthiness of the investment broker. Also, Serafino offered a hefty commission to clients who brought in new clients for him. We chose the financial planner and sealed our unfortunate fate.

In the beginning, everything went well because we kept our money in the safest investment that the bank provided. The money was placed in Ireland. Before September 2001, Serafino had suggested that Gianni and I invest our savings in the stockmarket. We both said no. I am not a gambler—I believe the stockmarket is too risky. Besides, I was making plans to return to the

United States so long-term investments with risks were not on the agenda. However, without our knowledge, Serafino had invested my savings and Gianni's money from the sale of his café, placing everything into the highest-risk stocks on the market. We didn't know this until six months after 9/11.

Since I decided to embrace the idea of buying a home in Florida, I collected as much information as I could find. *What would I do there?* I was too young to retire and I wanted to continue teaching. Where I settled in Florida would depend on where I worked. After I had lost the space in the Kennedy elementary school, I knew my future was shaky. I asked myself if the fight to stay in Conegliano and in Italy was worth the suffering. I never would be completely accepted. There were long, multiple lists of inconveniences in Italy. I missed so many things from the United States. I hadn't yet given up the battle, but I couldn't see what I was fighting for anymore.

We hadn't heard from Serafino for almost a year, which wasn't normal, so I decided to call him. By the sound of his voice, I could tell something was wrong. After a brief conversation, he spelled it out: our savings were gone!

The shock was overwhelming. Again I wanted to wake up one morning and find out it was all a nightmare. I desperately tried to understand how it had all happened. Serafino had had us sign papers for low-risk investments but had written in something else—"high-risk." I had to do something, so I began to climb the ladder in the bank, but at each level, the people got nastier. At some point they thought I would give up, go home, and forget about my life savings, but I didn't. The only step left was to bring a case against the bank, so I engaged a lawyer, avvocato Paolo Polato, who specialized in going up against banks that defrauded customers. A letter from him infuriated the top echelon of the bank. *How dare I challenge them!* In return, a lawyer for the Banca Nazionale di Lavoro sent a copy of the letter that would be presented at the inevitable trial. I couldn't believe anyone could go so low. The letter said I was a whore living with Gianni, a loose woman because I was a ballet dancer, and too selfish to ever give birth to children. The last remark hurt terribly, but the writer went on to say I profited from the 9/11 tragedy by suing the bank. *Can someone say such horrible lies without consequences?* Shocked, I looked at avvocato Polato for the answer.

"La gente puo dire tutto quello che vuole." (People can say whatever they want.) He shrugged it off like a piece of dirt that had fallen on the sleeve of his jacket.

Work couldn't erase the loss I had endured—and the sense of total hopelessness. The insecurity of the future hovered over me like a death sentence. I wanted to kill myself. Then I thought that I would first take down the financial planner who had ruined my life. But soon I realized that there were so many things I wanted to accomplish in my life that it would have to wait. Instead, I decided to concentrate on the things I wanted to do and forget about suicide or getting rid of a crook. At the end of our lives, our accomplishments are worth more than money. In the middle of this passionate reasoning, my father called me about a mysterious old letter he had found. The letter, dated 1895, was from Bridget Barrett, Nanne's sister, to her brother Richard. She mentioned her sister Mary and a Thomas Monihan, but apparently they weren't married yet. I couldn't wait to see it, so my father sent me a copy and saved the original until I visited.

***

With renewed energy, I resumed the genealogical research into the Bourke family and contacted the Historical Society of Bucks County in Pennsylvania. I wrote a letter, asking for any information that could help with the research on my family. About two weeks later, I received a letter from Roberta, a genealogist at the society, with a copy of a local census done in 1880. According to this census, my great-great grandmother was a widow by 1880. On the list were my great-grandmother and four other siblings. Now the pieces of the puzzle were coming together and a chronology was forming. Roberta also found my great-grandfather's family in the census. There I discovered that his mother was Ellen Bourke and that she was the same age as Bridget Bourke. *Could they be related in some way?*

"Where should I go from here?" I asked Roberta when I called her and thanked her for her help. She suggested the Historical Society of Schuylkill County and recommended I speak with Thomas Dempsey who volunteered there on Tuesdays.

"The best thing to do is find out if your ancestor is buried in St. Joseph's Cemetery," he explained on the phone. This was the primary Catholic Church in that area. Tom suggested I contact a very old woman by the name of Evelyn Marquardt, a legend in preserving local history. She had kept records of all those buried in the cemetery, which had been closed for years. Evelyn wrote to me before she died and said that, unfortunately, she couldn't find Bridget Bourke Barrett in her records. Evelyn sent me the copies of the records she had compiled. Tom and I continued to speak across the ocean, as we pondered where to go from there. His desire to help me solve my enigma demonstrated his dedication to genealogy and the Irish spirit of finding home.

***

"Ho bisogno qualcosa o perderemo," said Polato, my avvocato. (I need something or we will lose.) We had to give the judge more proof to have any hope of winning the case. The opposition never imagined I would go this far, especially after the humiliating letter that destroyed my character. But like a warrior, I knew I was doomed so I decided that I would fight to the bitter end. It would be worth it if I could give those bankers, especially Serafino, even one sleepless night. I had known many sleepless nights over this disaster. I needed to prove that I had planned to move to the United States to demonstrate that I wouldn't have put my savings into a long-term, high risk investment. *But what proof could I find?* Then I remembered I had placed an ad in the *Dance Magazine* classifieds, asking if anyone in Florida wanted to sell their dance school. I had kept every issue of the magazine for the past twenty years, so I knew I could find the ad. I did. The next day, I gave the information to Polato, who said we had at least a bit of hope now.

The day of the trial, we went to the court house in Pordenone. Avvocato Polato never smiled, and he must have been nervous that morning because he wore two different shoes! Outside the courtroom were the legal representatives for the bank. The principle lawyer that handled the case was a fat, dark Sicilian with a huge stomach. He looked at me arrogantly from head to toe, and I stared right through him. A look of embarassment came over his face and he looked away. This horrible man had written the lies and character defamation in that awful letter.

We were called into the courtroom. The judge sat behind a desk high on a platform, looking down at the lawyers and me at our tables. He read some papers carefully and then called the Sicilian lawyer and me to come forward. How odd it was to be standing in front of a judge in a courtroom in Italy. *What was I doing there?* I looked up at the judge without hope, as I had once looked at the face of Sister Catherine Daniel when I had lost my shoe in the mud. But this time I was the accuser, not the accused. Then the verdict was announced. The bank was found guilty and had to return my savings! Unfortunately, my pension was not included, but I needed my savings to start a new life in America. The Sicilian's stomach seemed to fall to the ground and he began to stutter. For the first time, I saw a smile on Paolo Polato's face. At that moment, we bathed together in the exhilaration of victory. I had fought the giant and won against all odds, just like David against Goliath. There is at least one Goliath in everyone's life. More important than anything else that day, I learned that there is always hope, even when things seem utterly hopeless.

My great-grandmother Nanne

CHAPTER 21

An Italian Castle in Russia

"Satisfaction lies in the effort, not in the attainment,
full effort is full victory."
Gandhi

I remember the day when I finally became an Italian citizen. The guidance of my ballet teacher Mischa had emerged indirectly through his recounting many years earlier. He was a dual citizen of both Russia and Iran, or Persia, as it was called then, with two passports. As a nobleman from a rich family in Russia, his future was questionable in the Soviet Union. He said the Persian passport had saved his life because it enabled him to leave Russia. With terrorism on the rise, I thought an Italian passport might save my life some day. Gianni and I went to Trieste to begin the procedure to obtain an Italian passport. Since I had no home in the United States, my address was the American Consulate of Trieste.

Two years later, the informal ceremony to be sworn in as an Italian citizen took place at City Hall. Rather than an office, the ceremony was held in a less-trafficked corner on the main floor. On the other side of the floor was the anagraphy window. The vice mayor, covered with ribbons and medals, came to initiate the procedure. Usually the mayor presided, but he had bowed out to avoid controversy with my opposition. Two employees working in the office were called upon to witness my transition from extra-communitaria to European citizen. Gianni stood next to me as the five of us clustered together. As the vice mayor read from a book, a profound emotion overwhelmed me. Years of joy and sorrow on my journey in this country—and all the personal and professional battles—struck me like a fist. At that moment, I envisioned my life in Italy as a movie video put on fast-forward after having gone backward. I suddenly felt weak. A fountain of tears erupted, and I quickly collected them with a handkerchief. On that day, I became a citizen of Europe with Italian citizenship.

Once I became a citizen, Ovidio and I went forward with a consentual divorce. We had been separated for ten years. A friend accompanied me to court for support. The building in Venice was the same one where we had been separated and now, almost divorced. Ovidio was called to stand before five judges in condemnation. All were seated at a long desk on a high podium, similar to the one in the courtroom in Pordenone where the bank trial had taken place. I stood as the victim in the back of the courtroom, with my friend holding me, which appeared more like protection than support. The scene in this ancient courtroom that had seen many trials was bizarre. In Italy, divorce was not common, so one judge made a sarcastic comment about this being the second divorce for Ovidio, as though he was a two-time loser. He shrank with embarrassment. Then the judge asked if I wanted alimony, and without hesitation, I said no. It was done. Ovidio had never been a husband to me, so it was really only the voiding of a bureaucratic contract.

***

Two performances of the *Nutcracker* were enough for the school in one year. The year 2003 would be free of performances, but I accepted an invitation for our school to participate in an international competition in Prague. We could bring three dances, so I decided on Clara's solo in the party scene, the Sugar Plum Fairy pas de deux, and the Snowflake group dance, all from the *Nutcracker*. All dancers invited to the competition had to promise not to ski or ice skate to guard against the risk of breaking something. If one dancer became injured, the entire group would be unable to go. The competition rules did not permit cast changes. The classroom was always empty in January and February because of the annual flu epidemic, but also for the ski vacation. The *settimana bianca,* or white week, as the ski vacation was called, was a tradition in every middle-class Italian family. Absence for the flu was excused, but the ski vacations weren't.

We rehearsed and prepared for the competition in Prague at Easter. In the meantime, Filetto was working on a spring show. She hired the Ballet of Moscow to perform *Cinderella.* It reminded me of what Gianni had said after our last performance of *Cinderella:*

"Cosa fa adesso, chiama il Bolshoi?" (What will she do now, call the Bolshoi?) That was after our last performance of *Cinderella.* It wasn't the Bolshoi but it came close. Fortunately, our school wasn't performing, so we didn't have to compete for the ticket sales.

On my bucket list was a trip to St. Petersburg and the Vaganova Academy. I decided it was time to take this trip in the summer during the White Nights Festival. The Russian Embassy needed my American passport for a visa, so I used my new Italian passport for the Czech Republic, which was not part of the European Union. The day arrived for our troupe to depart for Prague. There were sixteen dancers, with the minors accompanied by parents, siblings, and in some cases grandparents. We were an enormous group! Everyone wanted the freedom of driving their own car, which was frustrating for the hostess and translator in charge of us because everyone arrived at the hotel at different times. Flavio drove four of us in his station wagon on a nine-hour trip that crossed Italy, Austria, and a part of the Czech Republic. Our hotel was arranged with the competition. Because there were so many schools from all over the world, accommodations were on the outskirts of Prague. However, we were near a subway, which could take us directly to the center of the city.

The hotel was a tall edifice that looked like a new government building. Inside, the massive lobby was marble and imposing, with grand Bohemian chandeliers everywhere. Adorning the walls were gargantuan portraits of recent Czech political figures that we didn't know, mounted in ornate, gilded frames. In a striking difference to the enormous lobby, there was only one tiny elevator to take guests to their floors. After a long wait for the slow elevator, I arrived at the door to my room. I opened the door, expecting to find décor that matched the opulence of the lobby. Instead, I found a stark, white, sterile room with a cot in the corner. It was startling and could only be compared to a prison cell! A toilet, small shower, and a wash basin were in a space that probably had been intended for a closet. There was no TV and the phone didn't work. I met my dancers and their families in the dining room where they exchanged similar horror stories about the rooms. All meals were included in the hotel price, always buffets. The food was greasy, with fatty meats in heavy gravy predominant. Fruits and vegetables were non-existent.

The competition had so many groups performing and competing that two theaters were used simultaneously. One theater was in a small Czech village several hours from Prague. Early the next morning, a bus was parked outside the hotel, waiting to take us to the village. We were handed box lunches since we would be away from the hotel all day. Enrica's daughter Camilla was one of the dancers, and she opened the lunch bag to find a barely cooked, cold, greasy slab of meat wrapped in waxed paper. That was our meal!

Camilla looked bewildered.

"Cosa faccio con questo?" she asked. (What do I do with this?) I had once read that a slab of cold meat placed on aching muscles can soothe the soreness, so I suggested this to Camilla. She laughed and looked at me like I was crazy, but it was the only thing I could think of. It certainly wasn't edible.

We spent hours traveling to the Czech village. The landscape along the way was desolate, with only flat, treeless tundra. Finally we arrived in a town square surrounded by gray buildings. The most outstanding and impressive structure was the theater. There was nothing else for the townspeople. I was reminded of Klagenfurt, Austria, where I had danced with the Stadttheater. It amazed me that all over Europe, similar scenes repeated themselves, but this place was the bleakest. Rain showers added to the depressing atmosphere. The interior of the theater was a temple of worship for the arts. Carved Greek statues were placed in grotto-like recesses on every floor.

The day seemed endless, and the only café in the square was closed.

Francesca and Flavio danced the Sugar Plum Fairy pas de deux beautifully in mid-afternoon. The Snowflake group dance went onstage in the evening. Unfortunately, it didn't go well. Some dancers were nervous about performing in their first competition and in a foreign country. An exhausting schedule that day didn't help either. All of us were down about the performance. We arrived late that night at the hotel where a greasy dinner awaited us. No one had an appetite after such a difficult day.

The next day we were free, so we went sightseeing in Prague. The sun was shining, and visiting the "Paris of the East" transported us beyond the disappointment of the prior day's performance. On the third day, our young soloist, Giulia, was due to perform at the famous Vinohrady Theater in the Prague's historical center. The old theater had a long history and a gigantic stage. Giulia looked so tiny on this stage! Her angelic beauty and talent won the hearts of many. When it came time for the awards to be presented, we knew our group would not win the coveted Bohemian glass sculpture, but Giulia received an honorable mention for her solo and I received a recognition award for my choreography. We went home lighter from the bad food, which had given us diarrhea, and the empty spirit of disappointment. But I knew we had learned a great deal from the experience and that we would do better the next time.

***

When the school season ended, I flew to St. Petersburg for the Vaganova Conference. I had visited St. Petersburg and Moscow almost thirty years ago. Russia was then the Soviet Union, and St. Petersburg was called Leningrad. Back then, there had been thirteen airports in Moscow, and for reasons of secrecy, no one except the pilot had known at which airport we would land. Memories of that trip came back with clarity, as I replayed everything I had experienced decades before.

***

We booked a room at the big, ugly, gray Moscow Hotel, where I shared a room with Diane, an American translator of the Russian language—a bland room on a high floor with a snowy view of nothing. Each floor had a key lady, a type of concierge who watched over everything but who was really a KGB spy installed in the hotel. Even though it was late and snowing hard, we decided to take a cab to Red Square. There wasn't a soul in the square, and the falling snow made the whole atmosphere surreal. I started turning, arms open, as the snowflakes came down furiously. Bright lights fused with the snow, and Red Square became my stage. Suddenly, a tall, dark figure like a wall interrupted my solo. I stopped and looked up at a handsome, smiling, young Russian who spoke to me. Diane translated what he said. His name was Victor, and he said he came from a "closed city" in Siberia. The people who lived in closed cities couldn't travel to other Russian cities without a special visa, much less travel to other countries. This was his first trip to Moscow, which was considered an "open city." Victor took us back to the hotel in a cab, and then he asked Diane to ask me if I would go sightseeing with him.

"How will we communicate?" I asked.

"You'll manage," she responded with a smile.

The following day, he met me at the hotel and we went sightseeing together. I sometimes had the uncomfortable feeling that I shouldn't be in certain places, and I saw terrible poverty in a country that boasted that it didn't exist under communism, something that tourists weren't supposed to see. I remember waiting with Victor at a bus station on the outskirts of the city one night. Some young Russians from a region close to Mongolia sat there and stared at my boots. Their boots were layered newspapers tied with string! Much of the Soviet Union was off-limits to foreign visitors.

The first morning, we had breakfast together and we ate in a soup kitchen. Hot borscht was served up in a large, beaten-up, metal bowl that looked like a wash basin, along with a chunk of black bread. After this hearty meal, we were immune to the sub-zero temperatures. We ran through the snow, laughing, and no one watching us would have known that we were from countries that were engaged in a cold war. I was taking a terrible chance—the tour guide was furious with my disappearance every morning. The last day, Victor and I exchanged addresses so we could write to each other. At the moment we said goodbye in the hotel lobby, four men who had been casually reading newspapers jumped up and led Victor away. He didn't seem to be alarmed, and Diane explained that he would be okay.

"They are afraid he will try to leave with you, so they'll hold him until you are gone."

We embarked on the part of our journey to Leningrad from an unknown airport. The aircraft was an an old prop plane that was shared with Soviet soldiers. It was cold inside, so the passengers kept their hats and coats on for the slow, long, unpleasant trip. I thought about Victor the whole time, so I was almost numb to the severe discomforts. Except for Red Square, Moscow had been very drab, but Leningrad was completely the opposite— like a glorious dream with snow, sunshine, and beautiful architecture. It reminded me of the film *Dr.Zhivago*. The tour guide was happy that I stayed with the group on this part of the trip. We were warned not to drink the water and to use only bottled, even to brush our teeth. I followed the rules, but the heavy food at the hotel didn't agree with me, and I came down with diarrhea.

One night Diane and I had an experience that could have ended badly. While we were sleeping, we were robbed of our jewelry. Half-asleep, I had seen a dark shadow moving around in the room but had thought it was Diane, so I said nothing out of respect for her privacy. She informed me the following morning that she had never gotten up during the night. Diane was robbed of a gold chain necklace and I was robbed of a pair of gold earrings. We reported it to our guide who informed his Russian counterpart. The Russian guide was angry and accused us of lying. She said her people would never steal and that we had made the whole thing up.

This was my cloak-and-dagger experience in the Soviet Union in the nineteen seventies under communism. Victor and I wrote to each other, thanks to Mischa Katcharoff who translated my sentiments on paper. We even planned to meet that summer in Kiev because I was planning to go to Europe and audition for a ballet company. I bought a train ticket and had a visa to cross into the Ukraine, but his letters suddenly stopped—I never saw or heard from him again. I cashed in the train ticket for one to Venice, where a different destiny awaited me.

***

Now, almost forty years later, I was returning to Leningrad. The city had its old name back: St. Petersburg. Except for the name change, the different season, and the end of communism, everything was the same. My colleagues and I at the Vaganova Conference were treated like royalty, which was a far cry from the cold-war cordiality under the regime of the Soviet Union. There was no longer a key lady spy sentinel on every hotel floor, and accommodations had improved. One thing that hadn't changed was the water situation. Large tanks of bottled water were placed in every hotel room. The same advice was given: don't brush your teeth with tap water.

The conference group consisted of teachers from Europe, the United States, and South America. We spent hours observing classes at the Vaganova Academy. I was thrilled to be visiting the school where many of my teachers—Balanchine, Danilova, Doubrovska, and Vladimirov—had studied when it was the Imperial School of Russia. At that time, the czar would watch classes through the window of a door that is still the same today! The tiny museum in the Academy was a memorial to my teachers and the great dancers of Russia's past. Through the translators, many teachers asked me what it had been like to study under these famous dancers, especially Balanchine.

One night we were invited to a nightclub, the Troika, which I had been to on my first trip to St.Petersburg. I remember that we had dined on mediocre food and the show had been a traditional folkloric song, dance, and musical spectacular. The food was better now, and the show was a big surprise. The dancers were semi-nude—their performance would have been at home in Las Vegas. Other evenings we spent at the Mariinsky Theater to observe the famous Kirov Ballet whose dancers came from the Vaganova Academy. This was the same company I had been desperate to see in New York, and now I could see them every night! They performed Balanchine's *Jewels*. Times had certainly changed since communism. Everything western was now welcomed into the new Russia.

On the last day in St.Petersburg, we were taken to the Hermitage Museum. Once the Winter Palace of Catherine the Great, it housed one of the most incredible art collections in the world. We were able to avoid long lines of visitors when our guide escorted our eight conference participants through the side door. It could take days to see everything in this museum, but we had limited time so the guide presented the most important masterpieces.

"Is there a Gian Battista Cima painting in the museum?" I asked the guide.

She said there was one of his paintings, the *Annunciation*, in the Italian art section. Unfortunately, it was at the other end of the museum and we had no time to go there. I made up my mind to see it the following morning, before flying home. That night I never slept; instead, I stared out the window at the view of the Neva River. Beyond the waterway and the bridge, I could see the Winter Palace. The darkness of night came only for an hour. I thought about Victor. *Was he still alive? What was he doing now?* It was a lifetime ago—two young people, once separated by an Iron Curtain. Now all barriers were gone. Or were they? Did new ones substitute for the old?

After breakfast, I jumped into a taxi and went to see Cima's painting. A long line awaited me outside the museum where I patiently stood for hours to see one small painting. While waiting, we were entertained by a man with a small bear cub on a leash made of rope. I wanted to leave the line momentarily and cuddle the bear, but we had been told to avoid contact with animals, especially the dangerous packs of wild dogs that wandered the streets of the city. Once I had bought my ticket, I walked at a quick pace, almost running, to the Italian Masters room. I was chasing down the painting of a small Italian castle in a Russian Palace! Finally, I stood before the tiny *Annunciation*, and there, even smaller, was the castle of Conegliano in the background, just as Cima saw it in the 1500s. With pride and excitement, I thought: *This is my home.*

***

We prepared for our third *Cinderella,* which would be the last. Francesca was my choice for the lead, and looking back, I think she was ideal in the role. While Arianna and Elena were stronger dancers, Francesca was the classic, pretty, girl-next-door that the audience hoped would get the prince. I decided it was time to look for an alternative to using Casserotto's antique throne. It was too much of a risk. Gianni ran into a former client from his café and remembered that he owned a *bottega,* or workshop, that made baroque furniture. He asked him if he had a baroque chair that could resemble a throne on stage, because we were searching to buy one for our ballet productions. The artisan said he had a couple and that we could come to the bottega to see them. In his backyard, there was a separate garage-like structure that was his workshop. The space was freezing cold and had a dirt floor.

The frames of two large baroque chairs sat in the middle of the bottega. They were perfect thrones. One was gold and the other silver, and both were ready to be sold and upholstered. He explained that the King of Morocco had ordered eleven of these chairs but, in the end, had decided on only nine. He asked whether I preferred the gold or silver. I chose the gold and he promised to give the chair a second coat of paint. We worked out a very reasonable price, after the discount from the program publicity. I asked Corinto, my sponsor all these years, to upholster the chair as one of our sponsors. The upholstery was a lavish red satin, with a gold design woven into the fabric. On Thursday, June 3, 2004, we performed *Cinderella.* The day of the performance, Corinto's workmen delivered the throne to the theater. It was unveiled with wonder at the dress rehearsal for the ballet. Finally, we had our own throne, and though it didn't have the history of Casserotto's, it was admirable that it belonged to the same collection that graced the palace of the King of Morocco.

***

Many things seemed to rush together at once. I wanted to try things that I had never done before but always wanted to do. One of those was ballroom dancing. There was an Arthur Murray dance school in Treviso, so Gianni would visit his parents while I would take a private dance lesson once a week. As a ballet dancer, I learned ballroom dance quickly. From 2003 to 2004, I received awards in the waltz, foxtrot, tango, and rumba categories. Three months before *Cinderella,* I won the "Best Exhibition in the Waltz" in Verona. However, although I participated in competitions, I never had danced socially. Gianni took me to a local dance club one night. I was reluctant at first because Gianni did not dance, so I would have to find a stranger to partner me. That night, the "Miss Over" beauty contest was taking place in the discotheque. A representative came to our table and asked if I would like to participate. *What have I got to lose? It might be fun.* Three judges declared me "Miss Veneto Over Fifty" for 2004, eligible for the finals the end of September in Pesaro! At first I thought it was probably a ridiculous beauty contest for old ladies in bathing suits, but the finals came down to a talent contest, which intrigued me.

The father of a student had once told me that he was disappointed in me because he imagined a ballet teacher to be severe, mean, and ugly, with a cane in hand, ready to whack her students. It was an image I never wanted to become, so the "Miss Over" contest would challenge this idea. I wanted to dance again; a part of me danced in every one of my students, which made it more distressing when they quit. I had six weeks to prepare a short solo. *What would I do?* My ambition had no ceiling, and I decided to dance a modified variation from the ballet *Paquita* on pointe. There wasn't much time to prepare, so I put together a daily regimen, and my strength started to return. There were things I thought I would never be able to do again, but with constant work, my body responded. I practiced the variation on pointe before I taught classes, and curious mothers would try to peek through the crack in the door to see what was going on.

Finally, it was time to go to for the finals, so I packed a beautiful red tutu, tights, pointe shoes, and a black velvet gown, and hopped on the train to Pesaro. I wanted to prove to myself that I could still dance, though I would never again be sixteen and at my peak. Every region had a representative for each of three age categories, so there were many of us.

After a colloquil with the organizers, we rehearsed a walk on the runway. There was no stage, so I asked where finalists would eventually perform. The artistic director pointed to an area three feet by three feet. The flooring was flimsy plywood, covered with loose carpet squares that were not fixed to the floor. It was dangerous to walk on, much less dance on! I could visualize my pointe shoe getting caught in a carpet seam. *How could I dance in such a small space?* But in the end, I was not one of the five finalists chosen to perform. This happened for the best, under the circumstances, and did not diminish my delight in dancing again. I had proved to myself how far I could go and didn't need an audience to validate my performance. The journey is always better than the arrival.

***

My guardian angels on earth were my two English Bulldogs, Sissi and Andy. One night they probably saved my life when someone tried to break into the house. Their powerful barks protected me and sent the intruder running. When Gianni and I had adopted Sissi, the breeders had told us that there was one condition: we had to also adopt Andy, who was inseparable from Sissi. We had accepted without hesitation whereas most people had refused this agreement because Andy was handicapped. He had the "swimming puppy syndrome" and had difficulty standing. With our constant care as a puppy, we were able to help him walk—and eventually run. When they had first come home, I was terrified of them. After the Lupo experience during *Firebird,* I had become frightened of big dogs. Sissi and Andy looked ferocious to me. They often had mock fights in the living room, leaving bloodstains all over the walls. But after a few days, I abandoned my fears and fell in love with them.

Sissi, at twelve years old, was the first to pass away. *Do our beloved pets go to heaven?* A few months after Sissi died, I saw her in a dream. She was in the first apartment where I had lived, on Sixty-Sixth Street, many years ago. She walked toward the bedroom, which was illuminated by a strong white light, and I followed her. In the blinding light, I saw my mother lying on the bed, and she woke up and smiled. Sissi went to her immediately and my mother caressed her.

"You see, Barbara, dogs go to heaven too," she said. This dream gave me comfort.

Andy lived six months without Sissi. We stayed close to him, but we were no substitute for Sissi. One morning I found him dead in his bed. I wanted the power of God to touch him and bring him back to life, but this was futile. They were both buried next to each other in the mountains of Cansiglio, in a green field bordered by pine trees. I had said a tearful, emotional goodbye to both, individually, when each one had passed.

"*Ti amo per sempre*" was my farewell. (I will love you forever.) Each one was buried with an old pointe shoe of mine close to them. A part of my heart and soul was in this pair of shoes that I had danced in, so a part of me would always be with them. The shoes symbolized a love that would endure forever.

Vinohrady Theater, Prague, Czech Republic

Hermitage and Neva River, St. Petersburg, Russia

Sissi, Andy (white), with me

CHAPTER 22

Debussy in Barcelona

"The voice of beauty speaks softly,
it creeps only into the most awakened souls."
Friedrich Nietzsche

I recall, as a child, feeling like a prisoner at home when I was sick or on snow days. Instead of watching cartoons on television in my pajamas, I was captivated by old black-and-white movies. One program, *Million Dollar Movie,* would play a select film of the week over and over. Saturday and Sunday, the same film played all day. Most of the movies ended on a happy note, but there were ones that didn't. I wanted by sheer will to change the outcome, and I thought that if I watched the film enough times, I could somehow make the ending change. One in particular that I remember was the mysterious film *Portrait of Jenny.*

In this film, a starving artist meets a child named Jenny in Central Park. Every time he meets her, she grows older, until she is finally transformed into a beautiful young woman. He sketches her at every age and paints a final portrait. Tragically, she loses her life—the artist cannot save her from her destiny. His love for her lives on in the incredible portrait. I cried every time I saw the movie and would ask my mother how I could change the ending. She would laugh kindly at my innocence and inform me that, unfortunately, I couldn't rewrite the story. The movie remained in my memory, but the haunting music of of the film, Debussy's *L'Après-midi d'un Faune,* slept deep inside of my soul for thirty years, waiting to awaken one day. When it did, I choreographed a ballet to the music.

251

The first choreography I made for Dina and her school in 1989. In my mind, the melancholic music represented separation and the desperate desire to hold onto something. I thought of a mother separating herself from her child. The young girl must live her life and stand on her own two feet, so the mother's love releases her child into the world. The significance of its meaning was astonishing. *How did this reflect on my own life? Was it the terrible separation from my mother, brought about by her death?* Maybe subconsciously I comprehended that I would never have a child and I was losing my marriage. My own pain and suffering had awakened the music in me. An idea, a love, or whatever is born within us must eventually come out or it will wither and die. The ballet was a vehicle for all my emotional turmoil inside me.

A tall long-legged dancer, Martina, was my choice for the young girl, and I interpreted the mother. The nature of both dancers was an enigma, but I visualized the two as gracefull gazelles. The costumes were simple unitards, the mother in dark brown and the daughter in light beige. We performed *L'Après-midi d'un Faune* in Teatro Goldoni, Venice, and Teatro Verdi in Pordenone. The ballet was so well received that it was commissioned by Sandra for Teatro Toniolo in Mestre.

In January of 2005, I decided to repeat the ballet and bring it to the International Dance Grand Prix in Barcelona. For this new choreography, I went back to the original *L'Après-midi d'un Faune,* choreographed by Vaslav Nijinsky for the Ballets Russes in 1912, for ideas. Nijinsky's ballet was primarily about the faun, and he danced this role. I wanted it to be more about the nymphs, whom I envisioned as sisters. The oldest sister, or dancer, I chose was sixteen, with ages descending to fourteen. The youngest was eleven, and all three danced on pointe. Ironically, they were all named Giulia. The three girls had won full scholarships to the Teatro Nuovo Vignale Danza more than once, and the oldest Giulia had been accepted into La Scala Ballet School at age eleven. The youngest Giulia had won the award in Prague. The girls were beautiful in nude body stockings, with their hair let down, hanging loose. Flavio portrayed the faun, bare-chested with dark-colored tights and shoes.

The ballet begins with the three nymphs sleeping. From the start, the sentiments of joy, love, and fear are conveyed in their expressions and the choreography. The oldest nymph becomes protective of the younger two. Then the unknown enters their world, causing panic. The oldest tries to break away from the faun after sacrificing herself for the other two. A pas de deux slowly evolves into mutal confidence. The two younger nymphs rejoin them and shyly dance with the faun. In the end, the male figure is accepted into their circle. This acceptance symbolizes an inner peace that I had come to know and subconsciously reflect in my choreography. The ending is a far cry from that of *L'Après-midi d'un Faune,* which I had choreographed in 1989.

It seemed unfair to take only four dancers to Barcelona, so I choreographed a piece to the waltz in the third act of *Swan Lake,* where Prince Siegfried dances with the princesses. For this dance, I chose six of my strongest female dancers and a talented male student. When the Easter vacation came, we were all excited to fly to Barcelona. After Prague, the dancers were more seasoned and confident. Again we were a large group that comprised dancers and their extensive family members.

Barcelona was sunny and warm, with an air of spring festivity. The hotel and buffet meals were far better than those of our Prague experience. Again, groups came from all over the world, so the program was planned carefully to fit in sightseeing between performing. Our group successfully danced *L'Après-midi d'un Faune* and the *Swan Lake* waltz the first day. I had worried about the dancers losing expression on the day of the performance, but it didn't happen.

The following day, after breakfast, we visited the market by the port and Teatro Real where the Ballets Russes performed in 1917. I fell in love with Spain and the Spanish people. The next day was the finale of the competition. We didn't have to be back in the theater until nine o'clock, so we continued to tour Barcelona, visiting Antonio Gaudi's Sagrada Familia, or Sacred Family Cathedral. We made it back just in time for the awards ceremony at the Gran Palace Theater. A platform with a table full of sparkling trophies emerged from below the stage to the deafening music of

Star Wars. The Spanish version of the singer Wayne Newton walked proudly out of the wings as master of ceremonies and everything took a comical turn. The awards were presented, with "Best Ballet" being one of the last categories to be called. There were four prizes to be awarded in this category. There was a moment of suspense, when the hope of winning one of the coveted prizes hung in the air. I knew we had performed very well and was proud of everyone, but I had no illusion about winning. There were too many phenomenal ballet groups. But had *L'Après-midi d'un Faune* touched an empathetic chord in a judge? *Could we win?* Then the Spanish Wayne Newton called out the name of our group! The theme music from *Rocky* played, and from the back of the theater, I ran faster than Rocky had through the streets of Philadelphia. I jumped onto the stage and accepted the heavy trophy, and while I wanted my dancers up there with me, they preferred to stay in the back and applaud. Even though we came in fourth, my students had finally been recognized and I grabbed the moment for all of them. For the rest of my life, I will remember that night in Spain.

Crowds of people poured out of the theater into the narrow Catalonian streets. The winners and their companies commenced singing victorious songs in their native tongues, and shouts of victory rang out everywhere. The youngest Giulia sat on her father's shoulders and held the trophy high over her head. Her father was a former basketball player who stood six feet six inches tall, so with his daughter on his shoulders, holding the trophy over her head, they triumphantly towered over the mass of people. Everyone in our group had their turn in holding the victory cup like it was the Olympic Torch.

On the plane returning home, I stared at the mountainous cloud formations and reflected on the surreal experience of the days in Barcelona. Rays of the sunlight penetrated the clouds, came through the window, and danced on the trophy in my hands. *Did I dream all of this?* But as I held the heavy weight of victory in my hands, I knew it wasn't a dream.

***

After our success in Spain, everyone was ready to take on another challenge. A competition was scheduled for the end of June in a small town on the Italian coast near Rimini. The theater in this town, Teatro Bonci, was famous all over the world. In addition to its long history, Rudolf Nureyev had performed there, which made the theater stand out from others. Nureyev had put the place on the map. We brought the same ballets that we took to Spain.

Our hotel overlooked the Adriatic Sea, so the dancers spent every free moment on the beach. Fortunately, they didn't need to be pale for their roles because after just one afternoon in the sun, their skin was several shades darker. I chose the hotel not only for its proximity to the beach, but also because it offered air conditioning. But when we checked in, we were told that there was no air conditioning, and if we wanted it in our room, we had to pay a daily, eight-euro luxury fee. In June, the heat and humidity were unbearable, so I paid the fee. Most of our group didn't want air conditioning because they weren't used to it in their everyday lives. The rooms were hospital-like, almost as bad as the rooms in Prague. The worst part was that the bedsheets were wet! It didn't take long to figure out why after looking out the window. Down in the alley, between the two buildings, rows of clotheslines were strung everywhere, with limp white sheets hanging on them. But it was too hot and humid for the sheets to dry. Dryers were as obsolete as air conditioning, even in the first-class hotel.

Teatro Bonci was another baroque masterpiece of Italian theaters, completely carved in gold leaf. The gigantic, old stage was more than adequate in dimensions and only slighted raked. Because it was the end of June, more groups participated in this competitition. There was no air conditioning in the theater, and foreigners, especially Americans, suffered. Italians didn't notice this inconvenience because it was normal for them. Along with the heat was the unpleasant problem of mosquitoes inside the Bonci, so many of us were covered with bites. They thrived on the internal heat and dampness.

L'Après-midi d'un Faune was better the second time, and it was performed exactly as I envisioned it. The dancers were more professional after having won in Spain, so they were able to work on expression. However, we were up against stiff competition. A couple of ballet groups from America were very strong because they practiced many hours each day, while my students worked only three hours each week. Nevertheless, the experience of dancing in Teatro Bonci—and on the same stage as Rudolph Nureyev had once danced—was enough to take home with us, even if we didn't carry home another award.

The awards ceremony was held in the town piazza, with a warm breeze under the stars. The theater would have been stifling without air conditioning and with hundreds of people jammed in. We were not surprised when we didn't win for the performance, but we were shocked to be awarded a prize for "Best Costumes"! The costumes were meant to look like *no* costumes: nudity was the look. At least we had a good laugh at this. Later, it struck me with sorrow that this was our last competition together.

***

Every summer for eighteen years, I had returned to the United States to visit my father, but each year when I had come home, I had vowed it was the last time. A few days in New York would give me relief from an otherwise strained visit, but it wasn't enough. The physical abuse that I had been subjected to as a child had transformed into verbal abuse, which was equally devastating. The torture worsened every year. My stepmother became more and more hateful with age, and my father would apologize for her nastiness by blaming it on her diabetes. The mistreatment by both my father and stepmother made my visits overwhelmingly sad and stressful. During the year, my resolution not to return would break down, as kind words from my father over the phone would soften me. *Was I that desperate to have a father, or was I a masochist?*

The problem with my stepmother had plunged to its lowest depths. She was threatened by the fact that I was planning to return to the United States, even though my plan was to settle in Florida. But it still came as a surprise when my father told me I couldn't visit him again because his wife didn't want me to. He also suggested I forget about returning to live in the United States because it upset her.

"Maybe we could meet somewhere in Europe someday," he added.

This was the proverbial straw that broke the camel's back! I finally broke this abusive pattern. One month later, he changed his mind and called to ask me to come and see him. This time I told him *no*, and I didn't change my mind.

***

Before moving back to the United States, I had places I wanted to visit. Egypt was number one on the list, even before Ireland. As the situation in the Middle East progressively deteriorated, I believed it would soon be too dangerous to go there. Ireland was a peaceful country, and I wanted to have as much information as possible about my family before traveling there, which would take time. Egypt's proxmity beckoned me to visit. Gianni had always stayed home with Sissi and Andy when I traveled to see my father. Andy was the last to pass away before I went to Barcelona, so we were alone. I went to the local travel agent and booked the most expensive excursion to Egypt and a deluxe cruise on the Nile for two. It would take years for me to pay off the debt, but it was worth it!

One week before the departure, Al Qaeda bombed a discotheque in Sharm El Sheik, Egypt. A few Italian tourists had perished in the disaster and citizens were warned to avoid travel to Egypt. I was frightened enough to want to cancel the vacation, but Gianni knew how much the trip meant to me, so he convinced me to ignore the threats. In the end, we went. We never regretted the trip, and it turned out to be our honeymoon before our wedding. Once again, my Italian passport came in handy for traveling to the Middle East.

The day of departure came, and within two hours from Rome, we were in Cairo, another world. At sunset, the chant of the *muezzin* calling followers of Islam to prayer echoed through the city. While staying in Cairo, we spent evenings in the beautiful Egyptian gardens and smoked the hookah. We flew to Luxor at four o'clock in the morning, and I had to wake up one hour earlier to apply a strong Australian sunscreen. My skin turned blue until the protection was fully absorbed, but my legs always remained a bluish color, which frightened the Egyptians! The heat of the desert was so intense that all outdoor sightseeing had to be done before eleven o'clock a.m and after four o'clock p.m. Between those hours, we remained indoors, using the time to travel in air conditioning, eat lunch, shop in the bazaars, or visit museums and mosques.

We were ten Italians all together. Except for Gianni and me, everyone in our group looked like *Italian Vogue* in the desert. We were dressed in khaki shorts, hiking boots, French foreign legion hats, and Italian army shirts. Each of us carried a backpack filled with bottles of water we had brought from Italy in our suitcases. We took turns carrying the photo and video cameras, depending on who was using what. I even brought a pee cup for emergencies in the desert. We were ready for a long desert crossing! I had envisioned blinding sandstorms, snakes, and scorpions everywhere. To our surprise, the small mini-bus we traveled in had plenty of cold, bottled water, and we never had to walk far. There was always a portable public bathroom at every archaeological sight. We were definitely overprepared, and we looked at each other and laughed!

The security everywhere was startling, so we weren't afraid. Soldiers with machine guns were positioned on the top of our cruise boat. We lazily cruised along the Nile, and from our private balcony we drifted centuries back in time. Young Egyptian boys, wearing traditional, long shirts, or *gallibayas,* herded water buffalo through high grass in the river. In Luxor, we walked through an ancient temple whose age we found impossible to fully comprehend. We visited Hatshepsat's Temple in the Valley of the Kings, sailed a *felucca* in Aswan, and saw the most magnificent sights: Abu Simbel, the Sphinx, and the Pyramids of Giza. High up over Cairo, we said goodbye to Egypt from the plane window. We could see the Pyramids of Giza, looking like miniature LEGO models from the sky. *Would we ever be able to return someday?* My words are inadequate to describe the emotions I felt when seeing this ancient land.

***

When I got back to Italy, it was time to prepare for school registration. Before doing this, I had always spoken to my father by phone, but this time I couldn't find him at home. As the days went by, I became alarmed and I started calling at all hours. One night, my stepmother answered and told me that my father was in the hospital. A bacterial infection had attacked his heart. I couldn't ever remember my father being sick and he had never been in the hospital. My stepmother said that he couldn't talk because he had a breathing tube. I called every day, but his condition turned for the worse. I felt a sense of desperation because I understood he was dying. There seemed to be so much to say that had never been said. *Would we ever have time to talk?* I wanted him to say that he loved me and to acknowledge that I was his daughter. With panic in my heart, I thought I would never get this chance. But then suddenly I woke up to the truth: he had had fifty-three years to speak to me, and he never had.

After I had called every day to find out his condition, my stepmother said she would call me if there was a change. A week went by with no call, so I called her for news. I was shocked when she told me that he had died a few days before and his funeral would be the next morning! It was impossible for me to get from Italy to the funeral in New Jersey. Such was our estrangement that if I hadn't called, she never would have informed me of his death.

After the funeral, I asked my stepmother to send me some photos of my father. Her response was to send me photos of my grandmother. To send me a photo of him was to acknowledge me as his daughter. But he made the choice not to acknowledge me as his daughter long before he met my stepmother.

Here was a man who had once said that I was a mistake who never should have been born. I will never forget those words. But the bully I had known all my life was really a very weak man. I had told him the year before he died that I had forgiven him for what he had done to my mother. I understood that he had been weak when he disappeared and started a relationship immediately with another woman. I had watched death consume my mother every day and had felt helpless. I hadn't been able to fight death with a sword, but I had wanted to touch her with some borrowed divine power and make the cancer go away.

"Yes, I am weak," he had admitted.

"You are the strong one." I was surprised at this admission. Nevertheless, I am proud to have stood up both times to abuse—first the physical, then the psychological. It had taken me a lifetime, but I had finally done it.

***

Gianni wanted to return with me to the United States, where we could start a new life together. The immigration papers kept coming back, declining permission for him to accompany me. We planned to legally marry after we moved to America, but this was also denied. The American Consulate in Rome suggested we get married first and then request a green card for Gianni. I didn't want to marry in Italy because of the bad memories of my first matrimony. Gianni's family didn't accept me, so it would have been miserable. I wanted a happy wedding and imagined one on the beach. It was the end of November, but I made quick plans for us to fly to Florida at Christmas so we could marry on the beach, overlooking the ocean. A ballet teacher from my childhood, Joan Wolf, lived in Boca Raton with her husband Ken. Joan has always been a friend, teacher, mentor, and family, so I wanted her and her husband to be witnesses at our wedding.

The wedding dress was a problem, but this time I was determined to wear white on a white beach, in contrast to the dark navy blue suit, the black gondola, and the drizzling rain on the day I married Ovidio. White silk curtains had been donated to the school for costumes, so like Scarlet O'Hara in *Gone with the Wind,* I decided to make a wedding dress out of curtains. I asked Carla to make it.

"Ma sei matta?" she laughed. (Are you crazy?) *Who makes a wedding dress from curtains?* I asked her to copy a long velvet skirt she had made for the *Nutcracker,* and to make the top a simple, strapless bodice. Then she asked her usual question, "Quando ne hai bisogno?" (When do you need it?) In two weeks, we were leaving for Florida. It was the last thing she would ever make for me, and she didn't let me down. It was beautiful. She asked only fifteen euro, but I paid her thirty.

"Congratulations e auguri!" She hugged me and we said goodbye.

Finding white shoes was another difficult task, so Gianni painted an old pair of high heels. However, like the gold Bayadère ballet slippers in *On Your Toes,* the shoes never dried, so I packed them, wet, in a plastic bag. Two days before our flight, I came down with the flu and I didn't know if I would be able to travel. But canceling meant waiting another year, so I was determined to get on the plane. We had to first take the train to Milan, and I was burning with fever. It was below zero, but I was dripping sweat. We spent the night at the airport, sitting in the waiting room because we had an early flight. By the time we arrived in Miami, the fever was gone and all that was left was a bad head cold.

The official marriage ceremony took place at the Delray City Hall, with Joan and Ken as witnesses. Later, on the beach overlooking the ocean, Ken, who was a boat captain, performed a mock wedding ceremony. Their granddaughter dressed as a flower girl and dropped rose petals on the beach. The white wedding shoes were still wet, and sand stuck to them permanently! After dinner and a wedding cake at La Veille Maison, we spent the night on Joan's and Ken's yacht. At fifty-three years old, I finally had the wedding I had always dreamed of. One week later, we flew back to Milan, and the fairytale wedding was then only a beautiful memory. In Italy, preparations for the last ballet awaited me.

***

The last ballets the school would perform were *Petrouchka* and *Firebird.* The dancers were stronger than they had been twelve years before, so I wanted the chance to repeat the ballets and make the last show the greatest. Seventeen-year-old Giulia was my choice for the *Firebird,* after her astounding performance in Barcelona. However, she already had a busy career as a fashion model, which would interfere with rehearsals, so I was uncertain about giving her the role. But she wanted it badly and convinced me that she would work hard. There were moments in rehearsal when I could see that she had studied my expressions from the film made years ago and had copied them. She didn't disappoint her audience or me.

The day of the performance, I observed and directed the rehearsal from the back of the theater. I thought about how far I had come from my days with Ringling Bros. and Barnum & Bailey Circus. I also thought with sadness that it was to be our last show together and no one on the stage knew. Over the years, Filetto's army of volunteers had blatantly torn down every poster advertising our ballets. But word got around anyhow, and people often came from other cities to see us. We had a sold-out show, as if the people sensed it was to be the last. Sponsors who had supported the school for many years were present, including Signor Corinto who loved Stravinsky's music. My dear friend Ledo Freschi spoke to the audience before the show, saying fantastic things about the school and me. The ballets couldn't have gone better, and from the wings, I held back my own tears. I took my final bow in Conegliano, the city with the castle on the hill.

L'Après-midi d'un Faune

Our wedding on the beach in Florida

CHAPTER 23

The Bourke Castle

"The future is a door.
The past is the key."
Victor Hugo

The hardest thing I ever did was to say goodbye to my students. It hit me harder than the death of my father. Here were the children I wished for on the mountaintop in Greece. I was overcome with emotion one day when Paola's daughter Giulia gave me a lift home. The smiling little four-year-old who had walked into the dance studio was now driving a car! I had watched these girls grow up. We had a party at the school for students and parents to celebrate all the years we spent together. At the end of the farewell party, one student turned and regarded me for the last time. It was a look of both sadness and anger, because I was abandoning everyone. I will never forget that look. Then she turned away and left the room, crying. I felt sick and empty. *How could I leave them?* But we would find a way to reconnect over the years. They were all my children.

I had always lived like a gypsy, packing my memories and carrying them from place to place, so preparing the container for America was almost routine, except for the fact that my baggage had doubled in nineteen years. Touring with the circus all over the United States had taught me the art of packing. The *Tribuna* newspaper called me after word got around that I was leaving Italy. The reporter was a young woman who had taken Signor Basso's place at the newspaper. We met at the local café where I gave an interview. Without mentioning her name, I explained the problems

I had had with Filetto, tearing down our posters and undermining our work. Also, I told her about the local *Mafia Italiano* that had created a false case against me to take money from the school. I let everything out—it felt good. *Was the fight against all this worth continuing?* No! Not anymore. Italy is an amazing place to visit, or even to have a vacation home, but once a person decides to permanently live, work, and own a business there, she can expect all-out war. Also, I didn't know if my body could live through another winter. The cold, damp climate was destroying my health, and I couldn't bear to continue working with gloves, six sweaters, and boots on in the classroom.

However, there were many things I would miss: the church bells that chimed the time of day, gelato at Adriana's, and excursions to nearby Venice. The *colline,* or hills, were always a delightful break for Gianni and me. Autumn, my favorite season, was a colorful spectacular in the hills. We would visit Sissi and Andy where they were buried in Cansiglio, even when it was covered with snow. In the summer, Gianni and I rode his Lambretta scooter through the wine and prosecco countryside, when there were few cars around. There was a patch of forest that was cold, even when it was hot everywhere else. When we breezed by the trees, the cold suddenly hit us like an icy shower. We called this place *la doccia fredda,* or the cold shower.

Friends far outnumbered enemies. I would miss them, especially one, Rossana, who lived next-door. Her optimism had guided me through moments of total despair. I stood on her doorstep when Sissi and Andy had left this world and when my father died. She had taken me into her life and given me a shoulder to cry on. I carry her friendship with me. Sometimes we must take the next step, even if it is into the unknown. We are compelled to try so that we have no regrets. I left the door open behind me, but I wouldn't backtrack, not until I had accomplished my goals in America first. We take something with us after every chapter in our lives. If we don't, we have wasted time, not used it well.

***

Before leaving Europe, I had one last thing to do. Thirty-five years before, I had made a vow in my grandmother's kitchen. I was determined then to find the castles of my ancestors. I knew where the family began in Ireland and when my great-great grandmother had come on the famine boats, but I hadn't yet connected the dots in between. The performance of *Firebird* and *Petrouchka* were profitable. With the money I made from the ballet and the free flight I got with frequent-flyer points, I could take the trip I had promised myself. I was not going to America yet. I was going home to Ireland, the land of my ancestors. *Nan and Nanne would be proud of me,* I thought—*the first one in four generations to go back to Ireland!* Discovering who I am meant finding who my ancestors were. Who I am either *was* or *was not* shaped by my ancestors. Now I would fly on the back of my lucky dragon that would carry me through the sky, over land and sea, delivering me to the portals of my ancestors' castles.

From Venice, I departed alone, without Gianni, because I decided that I had to experience this myself, in my own way. It was an emotional voyage. *What if there had never been a famine? Where would we all be today?* I often asked myself these questions. However, like the Jews who had found sanctuary in Israel or the African slaves who had found freedom in the North, the Irish had survived their own kind of holocaust when they arrived, half-starved, on American shores.

It was gray and drizzly when I arrived in Dublin. I grabbed a taxi outside the airport, and the friendly driver began talking and asking questions immediately. I explained that I was an American with Irish roots and a descendent of the famine survivors.

"You're one of our displaced people," he said.

I had never thought of myself as a displaced person before, but it made me feel I belonged, like a lost family member who was finally coming home.

The taxi driver pointed out the statues along the river that were monuments to those who had died in the Great Famine. It was difficult not to be moved by the dark, life-size forms, writhing in agony with starvation.

Tears began to form in my eyes. I don't know if they were the result of the dramatic monuments I saw on the riverbanks or of the thought of being one of Ireland's displaced people.

The driver then pointed out with pride the pub where Bill Clinton had served and paid for drinks for everyone.

"He is quite popular in Ireland, Bill Clinton."

"He's one of us," he affirmed.

The taxi driver left me in front of a small hotel in the center of Dublin where I had reserved a room for one night, and he wished me a good visit to Ireland.

"Welcome home" he said, as he pulled away from the curb.

The hotel was small and the room was simple, overlooking the busy Dublin street and the park. As always, whenever I visited a new place, I put my bags down and, without unpacking, took off to sightsee.

Trinity College was my first stop, where I saw the delicate, beautiful Book of Kells, the oldest book in Europe. The next stop was the Museum of National Treasures. Certain historical artifacts stood out in particular, especially items pertaining to the invasion of the Vikings. An ancient Viking boat had been uncovered and was proudly displayed in the museum. In the National Gallery, I discovered the art of Jack Yeats. His magnificent early portraits had led to an inspirational period during which he had transformed his later paintings into a personal style all his own. The subject of his work was often the small, traveling circus in Ireland, which was one reason why I fell in love with his art.

On the way back to the hotel, I noticed a building resembling an old courthouse. It was a genealogy center. The place was filled with other displaced people like me, trying to find something or someone from the past. An enthusiastic Irish woman helped me right away. She asked me what family line I was following and what information I had so far. I told her all that I had found out about my great-great grandmother, Bridget Bourke, up until then; but I told her I didn't know who her parents were. Unfortunately, this was not enough. The key to the door to my past was both parents' names. The woman kindly told me that some people never

267

find the link to their family in Ireland. But knowing where their name came from gives them something to hold onto. A cloud of sadness passed over me at that moment. My past could remain a mystery—I would never really know who I was or where I came from.

I thanked the woman for her help. As soon as I walked outside into the gray afternoon, I took a deep breath of courage. *It is not over yet. There is always hope that I will find something someday.* With that determination, I walked back to the hotel and finished the day with a fish dinner. In Italy, fish was an expensive luxury, but here it was plentiful. During the famine, the Irish were not permitted to fish in the open waters. Had they been able to, a great many people would have been saved from starvation, changing history. There wouldn't have been a famine.

The next morning I prepared for my voyage to Mayo County. It rained lightly as I arrived at the tiny train station in Dublin. There were two destinations: Galway or Westport in Mayo County. I embarked on the Westport train at noon, along with a small handful of passengers going to local villages on the way. The rain intensified as the train made its way across Ireland. Though I had prepared myself for wet weather, I wondered if my trip was going to be hampered by constant downpours. I soaked in everything that I could see from the train window, just as I had done the year I had spent on tour with the circus train across the United States or on my regular train trips commuting in Italy, Austria, and Germany. Every village had an elegant, enormous church or cathedral, surrounded by modest bungalows, some with thatched roofs. The house of God overshadowed all else in the towns.

The green, velvet-like carpets of grass, rolled out flat at first, began to cover low hills. The landscape slowly changed. Young trees had been planted in lines in an otherwise barren land. The English had cut down the forests of Ireland centuries before, so they could take the wood back home. Because of the scarcity of trees, low rock walls, rather than wooden fences, provided boundaries to the fields; but the stone gave grace to the land and glory to improvisation. The land had been raped but it was now being reborn again with new trees. It reminded me that my final destination was a part of Ireland harsh enough to discourage invasions. Only the strong, icy Atlantic winds bit through this land in the west.

The sloping fields became more mountainous, less green, and increasingly rocky. I judged by my watch that I was an hour from arrival. There were two young Indians on the train, sitting across from an old Irish couple. I couldn't help hearing the Irish woman say to the two, "We have a lot in common; both our countries were ruled by England." At that moment, the weather began to change and the sun came out, though the rain continued. It was like a message of hope from God. I looked out the window, and as we twisted around the rocky hills, I could see in the distance an enormous mountain. *Could this be Croagh St. Patrick?* This is the highest mountain in Ireland, with the statue of St. Patrick, arms open, on its peak, dominating the shore region of Mayo County. It is a sacred place and a pilgrimage for hikers or religious followers. From here, it is said, St. Patrick sent away all serpents, and the island remains snake-free, even today. I couldn't see the mountain's top because there was a light fog hanging over the crest. Again, my eyes filled with tears of joy. I was almost there.

Without formality, the last train station was announced and everyone disembarked. A few taxi drivers looked earnestly for customers, and I walked over to one.

"Need a ride somewhere?" asked a thin, middle-aged man in a light brogue. He had thick gray hair, high cheekbones, and a dark gray, bushy mustache.

"O'Toole is the name," he said.

Before I could say yes, he grabbed my bag and walked to the cab. I could have managed to get to my hotel from the station on foot, but this gave me a chance to speak with O'Toole and to ask him for his number in case I needed a ride. Transportation was infrequent there, as were taxis. I hadn't driven a car in nineteen years and no longer possessed a driver's license, so I couldn't rent a car. After checking into my room, I spent the rest of the afternoon walking around the lovely village of Westport.

The next morning, miraculously, the sun was shining. After a rather hearty Irish breakfast, I called O'Toole for a ride, but he said he was driving a passenger somewhere and couldn't pick me up. The hotel arranged for someone else to drive me down to the pier where I would find the ferry for Clare Island. Though it was July, a chilly, strong wind roughened the waters of Clew Bay. It was difficult to imagine what it was like here in the winter. I looked at the sea in Ireland and thought about the Hudson River in New York—and how far my family had traveled to the shores of America.

From the ferry, I could see a ruined, tower-like structure. *Could this be Grace O'Malley's castle?* According to the map and guide, this was the castle of the pirate queen. I hadn't imagined it being so small and so close to the water. Disembarking from the rocking ferry was a challenge, and as I walked onto the pier, I could see the castle was exposed to the open air on many sides. Looking at the waves splashing on the rocky cliffs below the dilapidated castle, I was reminded of a dream I had had in Italy, a dream I had recounted to Rossana. Drowning in the sea, I had struggled to climb the cliffs and had made it to the top where there was a castle. The castle I now saw was identical to the one in my dream.

The tower-like structure was scheduled for restoration, according to signs. I walked inside the damp, cold ruins, covered with green moss, and picked up a stone from the ground. I slipped the stone into my bag as a reminder that I had stood there. I left the castle and proceeded along the dirt road that passed through green fields and low hills. As I walked, Clew Bay and the mountains of the mainland were on my left. Again, St. Patrick's mountain was the most outstanding object, though it was too far away to see his statue. Walking along the road, I didn't meet up with a single soul. The warmth of the sun was my only companion. The rays shining on the sea were like old friends, and I was reminded of the reservoir outside Nan's apartment. Now it was clear to me what we had been looking for as we had stared across the shimmering water in the artificial lake so many years ago. The water was both enlightenment and air to breathe. It gave us strength and a life source. Our distant memories had been searching for this: the castle at the edge of the water. I was reminded of the edifice of Hunter College on the other side of the reservoir. We had been looking out the Bronx apartment window, across the water, for our past.

Eventually, along the road, I found the abbey and small cemetery where generations of the family Bourke had been buried. Inside the tiny chapel, there was an altar with the family crest of arms, as well as the helmet and sword of my ancestor, Sir Richard Bourke. It is said that buried under this altar is the skull of Grace O'Malley. Her body had been hidden after her death so that her enemies wouldn't desecrate it. *Could Grace O'Malley be my ancestor?* I looked at the names on the gravestones, then quietly left the abbey grounds and headed back on the long road to the castle.

Small purple flowers grew wild everywhere. I didn't know their name, and maybe they grew in other places, but I had never noticed them until now, here on this tiny island. Again, I wanted to remember that I had been here, so I picked some of these strange flowers and put them in my bag. Even if I were to discover someday that they grew in other places, these would be special. Suddenly, I looked at my watch and realized it was time for the ferry to leave. If I missed this boat, I would have to wait until late afternoon for the next, and last, one. I began to run, almost out of desperation and fear, but in the distance I could see the ferryboat arriving at the pier. Before I even made it to the pier, the boat steamed away. I sat on a bench in front of the Pirate Queen's castle and caught my breath. *Why did I want to run away?* As though a great and powerful hand had touched the back of my neck, I heard a voice inside me saying, "Don't run away now. Let this place enter your soul."

The oppressive prison of mountains that had once trapped my spirit in Italy was now on the other side of a Clew Bay. I could breathe freedom. The challenge had been met and the obstacles symbolically stood on the other side of the sea. My family always sought and worshipped the sea, the same body of water that mixed with the ocean and connected the shores of Ireland to America. A drop of this water could travel as far as the Hudson River. The water from the canals of Venice could flow to Clew Bay, without impediment. But no matter how hard I tried to feel what my ancestors had known in this place they called home, Ireland was a stranger to me. I wasn't born here: They were. Their story originated here, but mine had begun in New York. The blood of the people who knew and loved this land flowed in my veins, but their memories were not mine. There was no way I could evoke their sentiments. I perceived that wherever it is that you open your eyes and take your first breath, that is the place you will always know as home. Traveling halfway around the world, I had finally found the truth.

I left my thoughts there and climbed the hill to the Hotel Belle View, a small pension with an incredible view of Croagh St. Patrick. It was the only place to stay on the island for anyone who chose to—or had been forced to because they had missed the last ferry. A group of tourists waiting for the next ferry enjoyed the breathtaking view with snacks and beverages. Inside, a man asked the waitress behind the counter for a cheese sandwich.

"There are no cheese sandwiches," she told him.

"But it says on the menu that you have cheese sandwiches."

"The boat with the cheese didn't come today."

The customer laughed, but that was the pace of life on this tiny island. Everything depended on the boat, and progress lagged for this reason. Things hadn't changed that much since my ancestors had lived along these shores. The last ferry finally came and I said goodbye to this mystical place, carrying with me a stone and flowers as a reminder forever. O'Toole picked me up at the pier, and took me back to my hotel.

***

It was my last day in Newport before heading back to Dublin, then to Italy, and soon back to America. The best was for last: the Bourke Castle. O'Toole picked me up at the hotel and we drove west.

"I don't know where this castle is, and I've never even heard of it," O'Toole commented. But I knew where the castle was located, even though I had never been there. The Bourke Castle, by other names, Rockfleet or Carrow, was on an unnamed road that led to the sea. According to the map, the road entrance was on the curve of a main road that connected a local village to Westport.

"There it is!" I cried. I noticed a small, crude wooden sign with an arrow indicating a narrow, rough dirt road to Rockfleet Castle. We took the bumpy road and arrived at a clearing. The castle stood alone and perfect on a marsh next to a canal that flowed to the open sea. The tower-like structure was connected to my distant past. Here is where the Bourke family had originated in Mayo County, Ireland. Here was the castle that my grandmother dreamed of, the one in the dream she had shared with me. I had arrived in more ways than one, and it had been a long journey of self-discovery. O'Toole photographed me from far away, in front of the castle. Then he waited in the car, allowing me privacy to experience this spiritual odyssey and reunion with my past. Again, I picked up a stone from the ground of the castle and placed it in my pocket.

I had taken many detours on the way to finding both this castle and myself. I had made a full circle and was now back to my beginning. I had chased my castles in time and found them, but I had really been chasing my dreams. I caught those dreams, held them, and then let them go. But I would carry their memory forever.

My hand grasped the tiny stone in my pocket to remind me that all of this was real.

"I'm ready to go home now," I said to O'Toole.

* THE END*

Firebird program with Conegliano Castle

Church and graveyard, Clare Island, Ireland

Bourke Castle

Made in the USA
Columbia, SC
20 January 2020